CONTENTS

Acknowledgments

A host of friends have assisted in the compilation and coordination of the files of the Fordyce Family....from the kind assistance of Malcolm Goodelle of the Historical Society of Cayuga County, New York, to Dr. F. Terry Hambrecht of the National Museum of Civil War Medicine; to Mr. Michael Rhode, Archivist of the National Museum of Health & Medicine and his Assistant Archivist Joan Redding; to Curator Ernestine Rountree and John House of the Mansfield Louisiana State Commemorative Area, to Reference Librarian Virginia Steele Wood, of the Humanities and Social Sciences Division of The Library of Congress, to the Montpelier Vermont Historical Society and Betty Post, Genealogist of the Mills family, all of whom so graciously assisted in research into the participation of Dr. Benjamin A. Fordyce and the 160th New York Volunteers in the Civil War; to Louise Gayton Coulson, the enduring link to the Fordyce lore; to Harry Flinn, Jr., who gave so generously a valuable document from his collection, to Cliff and Jan Kent whose artistic and technical skills have produced the written work, to Nancy Wettlaufer for her generously offered proofreading of the text, to George Wettlaufer for his technical skills, to Tabby House for their expertise and kind advice that are apparent in the finished product; to William Hecht, my son, who provided both research and inspiration to the editor to bring the writing to a conclusion; and to my dear husband, Marco Hecht, who provided the vital path to that attic treasure and created the pleasant atmosphere that made it possible to complete the project.

To each and every one of these friends and relatives, go my heartfelt thanks for their invaluable assistance, inspiration and encouragement.

And to the reader, may you find pleasure in reading of the events of those bygone days.

Introduction

The correspondence of Dr. Benjamin A. Fordyce, who volunteered his service in the Civil War as an Assistant Surgeon with the 160th New York State Volunteers, spans the days from July 7, 1863, until his return to his family in February of 1865 and illuminates his experiences during those memorable days.

They present a perceptive and vivid panorama of his experiences painted against the background of the conflict between two dedicated forces - The North and the South - locked in deadly combat for causes that each judged right.

Dr. Fordyce was plunged into the conflict as the Newspapers were reporting the fall of Vicksburg on July 4, 1863. Three days later, with the capture of Port Hudson, the Union campaign, initiated in April of 1862 by Admiral David Farragut and his squadron of warships and nineteen mortar schooners, had succeeded in opening the entire length of the Mississippi River to Union navigation and shipping, and cut off the South's supply line from the west. A major objective of the Union forces had been attained.

Meanwhile, in the east, with the fall of Gettysburg on July 4, 1863, and the blockade of Southern ocean trading, supply lines of food and materiel had been virtually cut off. The Confederate forces were nearly encircled. The Union could turn its attention to other vital areas - to Texas, Tennessee, Atlanta, Georgia, Richmond, Alabama. . .

From July of 1863 to July of 1864 Dr. Fordyce was stationed in Louisiana, where he participated in the Red River Campaign, was taken prisoner, spending ten weeks in a Confederate prison in Mansfield, Louisiana, where he served as Surgeon to the wounded prisoners. Upon his release he resumed his duties as Assistant Surgeon, accepting the assignments of responsibilities of Surgeon, and with the shortage of competent surgeons, performing the work of two or three surgeons.

In July of 1864 he was transferred to Virginia where he served in the camps and hospitals, caring for the sick and wounded in Sheridan's campaign. While in the hospitals in Winchester, Virginia, he performed amputations that are memorialized in the medical history of the conflict.

In February of 1865, as the war was drawing to a close, Dr. Fordyce' petition for resignation was finally accepted and he returned to his home and family, where he resumed his practice of medicine and an active life in his community.

Genealogical Charts

The Fordyce Family Tree

Benjamin Fordyce - Rebecca Horton
(1759 - 1819)   (1763 - 1840)
|
Dr. Benjamin Fordyce - Alpha Clark
(1797 - 1870)   (1796 - 1864)
|
Dr. Benjamin A. Fordyce - Emeline Slocum
(1823 - 1893)   (1826 - 1900)
(author of the Fordyce letters)
|
George S. Fordyce - Marguerite R. Utt
(1860 - 1937)   (1876 - 1946)
|
Benjamin A. Fordyce - Virginia Trembly Franco
(1896 - 1962)

The Family of Dr. Benjamin Allen & Emeline Slocum Fordyce

Benjamin Allen Fordyce, M.D.
Born: Jan. 13, 1823   Portage, NY
Married: July 9, 1845   Scipio, NY
Died: June 3, 1893   Union Springs

Emeline Slocum
Born: Sept. 18, 1826   Scipio, NY
Married: July 9, 1845   Scipio, NY
Died: May 30, 1900   Union Springs

Children

Sarah Estella Fordyce
Born: Jan. 13, 1851
Married: Dec. 29, 1880
    Jefferson Yawger
Died: March 11, 1930

Abigail Elida Fordyce
Born: Oct. 4, 1853
Never Married

Died: Dec. 9, 1931

George Slocum Fordyce
Born: Sept. 1, 1860
Married: Oct. 28, 1891
    Marguerite R. Utt
Died: Feb. 22, 1937

Chronology

Note - ** indicate occasions of special import in Dr. Fordyce' Civil War experiences.

Date	Dr. Benjamin A. Fordyce	The Civil War Era
Sep 15 1759	Patriarch Benjamin Fordyce is born in New Jersey	
1795	Benjamin Fordyce, migrates to New York State	
Jun 11 1797	Benjamin Fordyce' son is born; he becomes Dr. Benjamin Fordyce	
1803	Benjamin Fordyce builds the family homestead in Scipio, NY	
Mar 1 1819	Patriarch Benjamin Fordyce dies	
Sep 24 1820	Dr. Benjamin Fordyce marries Alpha Clark	
Jan 13 1823	Dr. Benjamin Fordyce' son is born; he becomes Dr. Benjamin A. Fordyce, the Civil War Surgeon	
1835	Dr. Benjamin Fordyce removes from Portage, NY to Scipio, NY	
1840	Dr. Benjamin Fordyce builds his cobblestone house	
1844	Dr. Benjamin A. Fordyce attends Geneva Medical College in Geneva, NY and qualifies in medical practice	
Jul 9 1845	Dr. Benjamin A. Fordyce marries Emeline Slocum	
Apr 1 1847	Dr. Benjamin A. Fordyce purchases a farm in Venice, NY and goes into practice there	
Jun 22 1847	Dr. Benjamin A. Fordyce satisfies the mortgage on his farm home	
Jan 13 1851	Sarah Estella Fordyce is born to Dr. Benjamin A. & Emeline Fordyce	
Oct 4 1853	Abigail Elida Fordyce is born to Dr. Benjamin A. & Emeline Fordyce	

Date	Dr. Benjamin A. Fordyce	The Civil War Era
Sep 1 1860	George Slocum Fordyce is born to Dr. Benjamin A. & Emeline Fordyce	
Dec. 1860		South Carolina secedes from the Union
Jan 1861		Mississippi, Florida, Alabama & Georgia secede
Apr 12 1861		Fort Sumpter, SC fired upon - the opening shot of the Civil War
Jul 21 1861		First Battle of Bull Run, VA
Feb 1862		Grant takes Fort Henry on the Tennessee River
Feb 14 1862		Ft. Donelson is taken by General U. S. Grant, signaling the Confederate loss of Kentucky
Mar/Jun 1862		The Peninsular Campaign, VA
Apr 6/7 1862		Battle of Shiloh, TN
Apr 1862		Admiral David G. Farragut takes New Orleans, LA
Aug 29 1862		Second Battle of Bull Run, VA
Sep 17 1862		Battle of Antietam, MD
Oct 1862		Corinth, MS & Perryville, KY: General Braxton Bragg retreats
Dec 1862		Battle of Fredericksburg, MD
Jan 1 1863		President Lincoln signs the Emancipation Proclamation
May 1863		Battle of Chancellorsville, VA
Jul 4 1863		The Battle of Gettysburg, PA
		The fall of Vicksburg, MS
Jul 7 1863	Dr. Benjamin A. Fordyce (Dr. F.) volunteers to serve in the 160th NY Regiment of the Civil War Union Forces, leaving his family in Venice, NY (Chapter 1)	
Jul 13 1863	Dr. F. writes from New York City as he awaits orders to take ship for Louisianna. He describes his experiences in the NY City Draft Riots (Chapter 1)	**New York City Draft Riots

Date	Dr. Benjamin A. Fordyce	The Civil War Era
Aug 3 1863	Dr. F. arrives at Camp Weitzel near Thibodeaux, LA (Chapter 2)	
Sep 4 1863	Dr. F. serves in the field as they move from Algiers to Berwick City, Centerville, Vermillion, LA	
Sep 19 1863	(Chapter 3)	Battle of Chicamauga Creek, GA
		General N. P. Banks opens the Texas Campaign
Oct 16 1863	Dr. F. in Opelousas, LA (Chapter 4)	Grant is placed in command of the Military Division of the Mississippi, putting him in charge of all Union Forces between the Allegheny Mountains and the Mississippi River
		Grant is promoted to rank of Lieutenant General and transferred to the Washington, DC area
Apr 9 1864	Dr. F. is taken prisoner at the battle of Mansfield, LA and interned for two months, eight days (Chapters 7 & 8)	**General Banks' Red River Campaign - a gunboat attack that ends in disaster for the Union
May 3 1864		Grant dispatches General W. T. Sherman on his march through the Shenandoah Valley
Jun 17 1864	Dr. F. is released from captivity and returned to the Union Lines at Morganzi, LA	
Jul 19 1864	Dr. F. arrives at Fortress Monroe, VA after transfer from Algiers, LA (Chapter 9)	Part of Banks' forces are sent to Sherman in Virginia; remainder to General E. R. S. Canby in charge of the Union Forces west of the Mississippi
Aug 8 1864		Admiral Farragut takes Mobile, AL
Sep 1 1864	(Chapter 10)	Sherman takes City of Atlanta, GA
Sep 19 1864	Dr. F. is in charge of ambulances and wounded during the Third Battle of Winchester, VA: he performs noteworthy life-saving surgery	**The Third Battle of Winchester, VA General P. H. Sheridan's victory for the Union
Sep 25 1864	Dr. F. is named Medical Inspector of Hospitals for his corps.	
Oct 19 1864	Dr. F. serves during the Battle of Cedar Creek, VA (Chapters 11 & 12)	**Northern victory at the Battle of Cedar Creek, VA

Date	Dr. Benjamin A. Fordyce	The Civil War Era
Nov 15 1864	(Chapters 13 & 14)	Sherman starts his march from Atlanta toward Savannah, GA
Jan 15 1865		The Capture of Fort Fisher guarding Wilmington, NC, the last Atlantic port open to the Confederacy
Jan 18 1865	Dr. F's application for resignation from service to his country is finally accepted and he is honorably discharged	
Apr 2 1865		The Confederate defeat at the Battle of Five Forks, VA and the resultant evacuation of the Confederate capital city of Richmond, VA
Apr 9 1865		General Lee surrenders to General Grant at Appomatox Court House, VA
Apr 14 1865		Abraham Lincoln is assassinated in Washington, DC
1866	Dr. F moves to Union Springs, NY to practice medicine.	
Dec 29 1880	Estella Fordyce marries Thomas Jefferson Yawger	
1886	(Chapter 15)	
Oct 28 1891	George Fordyce marries Marguerite Utt	
Jun 3 1893	Dr. Benjamin A. Fordyce dies in Union Springs, NY	
Apr 4 1896	Benjamin Allen Fordyce is born to George & Marguerite	
Mar 30 1900	Emeline Slocum Fordyce dies	
Mar 11 1930	Estella Fordyce Yawger dies	
Dec 9 1931	Abbie Fordyce dies	
Feb 22 1937	George Slocum Fordyce dies	
Mar 14 1948	Marguerite Utt Fordyce dies	
May 5 1962	Benjamin Allen Fordyce dies, signalling the close of the Benjamin Fordyce lineage.	

Echoes

The fall sunlight glinted green-gold in the living room at Four North Cayuga Street as we discussed terms with the real estate agent. It warmed the mahogany of the ancient roll-top desk.... and brought to life the portrait of Great Grandmother Emeline Fordyce.

How many stories of days gone by she could tell! Was it she who had written in one of the desk's drawers, "1895 - This desk is more than 125 years old." [1] Who could have resisted the welcome repose of that sun-drenched living room?

So it was that in October of 1954 we purchased the house that had sheltered the Fordyce Family in Union Springs for nearly fifty years, and that warmed our hearts and nourished our souls for another twenty-five, before it resumed its course with its adoption by the Lawtons.

George Fordyce had gone to meet his Maker some years before, as had Maggie, his wife; and there remained only Ben, their son of some fifty-eight years.

Ben's health was failing. His wife had been called to care for an ailing father; and it was left to him to move the few cherished possessions that they could use in their new apartment, leaving with us the house and the collection of Fordyce memorabilia that had accumulated over the past fifty years.

Ben lingered over his good-byes, however. He occasionally would remember something that he had forgotten to take. On one such visit, he ventured down into the cellar and there stood looking at the warren of rooms.... the coal bin, the cisterns, the derelict water system, the jam cupboards long since stripped of their bounty of preserves from the garden.

"We cleaned the cellar," he said, as he eased his long frame down onto the stairs. "I could clean the attic, too," he added tentatively.

"Oh, no Ben, that won't be necessary," we responded. We had visions of his shoveling its contents into a truck destined for the trash dump.

The attic was the realization of a child's dream. The sturdy beams up there soared skyward to a height of some twenty feet at the peak; and the chimney leaned precariously as it sought the sky. A window on the west and another that let in the southern sun revealed a treasure trove of furniture, clothing boxes, chests and trunks, that had been the residue of other attics of the Fordyce Family. Over all, time and a smoky coal furnace had laid down a blanket of dust and cobwebs. So closely packed was the melange that the magnitude of the cache could not be fully appreciated. The thrill of exploration beckoned. However, the burden of establishing a home for ourselves, the arrival of another child and the demands of everyday life delayed the exploration for nearly three years. It was not until one hot summer's day, when a thermometer would have reached 120°, that we found the time to clean the attic.

The gem of the collection in that dusty vault was in a yellowed pillow-case that hung from one of the rafters. Opened, it contained the correspondence between Dr. Benjamin Allen Fordyce and his Quaker wife, Emeline Slocum, during his Civil War Service as an Army Surgeon. Ben's grandfather's neatly penned letters, still in their envelopes, told the story. It was these letters that initiated a study of the Fordyce Family and brought life to the days of an early frontiersman and his progeny.... a story that begs to be kept for posterity.

The Fordyce Family was something of a legend in the community of Union Springs. Scraps of detail had accumulated to create a quilt of interesting pieces; but a background was needed.

Allen Hammond, a neighbor who lived next door, had known the Fordyces and was feeling the loss of their hospitality. Naturally, he was generous in supplying the details that he had cherished through his nearly three score years of life with Ben.... and with Maggie.... and with George, who was a Slocum cousin.

But, what of the vital statistics? The Cayuga County Historical Society provided the necessary link. A phone call to Louise Gayton Coulson, a local historian, provided a direct descendant of the pioneer, Benjamin Fordyce, who had migrated to Scipio, New York. Kenneth and Louise Coulson, both great, great, great grandchildren of the patriarch, Benjamin Fordyce, lived in the Fordyce homestead, on the farm where in 1795 Benjamin Fordyce and Rebecca Horton Fordyce settled when they came from Chester, New Jersey.[2] Mrs. Coulson gave unstintingly of her wealth of information on her ancestors from which developed the glimpse into the lives of the Fordyce Family.

Benjamin Fordyce had survived his service in the Revolutionary War where he had served with Captain Nathaniel Horton, Jr., who commanded a company in the Western Battalion of the Morris County, New Jersey, Militia. He served with Captain Horton at Haddonfield, New Jersey, in November 1777, at Elizabethtown in 1778; and he fought in an engagement at Aquackanock Bridge on September 27 of the same year.

The Fordyce Homestead - Built ca1800 Scipio, NY

In 1790 Benjamin Fordyce married his captain's daughter, Rebecca Horton. Some five years later they responded to the current call of westward migration and set out for the Western Lands of New York State.

In the Spring of 1795 Benjamin, with three of his brothers-in-law, traveled through the wilderness from their New Jersey homes to establish homes for themselves and their families in the Lake Country of New York State.

Benjamin Fordyce purchased sixty-one acres in Scipio from Elder David Irish; cleared some of the land and set about building a log cabin for his family. He planted corn before he and his brothers-in-law returned to New Jersey for their families.

Via the water route they traveled from Chester, New Jersey, to the little town of Aurora on Cayuga Lake. There were eight adults and ten children in the little band. Benjamin and Rebecca brought with them their two children, John and Eunice. They transported their possessions in wagons drawn by oxen and horses; and frequently it was necessary to clear a roadway to permit them to drive their wagons through the dense forests.

Life was primitive in those days; and a simple log cabin was their castle. On June 11, 1797, Benjamin and Rebecca were blessed with the birth of a son whom they named Benjamin for his father. Nathaniel and Rebecca followed later. They grew and prospered. Life, although strenuous and fraught with danger, was good.

By the turn of the century, their larger family dictated that they build a new house on the recently developed highway "so that they could see the travel." Legend has it that it was between 1800 and 1805 when the frame structure took shape; and succeeding years and generations added rooms and wings, along with charisma, to its sturdy foundation. The fireplace, with its large oven and cavernous maw, still stands to warm the occupants. It has survived the ignominy of having been closed and plastered over, only to be resurrected and reconditioned to cast its warmth upon succeeding generations.

The child Benjamin was a blessing to his fond parents; and in time his interest in others took the form of his becoming a doctor to their ills. Thus appeared the first Dr. Fordyce. In 1820 he married Alpha Clark, the daughter of Wheaton Clark in Scipio; and they lived in Portage, New York, where seven of their nine children were born. By 1835 they had returned to Scipio where in 1842 they built a cobblestone house that still graces the town.

Their second son was Benjamin Allen Fordyce, born January 13, 1823, in Portage. He followed his father in the practice of medicine after attending Cayuga Lake Academy at Aurora, NY, and Geneva Medical College in Geneva, NY. He carried with him the cards issued to attest to his qualifications. They bear dates of 1844 and 1845 and indicate his proficiency.

MEDICAL INSTITUTION OF GENEVA COLLEGE,

MATRICULATION TICKET, FOR 1844.

For *Benj. Allen Fordyce*

No. *137*   *James Hadley* Registrar.

☞—By a resolution of the Medical Faculty, every Student, before he can be
supplied with Tickets from any Professor, must enrol his name in the Album,
and provide himself with this Matriculation Ticket.

GENEVA MEDICAL COLLEGE, OCT. 1844.

MEDICAL INSTITUTION OF GENEVA COLLEGE.

Mr _B. A. Fordyce_

Is entitled to Tickets of all the Professors.

James Hadley Registrar.

SESSION OF 1844-5

MEDICAL INSTITUTION OF GENEVA COLLEGE,

CHEMISTRY AND PHARMACY.

By _James Hadley_ M. D.

For _B. A. Fordyce_

October 1844.

No. _57_

GENEVA MEDICAL COLLEGE

OBSTETRICS And MEDICAL JURISPRUDENCE

BY

C. B. Coventry M. D. &c Profr.

For _Benjn A Fordyce_ 1844

GENEVA MEDICAL COLLEGE.

MATERIAL FOR PRACTICAL ANATOMY.

James Hadley Reg'r.

C. L. Ford Dem'r.

For Mr. *B. A. Fordyce*

184*4-5*

MEDICAL INSTITUTION
OF
GENEVA COLLEGE
INSTITUTES & PRACTICE
OF
MEDICINE.

BY *Thomas Spencer M.D.*

1844-5
FOR *B. A. Fordyce*

GENEVA MEDICAL COLLEGE.

LECTURES
ON
General Pathology and Materia Medica,

SESSION OF 1844-5.

Admit Mr. *B. A. Fordyce*

No. *16* *Chas A Lee*

GENEVA MEDICAL COLLEGE.

Anatomical Demonstrations,

BY CORYDON LA FORD, M. D.

For *B. A. Fordyce*

No. *137* Session 184 .

MEDICAL INSTITUTION OF
GENEVA COLLEGE.

This Certifies that *Benjamin Allen Fordyce* has attended a **Full Course of Lectures**, at this Institution, during the Term of 1844-5; and that his attendance has been regular, and his character and conduct, as a Student, proper and respectable.

Geneva, No. Y., Jan'y 20 1845

James Hadley Registrar.

This is to Certify, that at a meeting of the board of censors of the Cayuga Co. Medical Society, Benjamin A. Fordice was examined and found competent, in their opinion, to practice Medicine and surgery, and they would therefore recomend the president to grant him a diploma.—

Auburn Jany. 8. 1846 —

Charles A. Hyde
C. C. Cadoff
Blanchard Fosgate

} Censors

Rec. Auburn Jany 8. 1846 of Beny. A. Fordice five dollars being amt. for diploma —

Blanchard Fosgate
Secretary

Let us go back once more to that attic retreat at Four North Cayuga Street in the little village of Union Springs, New York. Do you hear the creak of the steep, steep steps as we ascend? There under the eaves we find the leather medicine bags that accompanied Dr. Fordyce on his rounds; and tucked inside find the wallets crammed with receipts and certificates of his medical qualifications.

Draw from another pocket of the wallet a letter from his friend, D. W. C. Van Slyck, date-lined Cayuga Academy, Aurora, NY, and dated July 6th 1842. Is it not possible that this very letter, carried throughout his lifetime by Dr. Fordyce in his wallet along with his diplomas, was the inspiration for his following the medical profession? The letter reads in part:

"I expressed in my last a possibility of my attending Lectures at Geneva but I am not certain however I am quite confident I shall go then on to Albany though I rather think to the latter place - there are great prospects of my going to Geneva to live in the course of four or five months and if so I shall attend a second course there & graduate - write whether you intend to go to lectures next winter I should like to have you attend at the same place - one thing if you wish to avail yourself of it is in your power that is to attend the course at Geneva free of charge - & even obtain a certificate from the censors recommending you if you desire it It is nothing like degradation I may take the same course at Albany, one can save about $70 or $80. as his board is about the only expense - the Medical colleges are obliged to receive four annually such as the state censors may direct. I think you had better avail yourself of the opportunity if you have a mind to."

Open Dr. Fordyce' day book that chronicled his daily medical practice and read his comments on his patients' ailments and his remedies for their ills.

Now, let us travel back in time to the days of his early practice, prior to his wartime service, and observe the life of the young country doctor.

Shortly after completing his medical studies at Geneva, on July 9, 1845, Benjamin Allen Fordyce married Miss Emeline Slocum, one of his pupils when he served as a district school teacher. She was the daughter of Scipio's respected Quaker citizen, George Slocum, descendant of that family of Friends who had participated in the westward migration from the Atlantic seacoast to open the west to settlement.

A faded deed dated August 2, 1850, describes his purchase of a farm of some thirty acres in Venice Township. This was to be their home until 1865 when the family moved to Union Springs.

Sarah Estella was born to Dr. Fordyce and his wife, Emeline, on January 13 of 1851. On October 4, 1853, Abigail Elida joined the Fordyce family unit; and seven years later, on September 1, 1860, George Slocum Fordyce was born. The Family of Benjamin and Emeline Fordyce was complete, happy and busy in the life of doctor and farmer.

As for his medical practice, he first assisted his father, Dr. Benjamin Fordyce in his medical practice and then established his own practice at Stewarts Corners in the Town of Venice, NY, where he served the community for eighteen years. His gentle, quiet manner, his concern for his patients, his proficiency in the pursuit of his science inspired confidence in his patients; and they often came to him for counsel and advice in matters of a financial nature. At the same time, his wisdom in matters of business and politics earned him the respect of the community. Soldiers, far from home, frequently, left their money with him for safekeeping. He loved life and mankind and enjoyed putting to paper some of his experiences and observations. He received letters from other doctors at the front; he was intimately acquainted with the magnitude of the nation's conflict.

A stone in the family burial ground near the family homestead reveals that on November 13, 1862, he had lost a cousin, John Horton Fordyce, in the war.[3] Dr. Fordyce was well-informed on the progress of the conflict and the political implications of the division between the states. His sense of justice and responsibility to his country, dictated his decision to join the Union forces.

It must have been a difficult decision to leave family and friends, a thriving and active medical practice, and to set off for a destination from which he might never return. His concern was for his family...his fine Quaker wife, his two lovely little daughters, Stella and Abbie, ages ten and twelve....and Little George, then nearly three years of age.

Thus it was that on July 7, 1863, Dr. Fordyce boarded the train at Auburn, New York, to travel to New York City to join the 160th Regiment of New York Volunteers. On the afternoon of that day he penned his first letter to his beloved wife from Albany. Thus began a series of letters to Emeline and to Estella and Abbie, with messages to little George. It was these letters that had been so carefully cherished by succeeding generations until fate left them in the dusty attic at Four North Cayuga Street. They present vivid descriptions of the national conflict, of life in the South, of life on the home front in the North, with interesting anecdotes for the children, details of the rigors of life at the front, the grueling long hours of hospital duty, the discomfort, the suffering, interspersed with charming descriptions of pleasant interludes, and occasional philosophical soliloquies on the inhumanity of war.

Dr. Fordyce continued on to New York City and stayed that night with his cousin, George Fancher who lived at 239 West 54th Street, New York. He witnessed the race riots that plagued the city. He saw the hatred and the violence that brought death and destruction even to civilians. He wrote during the same time to his little girls, telling them of his visit to Central Park with its natural beauty.

On July 19, 1863, he left New York "to try the ocean," and to sail to Thibodeaux, Louisiana, where at Camp Weitzel he began his service as Assistant Surgeon of the 160th New York Volunteers. He saw duty at Camp Hubbard, near Thibodeaux, at LaFourche Crossing, the Marine Hospital in New Orleans. His letters bore date lines from Algiers, Berwick City, Centerville, Vermillion, Carion Crow Bayou near Opelousas, Vermillionville, New Iberia, New Orleans and Franklin....all in Louisiana.

In the Spring of 1864 he resigned his position; but his resignation was refused. In March of that year he received orders putting him in charge of the General Hospital in Franklin. He penned a letter to his family as he awaited transport on a steamer off New Orleans, near the mouth of the Red River. Then, ominously, on April 9, 1864, a statement dated at Mansfield, Louisiana, made the following declaration:

"I, the undersigned, Benj. A. Fordyce, Asst. Surgeon, 160th *NY Inf., swear and give my parole of honor that I will not in any way assist any force employed against the Confederate State of America until regularly exchanged and that I will not leave this town until ordered so to do."*

This terse statement reveals his capture by the Confederate Army during the battle of Mansfield under General Banks. It was not until June 19, 1864, seventy-one days later, that he was released and wrote to his wife to assure her that he was safe and to describe his incarceration during which time he had been caring for the sick and wounded in Confederate hospitals.

On July 19, 1864, he wrote to his wife from Fortress Monroe, Virginia, after having been transferred from New Orleans via ship. He had been moved to the Washington, D.C. area where combat was heavy. He penned letters to his family from Maryland and Virginia.... from such towns as Monocacy, Halltown, Berryville and Winchester as General Philip Sheridan led the campaign through the Shenandoah Valley. It was there that Dr. Fordyce' talents as a surgeon and hospital administrator were tested as he was called upon to treat the maimed survivors of the Battle of September 19, 1864, and later in the deadly battle of October 19, 1864, at Cedar Creek, Virginia, that signaled the ultimate end of the war.

After repeated applications for permission to return to his ailing family and to his responsibilities at home, Dr. Benjamin A. Fordyce was finally released from duty in February of 1865.

He returned to his home in Scipio, New York; and thus ended his War Years and the letters that we are privileged to read, thanks to the foresight of Emeline Slocum Fordyce.

Fordyce house on South Cayuga Street

In the Year 1865[4], Dr. Fordyce moved his family to Union Springs, New York to set up a practice of medicine. His two years as an Assistant Surgeon, had increased his proficiency as a competent physician and surgeon. He was a credit to his profession. He was forty-three years of age. His children were at the ages of fifteen, thirteen and six.

He purchased the grey stone, Greek Revival house on South Cayuga Street and placed his daughters in the Friends' Academy, Oakwood Seminary, to further their education. The girls later attended Howland College in Union Springs, where the Friends granted a degree to Stella in 1872, and to Abbie in 1874. Abbie continued her education in music at the College of Music of Boston University, graduating in 1877. As for "Little George", he later attended the Oakwood Seminary and then went on to study at Eastman's Business College at Poughkeepsie, New York.

Both Stella and Abbie were active in the social life of the community. On December 29, 1880, Stella was married in a gala wedding to Thomas Jefferson Yawger and went to live in his family home some three miles north of Union Springs in the red brick, Greek Revival house on the road to Cayuga. Newspaper notices of the wedding

Estella Fordyce Yawger

festivities indicate that upon their return from their wedding trip, they were entertained at a grand Military reception and serenade. Shortly thereafter, in 1881, Dr. Fordyce purchased the Dock at Union Springs, and supplementing his medical practice, went into business with his son-in-law, T. J. Yawger, while Estella's brother, George, was employed as Bookkeeper.

Although Dr. Fordyce returned to a successful and happy private life in 1865, the horrors of the conflict had been burned into his soul, as witness the message that he brought as he addressed the inhabitants of Union Springs celebrating Decoration Day in 1886.

Faded photographs of the Fordyce Family reveal the fragile beauty of Abbie; and one might ask of her romantic experiences. It is sad to find that Abbie did not marry.

Reminiscences reveal that love came to Abbie: a young artist offered her his heart. It was he who painted the oil portraits of both Dr. Benjamin and Emeline, his wife. But, Dr. Fordyce, the loving and protective father, did not welcome the thought of his daughter's marrying a starving artist, relegated his portrait to the attic and would not hear of the proposal. Thus dimmed the bloom of youth and expectancy that was apparent in early photographs of Abbie, to be replaced by a detached air of resignation. She devoted herself to

Abbie Fordyce

her music and her piano and influenced the lives of the young hopeful musicians of the community. Her love of children is apparent in the fact that she is credited with having translated children's stories from the German and published them in book form. Abbie's final years were spent at the home of her brother at Four North Cayuga Street; and when she had gone to meet her Maker, her tiny mutton-sleeved shirtwaists and bouffant skirts were packed away under the eaves in the attic.

The child, Little George, who is the subject of many of the letters between Dr. Fordyce and his wife, Emeline, was revealed as an alert and energetic child. His mother, it would appear, kept the image of his soldier-father always present in the child's consciousness; and Dr. Fordyce never failed to counsel his child in his letters, accompanying them with the affectionate request that he "eat an apple for Pa", that at least 99 kisses be bestowed upon him each day, and that his mother should bite his ear for his father, and most importantly, that he should be taught the value of honesty.

When Dr. Fordyce purchased the Dock at Union Springs, George, who by that time had completed his education at the Eastman Business School, became the bookkeeper for the Coal, Lumber and Grain Business.

George Slocum Fordyce   Marguerite Utt Fordyce

In 1893, during an epidemic of Scarlet Fever, George Fordyce contracted the disease. Dr. Fordyce cared for his son; and he, too, fell prey, dying on June 3, 1893.

Thus came to an end an era that had known the growth of a young country, its disruption by a cruel war, and its resurgence as it prepared for the new century. Gone was a vital force in the life of the Village of Union Springs. Stilled were his memories of the past. His alert mind would no longer influence the community.

It was left to George Fordyce to carry on the tradition of the family. He, like his father before him, was a public-spirited man, as evidenced by the offices to which he was elected and which he served throughout his lifetime. For five terms George Fordyce was Supervisor of the Town of Springport, starting in 1887 when he was the youngest member to hold office on the Board of Supervisors. During his last term he was named Chairman of the Board. He was at one time the Chairman of the Cayuga County Republican Committee. From 1898 to 1901 he served as New York State Assemblyman. From 1904 to 1908 he held the office of Sheriff of Cayuga County. Returning then to Union Springs, he served as Postmaster from 1908 to 1916. Other offices that he held included those of Justice of the Peace and President of the Village of Union Springs.

In 1891 George Fordyce had been married at Hopewell, Ontario County, New York, to a Union Springs native, Marguerite R. Utt, the daughter of William Utt. On April 4, 1896, Benjamin Allen Fordyce was born, to add another generation to the Fordyce Family name.

It was during this era that Four North Cayuga Street, Union Springs, became the home of George and "Maggie" Fordyce and their small son.[5]

Maggie was a dynamic woman....ebullient and generous; and the home became the scene of frequent entertaining. From the kitchen where ceiling-high cupboards lined the walls, issued delectable aromas in preparation for serving the guests as they met in the oak-paneled dining room. Ornate silver sparkled on snowy linen in the light from the brass chandelier suspended from the oaken beams overhead; and later, the rooms echoed to conversation over bridge in the living room.

But the pace of life was slowing. In 1937 George Fordyce, who had been in failing health, died. No longer would he sit and smoke his cigar in the cool shade of the wide front porch with the Greek columns that Ed Cater had added to the facade.

Maggie still drove the Packard car and baked biscuits for her neighbors. But life was not the same; and in 1946 she followed her husband, leaving Ben alone in the echoing rooms. It was then that he returned to his former friend, Virginia Trembly Franco. In 1947 they were married and efforts were made to refurbish the old home. The billiard room was transformed into a master bedroom with the family heirloom four-poster bed and its massive carved posts. Lost were the dark tones of the oaken dining room, disguised under a coat of green paint. Appearances were different; but....something had been lost. Age and health had failed the family; and no new, young spirit was found to breathe new life into the rooms.

Thus Ben found himself called upon to desert the old way of life that had been his for all the years that he could remember. The time had come to place the "For Sale" sign upon the lawn and to move to smaller quarters: the echoes of the Fordyce voices were stilled.

The Hecht Family moved to Four North Cayuga Street and their life was enriched by the spirit of the old house. It is hoped that the preservation of the writings of Dr. Fordyce and his Family will enrich the study of those years of conflict and perpetuate the name of Fordyce.

THE FORDYCE CEMETERY

Not far from the Fordyce Family homestead in Scipio is a small enclosure that surrounds the graves of many of the family members who have "passed on to the other side." It seems to indicate the survivors' desire to continue the living family relationship of love and sympathy.

The headstone of the first Benjamin Fordyce, who departed this life on March 1, 1819, bears the incised inscription:
Hark, from this Tomb
Mortal, I would not change my doom.
No, let my dusty relics rest,
Until I rise among the blest.

It is interesting to find that originally the last word of the third line had read *lie*, but was later crossed out with three scored lines and replaced with the rhyming word *rest*.

When Dr. Benjamin Fordyce died on December 10, 1870, his family placed a stone over his grave with the inscription:
He visited the poor when sick
Without fee or reward.

The untimely passing of Nathaniel Fordyce' first wife was marked by this epitaph:
Death cannot long divide
For it is not as if
The rose had climbed my garden wall
And blossomed on the other side.

And to John Horton Fordyce, lost on November 13, 1862, in the Civil War these words were simply inscribed:

Farewell, my friends, Farewell.

The Letters

Benjamin Allen Fordyce, M.D.
(January 13, 1823 - June 3, 1893)

A Note to the Reader:

In recording the Fordyce Family Letters, care has been taken to retain the spelling and punctuation of each letter: i.e. the use of a " - " in lieu of a period at the end of a sentence, the superscripted letters in recording dates, etc.

Mrs. Coulson's helpful and sometimes cryptic comments have been identified with brackets and her initials "LGC".

Comments by the editor are identified by the initials "LPH".

Chapter I
On to Battle

Let us travel with Dr. Fordyce as he leaves his little family - his wife Emeline, his daughters, Estella and Abbie, and son George, to serve his country. He takes the train to Albany, en route to New York City. During the week, while he waits for orders to Louisiana, he explores the city and describes for his children the beauty and wonders of the recently completed Central Park... describes his narrow escape from injury and involvement in the Draft Riots. He cherishes letters received from his family and prepares to "try the ocean", then pens a letter from Key West as he travels toward Louisiana on the troop ship.

Albany July 7th 1863

My dear wife

I am in Albany today at 3 1/4 P.M. all sound and right except somewhat sad - I left Mrs. Divine and Roxena at Fonda they were obliged to leave there we being on the express and wait for Mail Train as express does not stop at small places like Amsterdam - As I got off the cars in Albany judge of my pleasure when I saw news that Vicksburg actually surrendered July 4th - unconditionally - They are firing cannon here in Albany I think if I am any Judge of noise - Tonight they make a demonstration with cannon and Fireworks - they are now collecting money in this store in which I am writing for the purpose I have put up at the American Hotel on State St - have just retd from the Surgeon Genls office but he was not in and I could learn nothing definite there. I went to his private office but was gone out of the city - I left word that I would call at 7 P.M. today shall probably know then certain about the matter & will write you - I should feel very comfortable only for you and the little ones - You must keep up good cheer - Lee's Army is defeated and 28000 prisoners taken and the Albany Journal which I send you with this reports Long St. *[Longstreet?]* dead - Kiss all the children for me and tell the girls to kiss George for me fifty times - Tell them to be good and I will send them something first rate sometime and will remember them every hour in the day

I am on Broadway looking out and see a horse car now passing one continued noise and rumble of carriages teams & people is heard really my head aches with the noise - dogs growling people talking, walking, running, &c but I must close will write tomorrow

I am as ever most Truly your husband Benj A. Fordyce

P.S. As soon as I know that I shall be in one place long enough to receive a letter from you I will let you know

━━━━━━

To Dr. B. A. Fordyce, Care of George S. Fancher, No. 239 West 54th Street, New York City.

Venice July 8th/63

My dear father

We are all well and hope you are the same Abbie and I cleaned the office yesterday we took the Legers and piled them together and scrubbed the floor with sand and soap so it looks neater than I ever saw it before Last night when Mr Divine brought the news that Vicksburg was taken they fired the anvil and rang the bell and some of the men said that they were going to send for Mr Bennett to pull the rope and Mr Hoffman said that he had ought to be made to pull the rope so his feet wouldnt touch the floor *[Bell in the Baptist Church at Stewart's Corners. LGC]* Carrie has just come in panting and out of breath with your letter I have just kissed George one hundred and fifty times for you I kissed him so much that he began to pull my hair and pinch my cheek and say it hurts Stelle it hurts I asked him what I should write to Pa for him and he said tell Pa Abraham Linkum president he says you eat all the Backer out of his box Grandma is over here now and we don't feel bad a bit that you are gone since Vicksburg is captured and 28,000 prisoners. We had a swarm of bees today and Ma hived them. George says that the photograph in the parlor is Pas pograph. Aunt Maria *[Slocum, sister of Emeline]* and Uncle Theodore *[Jump, her husband]* have just gone from here they think they never saw a photograph more natural than yours Mother is not exactly suited with the frame - she thinks that she will change it for the $4 one. It is now nine o'clock and I must finish by saying Good bye for tonight.

———————

Venice, July 9th 63

My dear father

George has just turned all the Ink out of the bottle on the floor and stand - he took holed of the bottle and was a little spunky   spilled it all he says Pa has gone to Albany to war he don't call Ma anything but Em. Well our folks have just called Abbie and I to breakfast the second time and we must go. (After breakfast) I have just come in from the Cherry Tree I have been getting George and Frank all the Cherries they could eat and that was a good many I hear Abbie and George talking about feeding the Chickens. How we wish you were here to eat some of these large Cherries in the garden which I can see from the window where I am writing Pa we all want you to have some small photographs taken Carrie and Grandma say they want one very much indeed. When we went to call George to supper we found him clean up on the woodpile Well, I must close my letter for Ma wants to write.

I remain your affectionate daughter, Estelle.

PS. Pa, please keep my letter so I can see when you come home if my last ones are any better than my first

My dear dearest husband

We are all well but lonesome   it dont seem possible but what you will come home today it seems now as though you had been gone a year, as soon as you left I sent Firm[an] after mother Father came after her Friday I dont think that I can stay here any longer than until we can get the crops secure. This keeping house without a man, ain't, so funny. As Estelle has written all the news there is not much for me to write - we are expecting to hear of a heavy battle every day as the rebels cannot cross the Potomac as yet   Captain Mead was dangerously wounded in the breast he is in Auburn now Lieutenant Murdock rec'd a shock *[shot?]* but did not quit the field.[6] Venice raised three boxes of dried fruit three of bandage and clothing and $205 in money that is doing first rate. Your father *[Dr. Benjamin Fordyce]* and Theodore *[Jump]* just went from here. T. says he would let the black mare run in the pasture two or three months - thinks she will be worth more money for it   Mr Kniffin brought back that bill you let him have he said he took it to the bank and they said it was counterfeit   the name of the bill was Southbridge bank Massachusetts I did not take it but told him I would write to you about it   Firm finishes hoeing corn tomorrow - thinks he will begin the grass by the middle of the week   I have just put George to bed he says will pa shoot Congdons cow he said this morning will pa come to bed with George and ma won't that be pretty fun he says twenty times a day I wish pa would come home. It has been very hot and dry since you left until to day which is cool enough to have a fire no rain since you went away. Temperance meeting to night and the girls have gone. Oh Benjamin you can't begin to imagine how lonesome it is I miss you at the office barn desk and table there has but 3 waggons stoped here since you left   they were my father's your father's and Theodore. My throat feels quite bad I dreamed last night that you put your finger down my throat & said there was something that would have to be cut out if so I shall have to go to New Orleans to have it done. Now Benj....do all the good you can take all the comfort you can be sure and get you a Bible & write when you think you can read & I will ours and I will try with the help of the Lord to be a better woman take good care of yourself be careful about your diet and write about every thing you think will be interesting to us

Monday evening

I have been to Auburn today changed the frame bought me a dress cloak and bonnet. I have heard that Dr. *[Cyrus]* Powers *[of Moravia; in Civil War Service]* is sick & coming home as soon as you get to New Orleans there are 10,000 sick and wounded there I dreamed last night that I was to New Orleans with you doing picket duty you must send for me if you think best. Co. Col Stewart has gone to Port Royal with his wife I have heard of two different physicians that were coming here Dr. E. Mead and Goodel write what you think I had better do with the stock and place house & as it is so lonesome I cant possibly stay here. you know how the yard drifts in the winter and know one to break it out, it would be bad for the girls to get to school you must excuse bad spelling Composition I will try to better every time come home as soon as you can

From your affectionate wife, E. Fordyce

(PS) Dr. *[D.R.]* Pearl *[of Sherwood]* has gone to Gettysburg to take care of the sick and wounded

(PS} Henry Hallet, musician and Lewis Bothwell's son were killed at Gettyburg

239 West 54th St

Geo. L. Fanchers residence

New York July 10th 1863. 11.o'clock am

My dear wife

A few moments since I arrived at the residence of Cousin Geo. and am very much pleased with my reception - They appear really glad to see me which you know is gratifying to me - George arrived in town last evening from the west and learned on his way of my business, etc I find them all well and living in a beautiful situation; building of fine marble front, and finished and furnished in fine style - I am well have put up at Earles Hotel Canal St - I really wish you and the girls were here a spell with me - I have not seen anything of the city yet although I have been through 6th Avenue some five miles - There is altogether too much to see to enable me say I have seen anything - you know we used to say Bannon knows so much that he is almost an idiot - It is so with me there is all to see & but little time to see it I have not done anything at the business yet Will attend to it this P.M - I believe I stated in my last that I have rec'd all the papers and am ordered to report to the Med. Director at New Orleans immediately - I must obey orders you know and as soon as I learn what transportation will be given me and how soon I must leave I will write again and let you know - I think I shall remain here long enough to hear from you Write immediately on rect of this - Direct to Dr. B. A. Fordyce - New York City Care of Geo. S. Fancher No. 239. W. 54th St

The War News is still cheering - Mrs. Fancher and Lilly both send their love to you all - Be of good cheer - and see to things and arrange things to please yourself -

The accounts that are not settled have John call on and get into notes etc as soon as consistent Dont let out the office or let my books be scattered if you can help - My deep abiding love to you & George Kiss him for me & bite his ear a little nice for me. The girls I will write to on next page - Please express my strong friendship and affection for all my friends and let my enemies go down South and I will meet them there-
        Most truly your husband   Benj. A. Fordyce

---

239 West 54th St
Geo. L. Fancher's residence
New York City July 12th 1863
My dear wife and children

I trust you will not be surprised that I should write every day or almost every day - I went yesterday to the Asst Quarter masters to get transportation to New Orleans but found that I can not go probably for a week to come - Now Emeline if you would like to come to New York before I go come immediately on recpt of this; start so as to take the evening train from Auburn say Wednesday evening take a through ticket by Hudson River road and land at 30th st New York. I will be at the Depot on Thursday when you arrive - Lydia and George say be sure and write for you to come - If you feel that you can leave the children safe and comfortable be sure and come - Write by first mail whether you can come or not before you start, you will start in the afternoon to Auburn in cool part of day and come down in the night which will be best probably - If you come bring money enough for what you may need for purchases &c a satchel or trunk as you choose so you can bring a little more Maple Sugar - My can of catsup by knocking the trunk around burst but I happened to discover it before my clothes were injured and very fortunate too - Do as you think best about coming - be assured I should like to see you -

Now a little for the girls and my little George (I wish you could all come) I have been in the Central Park today - it is near George's house - the Park contains 980 acres of land and is the principal grand reservoir of the Croton river Aqueduct - The reservoir contains 112 acres of land besides many secondary reservoirs or little lakes. These are made crooked all dug out some places the rocks blasted out to make it deep enough. In the park the land is very rocky where the park is situated great rocks rise to the height of twenty feet above the surface of the ground Thus this kind of rock form hills all over the whole park - now some of these hills are graded down by blasting the rocks and drawing on earth and ground for carriage roads or for foot paths or equestrian roads that is persons riding on horse-back - I wrote above you observe wagons no common wagons are allowed in the park such as lumber wagons Peddlers carts or grocers wagons they are immediately ordered out and shown the way - There are fifty men who are styled Park Police who have no other business than to take charge of and overlook this Park they perform no manual labor only business is to watch visitors and see that they keep hands off - not one leaf is allowed to be picked from the thousands of shrubbery planted there by authority of the City Park Director - This shrubbery is so thick in different parts as to look like woods and so very close that you can not see through it, all interlaced or marked with the neatest kind of foot paths all graded and graveled in the finest order winding around in various directions so as to give the most extensive view and please the eye of the Visitor The carriage roads many times cross over the foot paths also over the equestrian roads by the most beautiful bridges made of brick stone and carved Marble of the most beautiful workmanship I ever saw - one was carved to represent birds of various kinds many kinds of fruits were carved on the corner posts of these bridges - some had iron railings gilded in different parts to attract attention Some of the bridges are 100 ft. through under them that men and women ride some are narrower some have jets of water running all the time under in niches the arched walls Their beauty is conceded by all visitors I believe to surpass anything in the world of bridge kind: one bridge is blasted out of or directly through the rock more than 200 ft - there are several of this kind but no others that I saw so large - In other parts were deer fenced in a yard looking happy - then in a cage there were five eagles and in others other kinds of birds of very beautiful colors one as large as a common hen with long tail feathers of scarlet and orange the body and tail feathers The wings bright blue with a tuft of orange feathers on the top of head (very large head). In the water generally of the park there are fish of several varieties except in the reservoir for family use in this there is probably no living thing The water looks as pure as the finest well water in there All under the roads are large sewers or Ditches made of mason work so that it can never be muddy these come to the surface every two or three rods and are covered with Iron grates - No water can possibly stand on it I should think the number of visitors yesterday on the grounds must have been 25,000 perhaps 50,000 - The whole of the roads and passages were teeming with human life and horses and carriages numberless to me. To Estella and Abbie from your Father - PS I will write in your names if ma comes.

Now Emeline, if you can come get your father and mother to stay with the children at our house and set out at once - pay no attention to your baggage except to take a check for it to N.Y. City - it will come all right - I am well and shall be pleased to see you.

Most truly your husband Benj. A. Fordyce

No. 239. West 54th St
New York City 5 o'clock A.M.
July 18th 1863

My dear wife,

You cannot judge of the pleasure your and the girls letters gave me
last night on my return from the lower part of the City - I have
returned from the Post Office a distance of four miles where I had
been thinking there might be some mistake in my directions to you
where to direct your letters - I had not heard a single word from
home before and thought I should be obliged to leave without
hearing from you, as I am to put my baggage on the Steamer
Continental at 3 PM. today and may not be able to come on shore
again in New York She is a noble looking Vessel and made her last
trip in 6 days - How glad I am to hear that you are all well and to
receive a letter from Estella and my little Abbie and also to hear
from my little smoker George. Has he got any Bakker in his pipe
and does he want a fire - I want to answer a few things in your letter
and will try & write a separate letter to the girls if I can - I am really
glad you did not start to come here - I should have telegraphed to
you next day but the wires were nearly all torn down in the city the
Rail Road track torn up every means of access to the city cut off -
The Hud. Riv R.R. trains stopped at Yonkers 15 miles above the city
till Thurs P.M and then there were but very few who ventured into
the City - I was at the Depot when the train came in and nearly
every train till I recd your letters - I should have written but I feared
you had started and mails were cut off - I will describe what I saw
of the mob after noticing some things you wrote to me about - Be
careful to have your haying done in as good weather as you can select
- Fortune has favored this city for two nights past it has rained in
torrents - Rainy weather is bad hay weather usually you know - Oh,
it is rumored that Charleston is captured and even published in
some papers - I wish I had some of your good fresh cherries; be
careful to have George spit out the pits - *[Pretty late for that advice! LGC]*
The money paid Mr. Kniffin - I cannot remember anything what bill
it was or how it looked - I think it was an eastern bill and it is my
impression that the name of the Bank was put on with red ink still
I will not be certain. If from his statements you think he had the
bill of me be sure and pay it taking the bill back, this will be just -

About the stock I think I would dispose of it, either at Auction or private sale; advise with your father about it; you can keep it mostly till fall I think and have perhaps better opportunities of selling it. Now about going to your Fathers to live act your own judgement about that - my impression is that it will be best for you if your parents will be satisfied with such an arrangement but be sure and have Firman move in our house should you do so - Sell or keep the black mare as may be thought best but be sure and dispose of the other horses - if you go to your fathers - Port Hudson has surrendered I will get some small photographs today and get George to send them to you - be sure and give one to Carrie and John & Nelson and anyone else you choose - remember my relatives - I shall get a small bible today - The Drs you say are coming there will both suit me if I ever practice in Venice again.

3-1/2 P.M I have just returned from the Steamer and learn that she will leave tomorrow morning at 7 o'clock A.M. - I have had the Photograph taken. They will be ready Monday and George and his wife who have been remarkably kind to me will keep one or two and send the remainder to you, either by express or mail I had 2 doz taken full size and 2 positions cost $3.50 the whole. I have just bought me a Bible and blankets &c Please give such of your friends as you choose a picture and if there is a spare one that you do not want remember Mrs. Betsey Whitman [of Genoa] - Estella and Abbie must each have one - & George Everything is quiet today and I should think it ought to be with 12000 soldiers and citizens to keep it so - All well armed too - The number of rioters has been greatly exaggerated and the character of them also They are [the] hardest lot of low mean Irish that any person can conceive of - They look as if rioting, stealing, arson and Murder would be but idle pastimes and pleasing amusements - The Herald calls them the people of New York If these are a fair sample of the people God deliver me from any association with people hereafter -

Now for what I saw and know - I intended to have sent a description to the Auburn Journal for Publication but did not seem to have time

Monday Morning July 13th - I got up as usual and went out on the walk at about 7-1/2 oclock - I soon noticed that there was a host of men coming down the old Bloomingdale road now Broadway (you can see it on the map I sent Abbie) from Central Park which I described to you in my last - They turned into 54th St and come directly towards me - Well I knew nothing of their intentions - They were dressed with pants red and blue shirts no vest or coat heavy ditching boots old Hats and caps and all their clothing very dirty their faces and arms very black and dirty sleeves rolled up each one or nearly all of them flourishing a stick of some kind and talking loud one or two going ahead yet mingling with the mass to give orders - Their numbers filled the street for two blocks and more were at this time from 500 to 800 in number - Well being a little inquisitive I wanted to know what the trouble was, so out I went among them. Says I, Hello, boys what is up? a strike? "By H—l says one to me, it's a schtrike at the Damd Draft." - I could see a little clearer then and thought at first I would keep quiet - Mr. Fancher came home soon after this and we concluded we would know what was done - so we sallied out and found they had crossed on 54th St to 8th Avenue there dividing into squads sending some to 9th 10th 7th 6th avenues others in other directions to all the public works, to compel the workmen & teamsters to join them - This they did in almost every instance.

Those who persistently refused to join them were sure to be seriously maltreated afterwards   Their houses burned or themselves beaten and injured in some very cruel manner - The mob at this time became organized with a full quorum to do business - The Cheers and yells that rent the air from this time always indicated their whereabouts in the day time and even in the night for the first two days and nights - The order was then given to proceed to the Marshall Office, No. 677 3rd Avenue and such yelling and swinging of clubs were enough to shock any native Indian - Down to the Marshalls office they went and Mr. Fancher and I followed them *[BAF never wanted to "miss any thing!" LGC]* hearing them tell what they should do - soon we came in sight of the building a fine three story brick block part of it four story made into five houses and occupied by a large number of families except this front Corner room which was used for an office and there the great offense was being committed of Drafting the paure mann because he has no money, say $300 to pay the draft so say the mob (no the Heralds and Worlds people) - Well they broke in and took the men operating the wheel & business and we saw them throw one out of a two story window and then pound him almost to death - By

---

this time they had obtained and torn up the books and papers and fired the building - This was done by pouring camphene upon the floor and among the papers and by applying a lighted match the building would be enveloped in flames in a moment - The mob then being several thousand in number would not allow a fireman to come near it to put it out till nearly the whole block was burned indeed only one house was saved - George thought we could go nearer with safety so we kept working along down towards the fire till we were within some twenty rods on an open space before the building - At this time Supt Decker of the fire department had so far quieted the (Heralds people) mob that they consented to let the firemen stop the fire - The engines run in immediately some five or six in number Now just at this instant when all was growing quiet some policemen some fifty in number injudiciously rushed in with clubs knocking the Heralds people over the head which made the said people very indignant, but they run finely and took a direction toward us, you better believe we ordered a retreat in double quick divesting ourselves of all cumbersome baggage; at about the time we arrived at a place where we thought it safe to halt we discovered that the Police had passed the entire center of the peoples line and that the people had formed around behind them most thoroughly armed and equipped with stones brickbats and clubs and had routed them completely and that they (the police) were making a rapid retreat directly toward us and the people following up their advantage most vigorously pelted them awfully knocking some down that we saw one of whom I afterwards learned was killed - We thought it would be prudent for us, at this juncture to leave the field to the combattants and you may rest assured we were quite peace-loving men for a time particularly when we realized that a ball from a revolver of the Police passed within two feet of us - We commenced a vigorous retreat but found ourselves wholly surrounded with the combattants lines - Then all we had to do was to escape by attracting as little observation as possible - We succeeded and then went to Dinner. We returned in the afternoon nothing daunted with our former risks - When we arrived we found Bulls Head Hotel burning set on fire because Allenton was said to be a Republican and had secreted some of the drafting papers which last was not true - They tried to break open his safe which contained some $25,000 but the fire came so hot they were obliged to desist - The money was found all right after the fire burned down - Then they went to the Negro orphan Asylum and gave them a few minutes notice that they must take the children out which done just in time to save all but one or two. It is said the firemen got one out - About this time they entered a negro dwelling in this vicinity and beat them brutally - The Heralds peoples boys going up stairs while their parents were beating the grown negroes and finding a little negro baby then they threw it out of a 3 story window on the pavement dashing it to pieces killing it instantly so a gentleman informed me who was there and saw it - But the Military I will not give any more particulars except to say that they burned a house directly across the st. from George's when I was sleeping and threatened the house in this block only through the wall from my room. I sat up two nights to help watch it - they did not offer any disturbance When I first went to the H.R. R.R. Depot after you on Thursday before the trains were running through a great big stout negro came running for his life into the door saying they were after him. He quivered like a beef knocked down for slaughter; no hat; barefooted, and they - the People - sacking his house - There were only two other persons beside me in the Depot at the time and they were acquainted with the premises - Says I, boys hide him and they did hide him and agreed to feed him, but the poor fellow could not eat a mouthful - at night when he could be removed safely he was properly cared for & is safe.

PS - Read this to your Father and my Father & tell them as soon as I have time will write to them - Yrs - Benj.

[letter ends here, but a piece of a letter - follows,-may be the end of this one. LGC]:

The Military, as I said before, quiet things down very fast particularly when they point their cannon loaded with "Grape and Canister (not blank cartridge any more) right towards them and fire when they see a pile of the People laying dead from one discharge they are apt to scatter a little - The citizens are just beginning to see the justice of shooting a large share of the Heralds People and how they the citizens boil with ill suppressed rage when they speak of their delays in putting down this "excitement of the People" (Herald) by shooting every one of them -

I could not with any safety put on an article of clothing having military appearances or — One poor soldier was pounded to death by this Union loving People. They became much excited about the draft. He had not done the least thing to imitate them, only wearing Soldiers clothes. But I must stop and write a letter for the girls.

Kiss George tonight for me 100 times.

Tomorrow at 7 o'clock I leave New York to try the Ocean - In a fine Vessel my stateroom and all right - everything very nice - I must stop - Remember me to all, my wife, whom I have any reason to respect I remain as ever most truly your husband.

Benj. A. Fordyce

On Board Continental Off Key West
Sunday July 26th 1863

My dear wife

Thinking I might get a line to you from here quicker than from New Orleans I avail myself of this opportunity of writing a few lines - I will give you a little summary of my progress thus far and reserved the particulars for my next letter - I am now in excellent health and spirits today indeed the best I have been since I left Venice - I came on board the Continental one Week today at 8 o'clock A.M. at 11 o'clock we moved off from New York Harbor This you know is my first salt water sailing - Weather very fine - Ocean still and quiet - yet I am satisfied from what observation I have had of it that there is considerable water in it -

Some of the passengers were sick in two or three hours but I felt quite well in that respect - At 3 P.M. saw a fine school of Porpoise - roll and tumbling in the water - but of the description part I will write when I have more time There are four surgeons beside myself on board Two belonging to the Navy who both appear to be talented men One quite advanced in yrs has been in the Navy twenty-two years is now reading at the other end of the table while I am writing Three others Captain Leuts and Ensighn are writing at the table with me - Our Lieut Kelly of the 160th is writing across the table from me he is now returning to service after recovery from a severe wound through the arm - A fine Irishman too I can assure you - Of the other Navy Surgeon he is young but a man of fine talent - two Army Surgeons on board I can not speak from my acquaintance with them, so highly of - I think I should rather remain in good health than to fall into such hands dangerously wounded or very sick - There are some twenty-five Military and Naval Officers on board with me - and generally a fine good hearted class of men Yet I have seen as talented men around my own home as a large majority of them - On the whole I must write how I like ocean life - I think I am getting too old to learn to be a sailor now - Sunday 19th got along well but could not eat much - more 20th about the same and paying one dollar 50 cents per day for board it was a bit dull to me - Slept middling well however - Tues 21st did not feel so well - all the others were sick who were not used to sailing by this time. *[Perhaps passing Cape Hatteras. LGC]* Quite a breeze day yet the Seamen said it was very fine weather - No land in sight - We towed a schooner to Key West - loaded with cattle and sheep - The schooner rolled so that we had to slacken our speed to about 4 miles per hour whereas we had been running 10 miles I did not really understand how they could call this fine weather - I felt a little qualmish At night relieved my stomach of my supper and felt better - *[Letter ends here -LGC]*

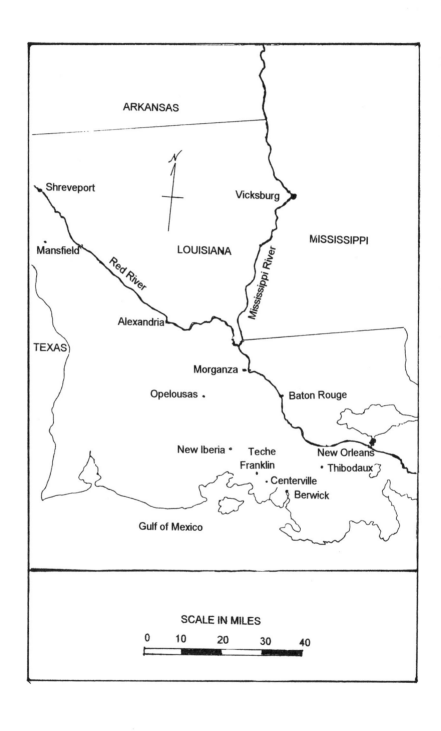

ARKANSAS

Shreveport

Vicksburg

MISSISSIPPI

Mansfield

LOUISIANA

Red River

Mississippi River

Alexandria

TEXAS

Morganza

Opelousas

Baton Rouge

New Iberia

Teche

Franklin

New Orleans

Centerville

Thibodaux

Berwick

Gulf of Mexico

SCALE IN MILES

0   10   20   30   40

Chapter II
Initiation at Thibodeaux, Louisiana

Dr. Fordyce arrives at his first assignment at the hospital near Thibodeaux, Louisiana and describes his surroundings and the scenes of suffering. From LaFourche he writes of the skirmishes that threaten; then describes the diet that he occasionally enjoys to supplement the meager fare of toast, tea and fruit from the bountiful box received from home. He describes his meeting and friendly relations with the inhabitants of the town. Dr. Fordyce receives a letter of advice from Dr. Cyrus Powers, a native of Moravia, NY, and former acquaintance now stationed in the service in New Orleans. A letter to Parents-in-Law Slocum graphically describes conditions as they exist at LaFourche Crossing, LA.

Camp Weitzel Thibodeaux La-
August 3rd 1863

My dear wife

I arrived here yesterday in first rate health - Be assured they were all glad to see me or I am greatly deceived by appearances - We have a comfortable building for hospital purposes - Dr. Armstrong is a very fine man has been alone through all the battles at Port Hudson. He is worn out and quite unwell with Diarrhea the great complt of this climate - I have seen Jo Wood - Elwood Fell - Capt. Corning - Beebe, Ogden, Jim Haylett's boy too and many others - all well - Dan'l Wing is dead, died at Port Hudson from wounds recd at the assault - Tell James Cannon that I have got Danls watch from the express office and find it all right - so Jo says - Tell him that I can sell it here for all it is worth and more too and that if he thinks best I will sell it and send him the money for it - I think this will be best as the cost of sending it back will be considerable I will do just as he shall direct - Take good care of yourself and my little ones - Kiss my little George & the girls often for me - I am very careful in my diet and attribute my good health to this - I cannot write a long letter because the man is waiting to carry this to New Orleans - I was mustered into service Sat Aug 1st but could not get mustered back of 29th of July but shall bring a bill for services rendered on Continental -

May not get any pay before 29th however - Shall find no difficulty in getting a horse at very little or no expense saddles etc -

I am doing well I think & the boys of the 75th are only a few rods from us the 114th N.Y. are close to us also - The officers are all first rate fellows they are all or seem to be pleased to get acquainted with me - They are all good - first rate fellows -

I must close. I am as ever most truly and affectionately your husband.

> Benj. A. Fordyce
> Asst. Surg. 160th N.Y.S.V.
> New Orleans La.
> To follow regiment

This is the address

My compliments to all.

/

Venice Aug 11th [1863]

My dear husband

You cannot judge of the pleasure your letter gave us yesterday Monday 10th It had been three weeks since you left New York and now you are safe in New Orleans or near there and five weeks to day since you left home - it seems five years - We are all well - I have spraint my ancle can hardly step on my foot and it is very purple - we are having a very heavy thunderstorm - the girls are on the bed hoops off and George is helping me write as he did you by putting papers and pens in the lamp - he has got your ruler, drawing it across the chair and says he is sawing wood - George says tell papa I am a naughty boy - We are having almost war at home - there are about

100 copperheads near Beardsleys corners that have commenced cutting down Union poles - they cut one at five corners *[Five Corners, Town of Genoa]* and last Saturday night were a going to cut the one at Beardsleys Corners - the union men met and organized a company elected their officers got the cannon from Genoa and when they came fired into them first with nothing but powder and then with shot killing two - William Kenndall, union man wounded in the ancle - I shall have to stop writing to night for George is altogether too much help -

Wednesday eve - I have heard today that the Beardsleys Corners riot is all a hoax but they are expecting trouble - I have had the oats cut today Firm, Curtain, and Mr. Kniffin cut them - they had to be mowed - I pay Curtain in pork, Kniffin in oats - the oats were flat to the ground, occasioned by the great storm we had *[May be the time of the "great July 21, 1863 flood" in Moravia. LGC]* Giles *[Slocum, her brother]* was over Sunday and offered me ninety dollars for bullet and colt two heifer it would be fifty dollars for bullet & colt $25 for the 3 year old heiffer and fifteen dollars for the yearling he said if I could get any more to sell them - write what you think is best to do - Mrs. Wilson has a fine boy Ira Fish has paid his bill it was 12 shillings *[$1.54]* - I heard before you got to New Orleans that Dr. Powers was going into a hospital as soon as you got there he would not be needed in the regiment any longer so I see by your letter that you are not agoing to be together (you know he wrote he wanted someone he could depend upon) I want you to write all the particulars was you much sea sick have you got to get a horse do you find things as you expected have you used any of your dried fruit do you want anything from home. I have had company today - Mrs Bateman Mrs Jennings & Divine Mary Strong Livina Baldwin we have had works folks or company ever since you left the neighbors think I had better stay here but I cannot keep house without a husband we should all go to destruction. Now Benjamin be careful of your diet do not eat to many (peaches and grapes) I think if that is a going to be your fare I shall soon go to New Orleans What about that Signor judgement - had we better collect it John has not settled any accounts since you left Tom Howland and Fish are all the ones that have paid me any money since you left. Harvey Low daughter is very low - not expected to live - the one that was sick when we were there - it is very healthy now not any sickness since you left Maidy

---

Bennett they say has lost her palate you cannot understand her any better than you can Dia Warring Thursday morning: every time George gets into the parlor he has to see Pa and kiss him he wanted I should bite his ear a little this morning for pa write how you like camp life and what you have to eat and how much it cost you to get to New Orleans I want to hear some of the particulars about yourself I have made 4 nice looking cheese our folks are perfectly willing I should go and live with them think they would not be contented to have us stay here this winter the girls could go to school much more. I sent you a letter last week directed it right except to follow the regiment you may not get it you must excuse all mistakes every letter I have written has been after bed time From your ever faithful wife

Emeline

(PS) the papers state that we can send mail down the Mississippi full as safe and quicker write what you think about it and how to direct we have received only six photographs how I wish you could see my flowers (people ride slow by the house so as to look at them) when are you coming home

———————

Hospital 160th Regt N.Y.V
Camp Hubbard near Thibodeaux La
Sunday night Aug 16th 1863 -

My dear wife and children

Not yet having heard a word from home since I left NY I feel sure you must have heard from me and no doubt have written to me

I am well and enjoy myself as well as any man can away from his family with the expectation of remaining away for a long time - I am very well situated at present in a large building (without windows or doors except such as we have put in since I came here) which we use for a hospital - By perseverance we have obtained iron bedsteads and ticks filled with husks for our sick and for ourselves - The good women of the country have furnished to the sanitary commission for the use of the sick cotton sheets shirts and drawers pillows and cases and dried fruits and thousands of luxuries for the sick which we begin to receive in abundance - You can have no idea of the great benefit it is to the poor sick barefooted sore, lame, soldiers, of our noble army - I arrived at the Brigade just after their return from Port Hudson - some of them barefooted with clothes worn out legs swollen with sores and poisoned in the weeds and bushes of the long hard marches they had made some with wounds just healing their numbers thinned by the casualties of that very memorable siege - some so sick that they are occasionally dying from the diseases and privations of that campaign - Yet when I talk with the men it does me good to hear the sentiments expressed from their great Loyal hearts and to see the glow of pride on the manly cheek when they boast that they were of Genl Weitzels Brigade which did so much of the hard fighting at Port Hudson and on the Tesche - No money could buy the remembrance of the part they acted in those battles from them - Regiments vie with eachother and even companies in claiming deeds of valor on those sanguinary fields - They count their losses nothing compared to the great gain to our countrys cause -

Aug 17 It was late last night so I went to bed on an Iron Bedstead with a good husk bed and mattress cotton sheets and good woolen blankets pillow &c as comfortable as usual at home much better than the old lounge on which I have slept so much - But much as at home I had just got fairly asleep when one of the soldiers in hospital was attacked with a severe convulsion screaming with pain waking all in the hospital and insensible himself - throwing himself in all shapes requiring three attendants to hold him - I gave him chloroform till his system relaxed and then we could manage him as easily as a child - We were obliged to repeat the operation in a short time - He is comfortable tonight We had a man die in our hospital last P.M He was an old drunkard and had been paid a few days before and of course the sutters gave him whisky for money this brought on incurable diarrhea the prevailing disease of this climate - He had been unable to do duty for two months before in consequence of Whisky but some of them will not learn anything - Peterson died in this way at Baton Rouge on the 4th July - We made arrangements to have his effects go to Wm Babcocks wife If I can arrange it will learn what there is and if can will have it forwarded to them - We had one man shoot himself by accident the first day I arrived here - ball passing through his liver, right lung heart & spine - One died suddenly yesterday in the 114th N.Y.V. The surgeon was absent I was called to see him he was dead when I got there - Post Mortem this AM found liver & spleen softened & enlarged c - I am invited to-morrow to assist in reamputating two rebels legs - about three & a half miles from here I have been to see them today - They are Texans one I think will die - I have bought me a nice dark gray 4 yr old horse saddle and bridle sound and smart as steel for $100. The officers say I have one of the best and certainly the cheapest horse in the Regiment - He is real pretty I can assure you and as kind as a Kitten - The boys say there is not a horse can outrun him in the Regiment - I think much of him for he was at Port Hudson - I have never been on his back yet but I have an orderly who is as proud of him as of his eyes he rides him every day - I do not seem to have a minutes time to ride - I look for easier times soon - I will ride him tomorrow or next day unless I am in duty every minute - I have a nice little nigger about 14 yrs old he blacks my boots cleans my room brings in my vituals takes off his hat when he comes in all right I can assure you - If he is honest I shall keep him and perhaps bring him home with me - I can get forty only say the word - Many of them are smart I must write you every thing I think of - I eat no meat - I have that dried fruit and it comes good I can assure you that Currant Jelly reminds me often of the friends who gave it - And the maple sugar be sure and save me some and I will send for a list of articles sometime that you can send me by express as safe and sure as you could send it to Auburn I had for supper tonight - Soup Chicken good too - toast bread some excellent cheese good butter sweet potatoes fried onions - Excellent tea sugar & milk - So I did not get up from the table very hungry - I often think of you all and many times wish I had all your photographs so that I could see something occasionally how you all look - There that little crosseyed George I fear he will grow out of my remembrance almost   If you can send me likenesses I should really like to see them - put them up very thin if you conclude to send them - My girls be sure & write me often - Write often Emeline - I work with a strong heart and hand almost every hour from 5 a.m. to 9 p.m. and am crowded all the time - I do not go out the hospital to see any sick in my Regt - I order them brought in - Give my love to all our friends - don't forget it for you Benj. A. Fordyce

We shall remain here probably two months or more - I have got a table and six chairs my trunk here - A Marble top wash stand all once rebel property but put in the hospital now. I will write every week whether I hear from you or not - Shall write to your folks soon

———————

Venice August 19th 1863

My dear father
Carrie was here last night and stayed all night. She has went away now. George is at my desk pulling his teeth he says he has pulled "too teef-fibe teef." He has been crying to get on the desk to get a pen. the other day we went to feed the chickens and George said "I always feeds my chickens anyway." the last lesson that we got in Geography was about Asia physical Geography. I think we will get through our Geography this summer although school is to keep only two or three weeks from this week. Julia Fanny is going to have a picnic down to the lake a week from today and I guess Fanny is going to have one too. George bothered me so that I came upstairs where I guess he won't find me right off. If he does come I will hide somewhere where he won't find me. Stell and I have played chess quite a good deal this week George has to play to Stell is more than a match for me I guess. The flowers are all in blossom the beds in front of the house look a great deal better than any of the rest because you fixed them. The china aster I think you ought to see there are double pink ones double purple and blue ones and double purple ones With white centers and double red ones and I dont know what all. but I must close my letter for it is most eleven o'clock and the stage comes in at eleven

Yours truly, Abbie Fordyce

Abbie and George have blotted this paper so she cannot write a very long letter and she says she can't think of anything more to write. Stella Fordyce

[half of 2nd pg cut off, including the "blots"! LGC]

———————

Venice   August 27th 1863

My dear father

Mother dont leave Abbie and I hardly any room to write in her letters so we are going to write ourselves I read Johns letter this morning from you saying you hadnt heard a word from home since you left New York and we think it strange because we have written five letters to you I guess when they come they will come thick and fast. Ma and Cynthia have gone Blackberrying and Abbie George and I are staying at home   George is lying on the lounge and Abbie has just come in from out doors George asks Abbie where she has been and Abbie says she has been to the brook and George wants her to go down there again so he can go with her and whip the water. I am not going to build up any fire today for fear of doing some mischief as I did when our folks went to Moravia   There is not any school today because Mr Manchesters people are going to have company. Abbie and I are not going to Sherwoods Corners to live we are going to live in the Office and pull teeth for a living and we won't pull black peoples teeth either but we will pull hogs teeth. I expect I will have to pull the first one for myself because I have got one that is decayed. Mr Mason was here sunday night and I gave him my photograph I have just come in from riding horseback I rode up east by Mrs Wheats and Mary Snyder was riding and she rode with me and we rode on a Canter nearly all the time. Aunt Maria and Addie and Libbie Howell were here this afternoon. Mrs Moe is dead and is buried tomorrow. Pa if you get to drinking with them Officers ...I won't claim you as my Father when you come home. Most everyone says you don't know how lonesome I am without the Dr I don't know what I shall do if any of my family are sick they talk as if they thought there never was such a man as you and I don't believe there ever was many.

Aug. 28th

George says he is going to ride on the water and is going to New Orleans to war where Pa is the Rebels won't get him he is teasing for pen and paper to write to Pa and I have got to get it as I won't have any peace I asked George what I should tell Pa for him and he says tell him I am a nice boy but I don't think he is he is so michievous he is pulling the papers in the desk all out. Mary Strong and Ma are going to Mrs Moe's funeral - it is in the universalist church at Genoa We have just heard that Mr. Peterson is dead That Fuchia that you and Ma got down to Mrs. Bennetts has got two blossoms and forty buds the blossoms are pink with a red center. The grapes north of the house are nearly as large as a plum and they are green yet You cannot guess how nice these flower beds look south of the house they are a great deal nicer than the other ones there are six kinds of Dahlias in blossom and we have got some sweet Mignonette that is in blossom and it is the sweetest flower I ever saw I am going to send a sprig of it to you in this letter we want to have this letter go out today so we have got to hurry. Don't fail to write every week.

From your daughter Estella

[Dr. Cyrus Powers to B.AF. LPH]

Marine Hospital, New Orleans, LA
August 29. 1863

My dear Doctor

I had hoped that ere This I should have been able to have gone up to your region and have seen you all, but lately our surgical force has diminished, while our number of patients has been increasing and I see no likelyhood of being able to get away at present. About two hundred of Grants men have been sent to this Hospital lately. Troops in large numbers are coming down from Vicksburg daily. I hear that the 17th Army Corps is coming. The 13th is already here and the two with Banks old 19th will make an aggregate of from fifty to sixty thousand men. Most of them will be off for somewhere soon, -probably Mobile. I suppose it is yet undecided whether Weitzels old Brigade will go, or stay. He is anxious to keep it with him when he goes, and I hear that he says that Gen Banks has promised he shall have it -

In how many places along the Railroad is the 160th quartered? Have you good accommodations at LaFourche Coping?

Dr. Becker received the three men you sent here Conklin, Shaw and Colman still, had I been in charge of the Regiment I should not have sent away either of them. They could all have been treated there, as well as here. I never yet sent a man to a General Hospital except when the Regiment was ordered to move and the sick could not be carried with us, and yet I have had as many as seventy in hospital fifty of them very sick. After a long and thorough trial of treatment if you are satisfied, that the man never will recover here he should have a furlough or a discharge and that should come from his Regiment - and not from a General Hospital. You are Acting Surgeon, and have the same powers, while in that capacity, that I would have if I were there. But discharge should be granted with great caution. Every soldier here has cost the Government one thousand dollars and his place - if discharged - must be supplied at a similar expense. Dr. Becker says a soldier had better be kept under treatment a whole year, if he will recover, and make a good soldier then, than to be discharged. Almost every soldier wants to be discharged and the Officers want to get rid of weak or ineffective men and between them both a strong pressure is brought to bear on the Surgeon, but his position is an independent one, and he should sternly set his face against the importunities. You may be constantly asked to excuse officers as well as men and to grant them Certificate of disability, but I am sure from what I know of you, you will only act from a sense of duty. I think the officers of our Regiment are as plucky and brave as those of any regiment I know of - and I feel proud of the 160th - yet the best of Officers and men will sometimes get homesick and discouraged, and then they seek the Surgical Dept to aid them in getting home. Probably all that have gone, should have gone - I have no reference to them, but only speak from general principles.

I am sure you will pardon me for these suggestions, and if they are unnecessary and uncalled for - you will rightly attribute them to good motives.

I hope the three men will be able to go back to the Regiment ere long, unless you should be ordered away, and in that case you will unqestionably have to send more sick men to New Orleans.

You seem to have made a very favorable impression on the Regiment - all that I have conversed with - officers and men - speak very highly of you.

Should Dr. Armstrong succeed in getting a surgeons [.....], which he strongly desires, another assistant surgeon will doubtless be very soon appointed to assist you. I think Col. Dwight and Dr. Benedict will see to that ere they return.

Have you made out the Semi-annual "Return" of Medicines and Hospital property yet, due July 1, and if so how did you account for the lost Surgical Instruments? Dr. Wilson has promised to send me a case of Amputating Instruments from Port Hudson, if he does, I will send them to you the first opportunity.

Give my best regards to Akin - and if you are willing - show him this letter -perhaps to avoid misconstruction, it would be best to show it to no one else. I have taken the liberty of writing it out of my most sincere regard for yourself and our Regiment.
Pray write to me long and fully.
Please preserve this.   C. Powers

────────────

La Fourche Crossing La.
Aug. 29th 1863

My dear wife and family

I rec'd your and Estella's letters of Aug. 13 and 25 inst and your, Estella, and Abbie and George of the 6th Aug on the 26th inst - the first mail - for some cause laid over - I was just as much gratified to receive it though long in coming These letters bring the first news I had received since I arrived in the Department of the Gulf from home - Really happy am I to learn that you are all well and that you often have company, often the neighbors fully appreciating your situation and the sacrifice I am making for the blessings they are enjoying - I am in excellent health but sometimes feel a little overworked - Mr Akin Lawyer Akins son of Moravia is my hospital Steward rooms with me; brought me the first two letters on the cars just as they were starting for Bayou Boeuf of the 25th He is a fine young man and did me the favor to run over the mail of the 160th

while the cars were taking on passengers at our station (La Fourche) - This station is about three rods from our rooms in the Hospital building - Every man in the Regiment officers and privates thus far have seemed anxious to do me any favors in their power - I hope I can fully reciprocate their kindness with attentions when they are sick or need my care and sympathies - We are having a little excitement here just now - The rebels are threatening to burn the bridge of the Rail Road just before our door and at Bayou Boeuf - Our folks are throwing out heavy pickets which have been driven in twice I believe - The rebels have an idea indeed they know to their cost in several previous attempts of the same kind that we have some fighting men here now Though our force is small they are now acquainted with what retreat means The officers are cool talk moderate and low but I feel quite sure I should not want to be of the rebel command that attacks them unless I had an overwhelming force - These are the men that stormed Port Hudson - We have once in a while a noisy officer full of boastful pluck but I can see they are often lame or sick when the prospect of real conflict is imminent - I hope I shall be able to do my duty fully if we are attacked - Yesterday a soldier while out in force on picket, while killing Mosquitoes accidentally caught his pants on the hammer of his gun and shot his forefinger off - I amputated it between the hand and the first joint - he went back to his company saying he could use the next finger nearly as well did not even ask me to excuse him so I am satisfied it was accidental - He was a hero at Port Hudson - We have some of the best Negro Regiments that ever raised a gun - They are a fine set of soldiers and are said to be great fighting men.

Today every thing is quiet Gen'l Banks has sent up a few baby Guns to parts where any demonstration can be made such as send 12 lb balls and shells - It is thought the simple sending of them will make that portion of the country very lamb like - I have just been eating my dinner we had a very fine baked duck such fresh beef sweet potatoes dry toast coffee tea and butter etc we live very comfortable but this is not a fair sample of our dinners and indeed any meals - We more often have dry toast tea and butter with some of those nice dried cherries or fruit you put up for me - I had a present of dozen lemons fresh from the tree a few days since - They are very green yet however - I had some fresh Peanuts just dug from the ground given me yesterday - The boys killed an alligator six feet long in

Bayou La Fourche about 20 rods from the hospital yesterday - I had a fine opportunity of seeing him - When it is cooler the inhabitants get any quantity of Oysters within a few miles of here - There are perhaps fifty Banana trees in sight from my window where I am writing They are very beautiful the leaves are from five to ten feet long and about one foot wide in the middle - They have a flower shaped like a long necked pint bottle hanging with the neck downward of a peach blow color - Thinking of it I have just been in to one of the neighbors gardens to dig a few Peanuts and pick a beautiful magnolia of which I will enclose you two or three petals. They will no doubt change before you get them - but I will describe the flower a little and you can form some opinion of its beauty. The flower now sits beside me in a bright pewter mug filled with water - Its petals are pure white and nine in number three below and six lying just above them, surrounded with green leaves, surrounding a conical center of the most beautiful purple capped with a large crest of solid substance of pale green and orange of the most beautiful and grateful odor I ever smelt - I hope the petals will retain the odor - the Tree is from 10 to 20 ft high those I have seen - I really wish you had a tree they are so beautiful - The Peanut growing like pea vines and are planted in rows and cultivated and dug like potatoes - There are sweet potatoes and figs in the same garden - The fig trees are about 12 to 15 ft high - the season is over for them now I bought a while ago a saucer heaping full of ripe ones for 5 cts-

The inhabitants treat me with as much respect as in any place I have ever been - One Doctor a fine looking man two thirds as large as Dr. *[Phineas]* Hurd *[of Scipio]* came to see me yesterday and before he left and although he is real secesh *[Secessionist - LPH]* and we both talked plain insisted so strongly that I had to promise to visit him and his family on his plantation some four miles distant. In fact I was really pleased with his open frankness   he was a union man and voted union till the President's proclamation of Freedom to the slaves - He says G-d D—m in that but will stand by everything else   He has 300 niggers and of course it worries him now when he has to pay them by the day - I am going to see him if I can in a few days   Then I will write you of our interview - I am not much inclined to yield all my sentiments to any man however - But he is so good-hearted that I can talk plain and will be friendly - He assures me that all surgeons are regarded as noncombattants by both armies which is indeed the rule here and are permitted to go & come except in the enemies lines as they choose - I will write to the girls soon again - and my little George, too - Tell George I got his letter and Estellas and Abbies too. Direct as before and write often all of you - Tell Abbie to bite George's ear for Pa - sell the pony and colt and heifer to Giles if you think best cattle are very high however I have bought a fine pony I assure you - My muster for pay is now in a few days if I get it I shall not need any money from home - I will write - Tell the girls to read the history through and if I can I will bring this pony home for them - He is gentle as a kitten Kiss George as many times as they are a mind to for me - save me some maple sugar - Give respects to Firman - I am glad you have done so well - Don't be too tight with hired help - My love to all relations neighbors and friends

Benj. A. Fordyce

PS You had better collect the Signor's judgment if possible - There never will be a better time to collect - Magnolia - I send one small leaf or petal - I do not consider it very warm here - not as warm as I expected - the evenings are cool and pleasant - I enjoy myself well I assure you - work nearly all the time

You may direct via Cairo, Ill I think they will come quicker Mr. Divine will tell you -

<hr>

Sabbath afternoon, Aug 30th [1863]

My dear husband

I thought as I and the girls were alone today I would commence a letter to you George has gone home with Cynthia. In the first place we are all well We went to church today the girls to Sabbath school Yesterday I went to church & society meeting or rather church meeting you never saw such quarreling in any political mtg or caucus one would get up and say you told me so and so and the other would say that is a falsehood they voted to pay a minister by taxing the taxable members according to their property E. Covey said he would pay $50 and Deacon Moshier the same I thought if he had so much money whether we had not better try to get our pay what do you think about it. they voted to call a council to settle their present difficulties they were principally secessionist pressure Alward was the man that they were all after and they closed their quarreling by prayer. I attended Adella Moes funeral it was at Genoa village. *[Or, Lodelia Moe, d. Aug. 26, 1863 in 23rd yr. LGC]* Mrs Worthington Smith inquired after you everyone thinks you had better come home they are afraid they will be sick they say it is so lonesome without you Your friends I mean John has not answered your letter yet he says he is agoing to today everything remains the same on the farm as when you left there has been several to look at bullet and the colt Mr Tibbits spoke to me this morning about buying the 3 year old cow he said he would see me again if Giles did not take her we have got two of the nicest pigs you ever saw John wanted to know what I would take for one I went a blackberrying the other day and have made 12 pounds of jam do you think I could send you anything by Captain Corning write to him and see if he would take charge of a small box for you I think however he had better take charge of your wife and son, do not say anything more about going to Texas will Dr. Armstrong resign when he gets home or will he go back again I heard from you today by way of Mr Ogden he wrote how glad they were to see you.

I think there is a family in Venice who would give all they possess if they could only see you Mr Dolson has just gone from here he has paid his little due bill it was $2.91 Mr S Whitney presented a paper to me with your name signed to it for wood and taking care of meeting house for 1861 the amount claimed was 75 cents 50 for wood, 25 for taking care of meeting house I did not pay it I thought you did not do business that way it seems as if folks were determined to get all the money I can get. Cynthia and George have come home he says write to pa in your letter that I am a nice boy he grows interesting every day he lives talks a great deal plainer and more sensible. I wish you could just come home to night and see us do not go any further from home Oh if you only keep well be sure and get some vegetables to eat and pickles lemons keep of scurvey - do not get vegetables that will produce diarrhoea. potatoes and turnips the papers speak of onions but they do not agree with you if I can only get another letter from you and learn that you are well and that it is healthier in camp it seems as if I should feel better about you do you see anything of your friend Dr Powers who wanted some one that he could depend upon Mr Fox on the hill was

buried to day he died with diarrhoea Mrs Lyman Murdock is esc[...]
again you will have to come home then - do you find things as you
expected can't you resign and come home if you want to   has Mrs
VanPetten or Babcock any children have they got them with them
be sure and season your fresh meat well with salt and pepper cook
a little pork with your chickens it will help season them be careful
about exposure to night air without plenty of clothing. On Monday
afternoon   The girls have just come from school with papers no
letter two weeks since I got one from you and this is the fifth one we
have sent you in that time   I hope you have got some of them   the
papers state that Gen Pemberton is dead killed by a Texas officer
and that Floyd is also dead Fort Sumpter a mass of ruins Gen
Gillmore throwing shell into the city charged with Greek fire
People think that Lee is agoing to make a desperate attack
somewhere most probably Washington I should think if they have
any troops to spare at New Orleans they had better send them this
way in room of Texas I see by the papers that Banks is agoing to
move in some direction cant you get a place in New Orleans hospital
and not have to go with the regiment (or resign) I see by the papers
that Jeff Davis is agoing to arm 50,000 blacks, promis them their
freedom and fifty acres of land. I have just settled with Adelbert
Wheat for work I supposed your account would ballance his work
he charged me 14 shillings a day for haying & cutting wheat he
helped about haying 2 days 1 1/2 day harvesting Your acct against
him was $4.38 I paid him one dollar and called it settled Curtain
only charged me fifteen shillings [$1.87 1/2] for a day and a half work
one day mowing oats half day drawing wheat he wanted pork for
pay. I charged him ten cents a pound. I can tell you it takes money
to farm it and take care of the little ones   we are not agoing to have
many apples pumpkins sweets more than any other I shall not have
to stay here to dry apples I most wish that Firm was not a comeing
here I could go over home and stay as long as I care to then come
back again and stay a while   write what you think I had better do
with stock   when you think you will come home   if there is any
prospect of the war closing It seems like fall weather had the doors
shut and fire for two days   it does not seem as if we could live all
this long winter without you the evenings are so lonesome I think
I shall go over home in October without your advice is different are
you agoing to have money enough have you rec'd any pay yet If you
want any money from home let me know & how to send it do not

deprive yourself of things for your comfor I hope you will not swill their liquor down I have no fear however Estella is very busy reading a story called the Island Princess she hardly looks up or speaks Abbie is cutting paper they are talking of having their school picnic next Saturday George is three yrs old to morrow write all the particulars of camp life if you like as well as you expected be sure and send us a letter every mail whether you do anyone else or not Mother and Father send their love to you they comfort me some saying the same one watches over you there as did here I do not suppose you can make sense of my letter

Emeline

PS Write to George about your photographs there has only six come yet I answered his letter informing him that I have got those that he sent.

Your wife Emeline

Scipio, Sept 1 1863

My dear husband

I have just got to your Fathers Mr Adams that bought Mrs Pierces place come here and wanted I should write to you She claims that she cannot give a good title and has notified him to leave trying to cheat him out of his crops and ditching that he has done amounting he claims to some 14 hundred dollars he wants to know if you heard her say that she had 90 acres of land that her father gave her & what the surrogate told you about her giving a title Mr Adams said she told him that she had 90 acres of land write as soon as you get this as he is notified to leave in one month Your mother say write that we are all well Estella Abbie & George and myself are at your fathers I must close as it is mail time I hope you are well I put a letter in the [Post] office at home before I left John takes one to Auburn today for you see if you get them all at the same time writ every mail Captain Corning has been here

From your wife Emeline Fordyce

Today is George birthday

LaFourche Crossing La.
Sept 2nd 1863

Father and Mother Slocum

Dear Parents - I have waited since I arrived here some little time thinking to obtain more information of the inhabitants and country that would be interesting to you before writing - I arrived here as Emeline has probably informed you safe and in good health and so remain -

The Regt appeared glad to see me and I have every reason to believe they were so - The Surgeon who was with them and had been through the march to Port Hudson and back again was worn out, sick and obliged to go home fore his health - They were without assistance in the Med line when I came and there is now and was then a scarcity of Surgeons in this Deptment - This is the Deptment where some of the fighting has been done too - No Regiment that I am acquainted with, has more than one Surgeon with them - They are entitled to three each - I am well pleased thus far with my situation although I have more to do than is agreeable in so hot a climate - On the whole I have suffered no more with heat here than I have done in Venice - I think from Emelines letter it has been full as warm with you as it has been here - The thermometer has stood the highest in the shade last week 92°. This is not as warm as we often have it at the north - We have frequent showers the rain pours down rapidly but is very warm when the water falls - You can almost see the sugar cane and corn grow when it rains - Some fields of Sugar Cane contain from fifty to one hundred acres that I have seen growing here - It is now about nine ft high When I came here on the 3rd Aug. it would average two and a half feet high - It is very sweet now - They will on the Government Plantations begin to cut it next month - The Govt Plantations are those deserted by rebels and taken and worked by the Govt giving Negroes and others extensive employment - Immense fields of corn are now ripe - Some fields were ripe when I came here - This I speak of is mainly lands cultivated by Govt - The inhabitants who are native and remain here are the most miserable set of human beings to develop the resources of a country any man ever put his eyes on - The Negroes excepted, nobody will work - The whites are generally too lazy to keep clean - some exceptions of course - The Negroes are as a general thing so far as I am able to learn willing to work for small wages and are honest and faithful - This is my own observation - The whites here say the negroes are lazy, lying, thieving and every thing else mean - To illustrate that they know they lie - They come in and tell me they would be glad to have the Union restored immediately and would stand by it if slavery can be secured and protected and Presidents proclamation withdrawn freeing the Slaves - When assured that this boon will not be conceded then they complain that the Government is ruining them by taking their property without which their country has no value - to me it seems a very humiliating admission that the whole value of the country is in the lazy negro at last -

This country looks to be suffering from the real ravages of war - The fine buildings Planters houses are burned to the ground or literally gutted sash Doors and even partitions taken out and burned for firewood and to get nails to make shanties or for any purpose they choose - The country has been first in the hands of the rebels of course and when the Union troops came to occupy it - The rebels in retreating burned RR bridges and public property everywhere to prevent it falling into Union hands - The bridge over the Bayou before the door of the building I am in has been burned three times 1st by the rebels then by our men then again by rebels. Now trains run over it every 3 or 4 hrs probably carrying Union men mostly, occasionally a lot of Prisoners - Yesterday I saw a negro recruiting colored men for the First Louisiana Regiment - This Regiment was the one so awfully cut up at Port Hudson. This Negro's Name is Lewis - He was wounded in the leg and relieved from duty in regiment and sent out recruiting - I thought I had seen men that could make a patriotic appeal to their countrymen before, in behalf of our country and the interest and necessities that should impel men to do Military service for their Government but when I saw this colored man who has been wounded at Port Hudson had two brothers killed in the same battle another and his last and only brother now in hospital with his wounds received in the same battle A man who was born a slave and had been a slave till within a year past who had left a wife and family of children to fight for a government that had never guaranteed to him a single right above that of a hog or a horse till within one year past - when I heard him appeal to every strong bodied colored man he met; with an earnestness that secured seventy three in three days entirely alone and took them into quarters - hurrying from place to place, inviting, urging every man he met to come right along and join the army pointing to his own sacrifices that he had already made and the inestimable privilege of owning himself and family as the reward - I admit I felt ashamed of all the feeble efforts I had made to recruit the army - I felt satisfied that an element of strength has been developed and brought to the aid of our government of which we had no adequate idea - In my opinion this element now so thoroughly aroused in the colored man is never again to be brutalized; It begins to realize its own strength and the fullness of its power - Could you see the joy expressed and the willingness to do anything to get a living manifested by the blacks it would gratify you beyond measure - I must stop will write more next time - Remember me to all and write to me.

Yours truly Benj. A. Fordyce

PS I remember yesterday was my little George's birthday I tried to think of something to send him It is difficult to find anything here and I am quite a distance from New Orleans so I send him my love and remembrance - and my love to all friends - remember me to my family - give my respects to Slocum Howland *[Father of Emily Howland and Wm. prob. her brother. LGC]*

Chapter III
Destination Texas

*Dr. Fordyce entertains his children with an explana-
tion of the culture of Cotton and the beauty of the
area, Algiers, LA. In the same letter he tells his wife
of the planned expedition to Texas and the conditions
under which he travels.... then compliments her on
her conduct of the farm home. Read of the failed
action at Sabine Pass and its effect upon the discouraged soldiers. From Berwick City come descriptions
of preparations for battle. At Centerville the doctor
indicates their destination, Texas, to be only seventy
miles away. He describes the fears and misappre-
hensions of the local slaves and deplores the activities of the Copperheads.*

<hr>

Algiers - La.   September 7th 1863

My dear wife and children

I today received your letters of Aug. 22nd and 27th also one from
George Fancher of the 22nd containing two Photographs that the
boys say look very much like me and one of George himself -   He
said he had sent you part of the lot I had taken and would send you
the remainder in a few days - If you think they are good enough you
can send to George if you wish and get one or two doz more - Well
Emeline I am in excellent health sitting under the wharf on the
banks of the Mississippi in the Village of Algiers across the river
about a mile from New Orleans and it is about 8 oclock in the evening
and the finest weather you ever saw - The days are very warm the
nights cool with heavy dews so heavy indeed that the eaves run some
mornings - I have slept on the dock two nights now expecting to sleep
here tonight - I have plenty of nice blankets and sleep first rate I
have a Mosquito bar and everything a soldier needs or can carry -
The weather is not as warm as it has been in New York City - It has
not been any of the time since I have been here - You write that you
would like to come here - It certainly would be pleasant for me to

have you here yet in my opinion it a very improper place for a lady
- Col Van-Petten told me only a few days since that [he] would give
a great deal if his wife was at home - Now to illustrate the Regiment
recd orders to move from LaFourche to Algiers last Monday - they
did not get transportation till Wed - I was not notified to move my
hospital till Friday got transportation Saturday Morning and when
I arrived here found the Regiment gone to sea on a secret expedition
without a surgeon - the Col. complaining on account of it - Of course
I am left behind in consequence of no fault of mine - I am now waiting
transportation to the Regiment - I have just recd orders what vessel
to take yet do not know where it is going - It may be Texas, this is
my opinion and my hope - The climate is fine in Texas and water
excellent and the country rich - Our regiment is not the only one left
thus the Surg of the 75th is in the same fix and the 8th Vt all here
with me - we shall be off tomorrow I think - I shall write at the first
landing where I can send to you - I had time today and went to New
Orleans and got a months pay - I have sent you by Express Eighty
dollars - It will come to Auburn and you will be notified when it
arrives and must receive it yourself and receipt for it - I have paid
all the charges on it -

Be sure and write me what to do with Danl H. Wings watch in your
next letter - Direct all letters as you have your last they will come
all right - Do not send me anything in a box till I write again - I have
seen considerable service I can assure you already My labors are
more difficult than they would be if I was familiar with the Army
Regulation - I think I give general satisfaction, however I hope to at
least - I have performed several operations - Amputated one finger
and one leg and assisted in cutting off three other legs - We had a
colored man run over by the cars both legs being severely crushed
he was brought to my hospital - I sent for the Surgeon of the 75th to
help me - we cut off both legs. He one and I the other one above the
knee, the other below - The man was real comfortable when we
brought him on the railroad forty miles to the General Hospital I
think he will get well with good care.

I am glad to learn that you are getting along with the work so well
- but I must beg of you not to write me another discouraging word -
I have come here from true Patriotism shall take every reasonable
care of myself and hope to live to return home at some future time

a wiser and more valued surgeon far [more] than I ever could have been at Venice - You can do just as much as I by taking care of the little ones at home watching their health improving their minds Your Patriotism will be just as useful as mine and in many respects far more agreeable -

I think of all daily and know that you are comfortable and ought to be happy as any body in your situation - I am very thankful for your letter and for Estellas and Abbies and my little Georges too - It makes a green spot in the scenes of military life to receive a cheering letter from home - I shall keep all my letters from home - I have a fine opportunity to enter a colored Regiment as Surgeon with increased pay and if I find I can get home just as soon think I shall accept - if I can pass - Write me what you think about it - I am finely situated now - Dr. Powers is quite sick not dangerous but his health is quite poor - Jaundice and Diarrhoea I take Quinine about 5.grs daily - am hungry each meal drink Mississippi water sleep out doors - Drink no whisky and am tough as ever - I expect to see some fighting now soon - Charleston I suppose has fallen or must in a few days - Abbie and Estella both improve in writing - let them write as often as they can - Tell them to set down anything they think of and when they get ready to write send it all along - Kiss Geo and the girls for me, bite George's ear, tell him not to wet his pant - Give my love to Carrie, John, Mary and Lovina Nelson and all the rest keeping the Lion's share for yourself   Benj. A. Fordyce

Sept 8th A.M.10 Oclock - No orders yet - I am well & happy as a clam - boys constantly coming for assistance   I being the only commissioned officer here on duty   about forty of the Regt to look after   Yrs B.A.F. - love to you all   remember me to your and my parents

===========

Algiers Sept 10th 1863

Estella and Abbic - My dear children - although I wrote you a letter yesterday from this place I have just received one from you although I am on board the Transport Sol. Wilde bound for somewhere yet she not having sailed just gives me time to receive your letter written while Ma and Cynthia were off blackberrying and George pulling the papers around the Desk, containing the little flowers you sent me - You cannot think how cheering your letters are to me my dear children and how much pleased I am to see your improvement in writing You have given me so much information of neighbors and all about everything that I should very much miss your affectionate letters - you admonish me not to drink whiskey with the officers I thank you for this I have not drunk any liquor, or not in all more than two tablespoonsful since I have been here - I really think I am exercising a good influence on the officers by my very abstemious habits at least they appear to respect me for it - I am sorry to hear of Adella Moe's death - Tell Ma to give my sympathies to Mr. and Mrs. Arnold in their severe affliction - Write me everything you think of about Mr. Congdon - Mr. Alwards - John Strong - I have had no letter yet from John - Write me of all the neighbors and of Grandpa Fordyce Grandpa Slocum and all of your uncles and aunts and everything cunning little George says and does and Kiss him and bite him a little for me occasionally - watch him carefully that he may not get hurt or eat anything to injure him - How I wish I could kiss and bite him a little myself and all of you When I see little girls and boys I always think of you

There is the most delightful vegetation here to look at you ever saw - I saw an Oleander yesterday that was twenty feet high growing in front yards as common as any of our evergreens - it was full of flowers too I have seen some very pretty cotton fields - The Cotton looks growing very much like that large orange colored flower of Ma's that blossoms late in fall Some of it grows eight feet high - some of the blossoms are yellow and some purple or lilac colored There is a large oval bud in the center that expands very much like a butternut with shucks on in shape and size - This as it ripens bursts open like a chestnut burr exposing the fine white cotton to view - when fully open the cotton is all picked by hand out of these burrs and put in baskets that are carried along generally by the slaves - The plants have ripe bolls green ones and flowers at the same time so that they pick it two or three times a year - This cotton when first picked contains all the seeds - This has to be carried to mills or cotton gins where it is cleared of the seeds when it is fit for market it is put in large sacks as large 5 or 6 bags full of wheat each then it is sold - It now brings here from 60 to 68 cts a pound and is in excellent demand

My little black boy Jo is just one of the nicest little niggers in the world - talks French like fun - You would laugh enough to split you to hear him talk English - He is on hand early in the morning to black my boots to keep flies off me or anything I want - He is going with me on the boat although he has found his mother and brother and sister here in New Orleans Still he wants to go with me - I have a man that takes care of my horse also I shall have to leave my horse and man at the Govmt Stable in New Orleans and send for them afterwards - I saw George Robinson the other day he inquired particularly after Ma and you girls - He is well tanned up - has charge of a Negro Regiment here and is very anxious for me to take Surgeon with his Regiment - I do not wish to take any place that will keep me too long from home - Estella you write a very good letter and so does Abbie - Abbie has improved very much in writing too - I cannot write much more to you girls - I must write some to Ma yet I write for you all every time - you won't forget to write will you -

From your Father, Most Affectionately, Benj. A. Fordyce

(PS) Your letters are directed right now - and will come - I have rec'd 5 or six now in all.

My dear Wife,

I must write a little to each of you I am called to dinner now - Dinner at 1 PM I board on board the vessel with the Officers - we had for dinner corn beef boiled sweet potatoes, Irish potatoes, bread, butter, puddings, pie and pickles - This is extra living for a soldier, now but Officers diet in this style closed with Claret Wine - This is a pleasant and acid wine about like cider just worked only sourer - Be sure Emeline and have everything straight on letting the house if you conclude to let it If you let it be sure and sell the stock and lock up everything belonging to you - be careful of fire - Get John to see to divisions of corn or your Father - I have an opportunity of seeing more of the world than ever I had any Idea of before and if I live to get home, shall have a great deal to tell you that you and the children would never have known - I will try and write something of interest in every letter - Give my love to all who may feel an interest in me and I must close - we may go in an hour or not till morning.

Your husband,   Benj. A. Fordyce

Algiers   Sept 14th 1863

My dear wife

I rec'd both of your letters one sent from Venice, the other from
Scipio dated Sept 1st have just rec'd them I am pleased to hear that
you are all well and to hear from Fathers that they are all well - You
write to me of Mr. Adams matters asking what was said at the time
Mr. Adams bought the premises - Mrs. P. did represent that she had
title to part of the land all the time that I heard the conversation -
If I recollect right however the contract is for land Deeded to Pierce
by Chas. Silcox which might cut off that claim - She assumed all
rights in the matters that Pierce ever possessed in connexion with
her and conveyed the same agreeing to give possession which was
in part fulfilled and on which agreement Adams made the first
payment of purchase money fulfilling in all particulars so far as I
know on his part - The Surrogate said she could contract for a sale
but must get authority from Superior Court before her Deed would
be valid - That such a sale could be effected and made binding and
legal but would be attended with considerable expense and trouble
- Yet that there was no doubt that it could be done if all parties were
agreed - The agreement was made and in writing and at Mrs.
Pierce's urgent solicitation - Mr. Adams will recollect that I called to
see him on or about the 31st of Mar last. This was at Mrs. Pierce's
solicitation - on the same day I saw the Surrogate and talked with
him about it, at that he thought it advisable for her to sell and
dispose of part of the real estate, if she could do so to advantage -
This is all I know about what you wrote to me about that comes to
mind now - Any further information desired I will write on recp't of
a letter.

I received a line from Ira Fish [of Venice] on the 27th August asking
a letter from me so that he could receive it the 26th of August - It
was difficult for me to get it to him so I did not write - please excuse
the matter to Mr. Henry Taylors folks for him so that he will see it
was no fault of mine that I could not be of service to him - I have
received no letter from John yet - I should like to hear from him -
Tell Father to write to me - I wrote quite a long letter to him - Also
one to your father - I has as yet rec'd no letters from anyone except
George Fancher and my family - I have had but very little time to

write to any one else - I have now been interrupted some eight or ten times thus far in this letter - Five or six times by the men and twice by the Colonel - so you see I have abundance of time to write - By the bye I have got off the Sol Wilde by orders - The expedition I wrote you of in your Estellas and Abbies letters proved a failure - They went to Sabina Pass by the Gulf and attempted to land but having no small boat could not get near the shore went up with two Gun boats the Clifton and Sabina shelling the shore along finally came opposite some masked battines that had not fired in return at all until the boats were exactly opposite their guns then they fired and disabled both boats in less than two minutes and took all the men prisoners in spite of our forces on board the other boats which must have been 10,000 but were perfectly unable to help them on account the shallowness of the water the large vessels could not approach within five miles of the scene of action - Two companies of the 75th NY were made prisoners Co. B and Co. G. You can not think how chagrinned the whole Army were at this comparatively little disaster - The vessel I was on was detained untill the whole expedition returned - Such a lot of sick men I never saw before probably more from chagrin by half than would have been if the expedition had been successful - I prescribed this morning for more than eighty sick men - I am now writing in a large field covered with tents nearly the whole 19th Army Corps are in this vicinity - There are probably 100,000 men in this Department now - This field contains more than 15,000 troops tonight - I have received orders today to make a requisition for medicines and Hospital stores for a 3 months campaign - We shall probably move in a day or two - I am rather pleased with the idea - It was providential I think that I was not along on the Sabine expedition - I had met every order and there could be no cause of complaint on my part - You can not think what a beautiful sight a field full of soldiers in tents is - particularly in the night. The light in each little tent and all as still as meeting [church] except an occasional shout from the boys - or the Sentinel or Change of Guard - I enjoy myself well because I am well and have entered the service from a sense of duty not of gain - You must manage affairs as will be most pleasant for you and the little ones - If you want to keep the house keep it but sell the stock so as not to be annoyed by it - Keep Cynthia with you she is a good girl and will be a great deal of company for you - but do as you think best - The campaign will probably be to Texas but I do not know which way yet - I am writing at twilight - my orderly waiting to carry this to the office

I have much to write but must stop now - have just had to stop and ext a tooth and sent them away to wait till I finish writing - my supper is ready and must close - will write again if I can before we move - Remember me to all - don't forget my little Geo & the girls - All will be for the best - Write and direct as before.

Yours affectionately   Benj. A. Fordyce

(PS) Elwood [Fell] is here in my tent - and well, I see him every day - give compliments to Moses and wife *[Fell, of Sherwood. LGC]*

Berwick City, La.   Sept. 18, 1863

My dear wife and children

You observe I date my letter at a different place today from my former letters - This place is across the Bay from Brashear City - Berwick City is a place about as large as Stewarts Corners - never quite so populous of white persons - Brashear is a little larger than Berwick, say 1/4 as large as Moravia with some very fine buildings or which once were good buildings - The bay here is about one third mile wide and some forty miles from the Gulf - We came over here yesterday on a steamer from Brashear - We slept on our blankets on the ground three nights at Algiers. The only inconvenience was the extreme heat in early evening and cold dewy damp air later in the night - I slept well however - Last night I slept in a nice building but took a little cold - my head aches some today as it always does when I have a cold - The weather changed in the night to cold and I had worked hard the day before to get the hospital stuff over the Bay and was very sweaty besides having a good many sick men to look after and take along - How long we shall remain here I do not know - perhaps till next Monday - I know too as well as anyone here about me Gen'l Franklin has arrived today I learn - Yesterday our pickets were fired upon by the rebels - In about two minutes after our folks sent a large shell over in their neighborhood and after that the quiet was almost painful for its stillness - No further stir was made among them all was quiet - I have been sharpening instruments today - and making all preparations I can for my duties - The other surgeons think I learn fast in the way of providing for self and sick - No Surgeon in this regiment before has ever had a team to carry things along with them - I told the quartermaster I must have it - He said he could not do it - I said it must come - I went to Hd Quarters and had my order approved and now I shall have a team - I have no good overcoat - this is the only inconvenience I suffer except want of drawers - I shall be obliged to get one, I guess. I sent you eighty dollars about ten days ago - I have now by me some over thirty dollars and have lent out fifty dollars - I can get along very well as well as any of the Officers because I pay out no money only for things that will make me more comfortable or to eat - If you send me a box put in my drawers and seal everything tight in the vegetable line and send a firm box either by some person of the regiment or by express - Anything you wish to send me of eatable kind will be very acceptable I can assure - If you can send some butter put it in Tin cans of about five pounds each and seal it tight - I pay for butter when I eat any from forty to fifty cents a pound - If it is sealed it may lay in the express office safely two or three months without injury if I do not get back to New Orleans in that time - We are going to Texas without doubt in large force by land - My team is not here yet - I think will be tomorrow - May not have another opportunity to write in some time but will write every opportunity - Give my love to all - retaining a large share for yourself - Don't forget the girls and my little Geo. Good bye Benj. A. Fordyce

(PS) Direct all letters as before till you hear from me to the contrary - They will reach us after a while - There are here now more than 20,000 soldiers on this side - enough to go most anywhere - They are fighting men & will arm a cannon as well as many could a rifle - They shoot two or more miles with rifted steel barrel cannon -

---

Camp in the field - 2 mi. east of
Centerville La. Sept 29th 1863

My dear wife and children

I recd your letter in which you all wrote dated Sept 13 with great pleasure I can assure you - When it came the Col. and I were playing

Camp in the field - 2 mi. east of
Centerville La. Sept 29th 1863

chess in his tent and having a good sociable time while it was raining like suds as it had done the night before - I had just finished a set of wooden chess men and we were initiating them into play when in came our mail carrier with four letters for me - one from you and the girls two from John B. Strong and one from Dr. Armstrong my associate in the Regt who is now at home in NY State for his health - *[John B. Strong married Mary Foote, dau. of Jared Foote and Eliza Ann (Clark) of Venice; Eliza Ann, sister of Alpha (Clark) Fordyce, mother of BAF. LGC]* - Your excellent letters do me a world of good - And John wrote me some excellent letters which I shall answer as soon as I can get a little time perhaps tomorrow - You write about the Phebe Pierce and Adams difficulty about their land trade - I am of opinion that I can have no trouble whatever about it - let it be settled as it may - All we Mr. Fish and I are bound to, is that she will discharge the duties of administratrix faithfully and take good care of the childs interest therein - Don't everything appear as though she is looking sharply to those interests sufficiently so to clear her bondsmen - We are not bound to take care of Adams property we have nothing to do with his contracts further than witnessing them - I knew when the contract was made and told Mr. Adams that It was a long tedious process by which Mrs. Pierce could give any title to the land but that if she went in earnest to work she could get him a good title - Whether he can compel her to give him a good title by any contract that can be made with her I have my doubts - She has so agreed and ought to do it - In any case I am not liable for her miscarriage as long as her interest will be sufficient to pay damages - My opinion is she can only be held for private damages even if the court decide that she has no right as administratrix to convey real estate in the way contracted for - In that case it would be held that Adams should have ascertained that fact before advancing money on the purchase and required security which he did not do —

You need have no fears about this matter - That you are well and the children well I am really happy to learn - You write there is a good deal of Dysentery prevailing about you - We have a great deal of it in the army - As yet I have lost no cases - I give a full dose of salts and follow after the operation with pills of Acet Lead 3 grains opium 1 grain Ipicac 1/2 grain for adults repeated every 4 or 6 hrs till discharges are checked keeping the men as still as possible - This treatment is successfull - This is the same I have always used of late years with vegetable astringents - I have fine opportunities to test the value of a remedy - Other Surgeons are not having near as good success in my opinion - Their men came with us perform the same duties, have the same food but are more often fatal - More are sent to hospital in proportion and more have to be carried in Ambulances-

We are now on our way to Texas with a very large force - We are now about seventy miles from the boundary of Texas - I went out yesterday in company with Col. VanPetten and several others some four or five miles beyond Centerville to see how the country looks and follow a lot of cavalry who went in advance to pick up horses mules and cattle - We called at several places along the route - It is now 10 o'clock P.M. I will retire to bed in my large covered wagon and give you the particulars in the morning - It rains quite hard

Wed. 30th Sept. A.M. - It has rained all night but I had a good nights sleep and was dry all right - The camp are not all so fortunate, yet the boys feel well this morning and have just started out on picket about a mile from camp in the rain - They go off cheerful while I sit in the cool wagon and write to you - Well about our excursion - we talked with slaves and men everywhere we went - We stopped at a fine plantation, where things had not been disturbed by the convulsions of war so much as to lose its natural or common appearance - The slaves about sixty adult slaves besides lots of little niggers - They flocked around us and appeared greatly delighted to see Yankees - The niggers gave me my pocket full of Pecans. They told us how they had been told Yankees looked formerly before they had even seen any of them - They - the masters - said a Yankee was a great big baboon as tall as a man with but one eye and that in the centre of the forehead with a sharp long horn on the top of the head and an enormous long tail and would eat niggers or anything they could get hold of - That they were nearly black and the most awful looking Animal in creation - When the Army first came down here the soldiers and officers tell me they could see negroes peeking around corners and behind trees - finally one more bold than the rest would come up to the soldiers and after looking around awhile would inquire Whar be de Yankees? When they were told all the soldiers were Yankees, "My dem looks better dan our folks! - Massa say they hab long tails! Dey look jes like White folks! - This was one of the impositions practiced on the Negro - Another now is that the

Yankees know they cant whip southerners and are catching the negroes and putting them in front of the battle to have them killed off - This is to frighten them to run off when the army approaches - but it don't all work - the negro regiments are rapidly recruiting and are a strong healthy set of men -

Dr. Lester made me a very fine visit some few days since - He has recd the appointment of Surgeon in Goerge Robison's colored regiment - This is a very fine situation for him and gives him full Surgeons pay - He appears well and is well - I joked him a little about Venice girls He seemed to enjoy it - There are a good many persons here in other regiments that I knew before leaving home - Young Dan VanLiew is in colored Regiment with George Robison, also Haights son in Auburn and Young Halsted and several others I do not remember - Edgar Nye is nicely situated having 1st Lt. pay in commissary Department which is about $100 per month - He is a good officer I am informed but whether he saves anything or not I do not know - One great difficulty with officers is after a campaign, they think they must spree it for three or four weeks as soon as they get their pay - This generally uses up all they have earned and leaves them in debt -

We shall probably move from here before long - I have considerable doubt about the French attempting any interference with us - The Army that will concentrate in Texas will in my opinion be 100,000 strong - We are not going out for mere fun - The men engaged both officers and soldiers are earnest Union fighting men who have seen service and mean what they say - There are intimations that Texas will submit before the army enters the State - They do not want the devastation visited on them that marks Louisiana - Their only remedy is actual submission - disbanding their army & returning to the Union or suffer the alternative of devastating war - This must and will come -

What difference between the men in the army who are perilling their lives and fortunes suffering the privations of storm and marching constantly exposed to death by disease and from the enemy to the miserable Democratic copperheads at home who are constantly blowing for peace - When there is no possibility of obtaining peace except by reducing the country to the condition it was before they had the powers to so misgovern it - There is no punishment so severe that it ought not to be visited on them - Miserable Knaves and Cowards - When the army returns after securing to them their rights in a free government that they have jeopardized themselves - I hope I may not be permitted to see the awful punishment that will be visited on them - Mark these men do not lack courage to do anything and such a retribution as awaits those who have openly or covertly opposed the efforts of Govmt to restore the Union will be awful to witness - I have written too much already but the awful unjust course that those who have remained at home have pursued in regard to the efforts the government is making to relieve the country from the awful scourge of dissolution has evidently prolonged the war already more than a year Is any punishment too severe for them?

In regard to your matters at home try so to situate yourself as to enjoy yourself in the best possible way you can with the children - My impression is that your own house will be most satisfactory to you - When I can come home I do not know but will try to be home on the 1st of Apr. next-if possible unless a few days or weeks shall in all probability close the war beyond that time - I am of opinion that the war will end before long perhaps before the 1st of Apr. or even 1st of January unless some foreign power interferes - The result must be favorable and soon too - but little or no resistance is offered to our progress here where before every mile was contested when the army went up - We are taking prisoners almost every day - They have got but one that I know of from us - that a guard placed over a rebel's property beyond our lines - Our man was taken in this way - Such things show the damnable manners of the rebels - Now here were some of their own women left by their valiant nigger driving husbands who were in the rebel army asked protection from our soldiers while we were encamped here - This was granted by our General and a man sent to guard the premises. This man was taken prisoner the same night - The women felt the bad faith with which they had acted and tried (so they say) every means to get him back but in vain. This all works just right - They will get the protection woolens give to lambs, if they serve us this way - We have taken quite a number of prisoners-are getting some every day - The day I went there were thirty above us mounted-our men goes after them but they were a little too fast for us - The cavalry brought in a large drove of mules horses and cattle all safe and right. Well, enough of this.

How is that little bit of George come on - does he ever think of Pa or say anything about him does he want to pile on to Pa's head when he is pacting - John in his letter says Geo is full of the white horse and Frank runs away 1/2 doz times a day - Abbie says she is most through the Geography - have them continue studying till they get through - Be sure and be good girls and watch George and send your photographs when you can in as convenient a form as you can - I enjoy seeing them very much - Keep charge of your own matters as far as you can and do not deprive yourself of anything for your comfort - be sure and enjoy yourself as well as you can - I am here from purely patriotic motives but determined to learn all I can and save all I can of my earnings - If God spares my life and health I shall return to you as soon as the country is restored to the just position such a government and such a people are justly entitled - Probably not to remain at home much sooner if my health continues good -

You may do as you think best with all the produce of the land - Be sure and collect debts that ought to be paid and look to interest on Mosher Mortgage and judgment but do not wrong anyone - Obtain as easily as possible only our just dues - Your own and the children's comfort health and happiness is my greatest anxiety - Nothing would so unman me as to hear that any of you are sick - I am seeing and learning much of this country that will be interesting to you when I get home - Orange trees are loaded full this year - They are not ripe yet - the trees are as large as good sized apple trees - Good bye all - will write every opportunity - direct as before.

   Your Husband and Father Benj. A. Fordyce
(PS) Be sure and have the children write.

(PS) I send one little flower from a garden here. There are many beautiful flowers here. I am glad you look so nice. Remember me to my parents and Father and Mother Slocum and all Friends.

[Note on envelope]: Send me papers often.

Chapter IV
Teche Country

From Vermillion, LA Dr. Fordyce describes the beautiful Teche Country and continues with details of the battle that had taken place that day. He requests his wife to purchase a Surgeon's sash of green silk for his protection as well as identification of his rank. From Carion Crow Bayou, near Opelousas, LA he describes the organization and activities of the hospital where he is serving and which he supervises (a responsibility not usually delegated to an Assistant Surgeon). He describes in detail his observation of the battle that had taken place on October 15th. He has preserved the letters received from his family at home. Back in Vermillion after a 40-mile march, the doctor tells of the capture of a regimental foraging team sent out for food. Read again his comments on the activities of the Copperheads and the deplorable conditions of the local blacks and the unwavering dedication expressed by a black ambulance driver in the Northern regiment. He describes the humiliation visited upon the starving family of Governor Mouton.

Camp in the field, near Vermillion, La
Oct. 9th 1863

My dear wife and children,

I rec'd your letter from yourself, Estella and Abbie, dated 24th Sept and read it be assured with the greatest pleasure - I am really glad to hear that you are all well and have got along so well and that George is getting to be so nice a boy and that the girls are reading their History so fast - The money shall be forthcoming when you get it through if I live to see you - I have just eat my supper and am feeling very comfortable - We had nice fresh sweet potatoes Beef Liver fried in Pork gravy fresh chickens cooked with broth and some excellent pickles and good tea (no milk, however) - But I think I shall not starve with such diet - All our Regiment had just as good victuals - We do not always fare so well sometimes we have only hard Tack (hard crackers) and tea or water - generally we live first rate - I can stand living that any man can - I never was more healthy in my life - I sleep in my wagon and enjoy it first rate of course I occasionally think of home and some little comforts I used to enjoy there - On the whole I enjoy the service much better than I expected - We are now passing through the finest country I ever looked upon in my life - From Franklin to Vermillion and the officers tell me it is still better clear up to Alexandria and even further up - Such beautiful plantations, I never saw or dreamed of before - (My little nigger Joe has just filled and lighted my pipe I thought I must tell you before writing further) - Such a country and then to see it subjected to the ravages the awful devastating ravages of civil war is enough to chill one's blood and make one doubt substantially the humanity of our race - But so it is - our country must and shall be saved cost what life and treasure it may -

We are now on a bayou passing up through what is called Teche (pronounced tesh) country - Today our advance forces were opposed by the rebels and a battle of an hour ensued at about one o'clock P.M. - Our Reg was in the rear of a large Army but we were in plain hearing of the conflict - The rebels burned the bridge day before yesterday on which we expected to cross and were posted in force across the Bayou - As soon as their position was made out by our forces our Cannon was brought to bear on them and I suppose they something more than in—) [?] for several of our men were wounded and whether any were killed or not I have not yet learned - Major Cowan on our side was quite seriously wounded in the thigh - He belongs to the artillery and is an excellent officer and will be greatly missed in the service - Our cavalry pitched in and crossed the bayou under our cannon and came near capturing the whole lot - We got ten prisoners (perhaps more) and the way the rest skidaddled was really laughable - it is said by those who could see it - One Brigade is the Reserve Brigade and are not put in the advance - Probably when real fighting is required some help will be needed for us - It is said we shall be all mounted as infantry and Cavalry (our Brigade) - This has been talked of for some time past and I am informed tonight that it is expected by our regiment and in fact by all the Brigade that it will be accomplished - I do not know how I can stand it - But I am in for almost anything - I find I can ride on horseback much better than I expected - I have a very fine horse - I shall not go into a colored Regt at present - Geo. Robison with his Regt are with us on the expedition - I think I shall go to Texas without doubt - We have but one Parish to cross now before we reach the State line - I am pleased with the expedition and its excitement - hope I shall come through it all right - I have not yet obtained me a Surgeon's sash of green silk - I tried in New Orleans and could find none - I ought to have got it in New York. If you can get me one in Auburn I shall be glad to have you send it to me - They cost from $10 to $15 a very plain one will suit me - I am not very proud have never dressed up since I have been in the Army - I dress in plain citizen's clothes except the band on my hat - the Sash is a protection in battle for the Surgeon in all enlightened Countries - I think I had better have it - perhaps you can enclose it so it will come direct to me in a small package and send it by mail put in a firm linen case and pay postage or a paper box very small it will come safe - A large box will not come at all, because officers are not allowed to carry much baggage - The box of eatables you choose to send may be sent to New Orleans to my address of the 160th NY Vols without the words, (to follow regiment) on it - The little box with sash and photographs should be marked to follow regiment as I have before directed - We shall probably stay in camp here a day or two - Remember me to Jonas Wood [of Venice] and family and express to them my anxiety for Freddy - I think it wise to change climate with him for this winter. If I had any conveniences for taking care of him I should like to have him with me for this winter - The climate is the finest I ever saw - The nights are quite cold however and a person in poor health should have good shelter - He could see a great deal here - Give my love to all our friends - Remember me to Henry *[Emeline's brother. LGC]* and his wife - you tell me Henry is very kind to you - I can but express my gratitude for it - I hope you will not fail to express to him my deep and abiding sympathy for him and his family for the loss of his darling little girl-

I cannot of course express the great anxiety I felt for her recovery, but it was not to be - A Superior Power willed it otherwise and we must submit -

---

Chapter IV - Teche Country

85

I should be pleased to hear from Giles by letter - I have so little time to write letters having everything to look after in the Medical department for the Reg't - I have not written but few letters except to you - These I shall continue writing - Tell Giles Henry and Theodore not to be particular but write to me and don't fail to have the girls write in every letter. They write excellent letter, getting in all the little matters about Geo. &c &c that pleases me. I must stop or the mail will go as it leaves at 12 tonight and I must carry it to Head Quarters it is now 10 oclock P.M. all are in bed - Write often - Most truly your Husband   Benj. A. Fordyce, U.S. Army.

============

Camp at Carion Crow Bayou 12 mi. south of
Opelousas La. Oct. 13th 1863

My dear wife and children

Having about 5 minutes to write to you I gladly embrace the opportunity - We will probably advance towards Opelousas tomorrow - I am in excellent health and spirits - Last night we had a fearful Thunderstorm commencing about 12 o'clock and it rained in torrents - I had slept in tent for a night or two before but concluded to sleep in Wagon and was very fortunate in doing so & thus escaped getting soaked - The weather is generally very fine & country delightful - The plantations are generally 2000 or more acres each and some of them in the most beautiful condition - Generally their improvements have been greatly modified by the passage of the Army through - The mail man is now waiting for my letter so I must close

We took a rebel General last night, Gen'l Pratt and several others We rather expect exercise every day in the way of fighting I think we have excellent Generals & must succeed - I am well My love to you all and everybody Yours truly,   Benj. A. Fordyce, 160th NYV

Send me 2 woolen shirts & a good navy flannel pair pants & vest in box if you get this in time   Yrs Benj -

---

Camp in the fields, Carion Crow Bayou La.

Oct. 18th 1863

My dear wife

I rec'd your letter of the 1st Oct. night before last at this place You can hardly imagine the gratification it gives me to hear from you and that you are all well and enjoying yourselves - I wrote a few lines to you a few days since but had little time then to give you any particulars - We are encamped in a beautiful place here and have remained here a week today - Had 2 little skirmishes with the enemy - We shall probably move soon but which way I do not know - It is reported here that Sabine pass has been taken by Genl Heintzelman - If this rumor proves true we shall probably return to New Orleans and go to Texas by water or possibly to the assistance of Rosecrans - Whatever course is taken I am quite at ease about the matter simply following the Regiment as Military rule requires endeavoring to discharge my duties with promptness and decision - Dr. Powers is yet at New Orleans he thinks his health is not very good and it is not - nor in my opinion it will be as long as he remains in hospital in New Orleans - Dr. Armstrong the other Asst Surg. of the Regt is expected here daily as his leave of absence has expired - I shall have help then. I have a good hospital tent now the best tent in the Regiment - We are obliged to have a large number of attendants in the field - I have an Ambulance turned over to me with colored driver - In brief to give you a list of the necessary domestics in the field Hospital of a Regiment - Surgeon usually of course is first and has charge as absolute as any other military officer in his command and gives receipts for and becomes responsible to the Government for all the Medicines, Instruments, Wagons, horses, mules, tents and everything belonging to the arrangement, all the provisions and furniture and everything in any wise pertaining which property is of perhaps $3,000 value - Commands everyone under him - Then the Steward who makes reports and is an overseer of all arrangements, provisions, medicines, &c under charge of Surgeon - Hospital Warden who administers medicines and directs the cooking for sick and dresses wounds with Steward - Two Cooks whose business you know - Two nurses to take care of sick - Orderlies, one for each Surgeon to take care of horses One woman (colored) or man as may be selected for washing for hospital - One driver of four mules for baggage wagon - One driver for Ambulance two mules - One servant for each Asst Surgeon - two for principal or Surgeon in charge of Regt - Every man and woman of the above are kept as actively occupied as they can wish - They have little time for mischief particularly when the Regiment is sickly or on the March - I eat at the same table with the attendants and of course have the same fare - This is unusual with officers of my grade to mess with attendants - but I prefer it for the present - I pay for my board $9.00 per month and have such extras as I am disposed to furnish. We live most of the time as well as I could ask (if I could only learn my cooks to be neat) - All the above are detailed men from the Regiment and are liable to be returned to companies if they are incompetent for their duties except the Hospital Steward he is a non commissioned staff officer and is liable to discharge if incompetent - Everything is quiet and pleasant in my Department - I have sole charge of the whole Hospital arrangement and have had since my Arrival here I have work enough I can assure you - I have bought me some cotton flannel drawers and an infantry overcoat, so I am comfortable - I should like some flannel undershirts of large size and a couple good strong cotton shirts with Linen bosoms and wristbands - Flannel shrinks so much by washing that mine have already become too small - Yet I wear them - If you can make and send me some by someone in two or three months if you have opportunity that will answer every purpose - I have had two of my handkerchiefs stolen, have enough left -

I was so situated that I could very plainly see the battle of the 15th inst - Our camp is about two and a half miles from place where the fighting was done - Early in the morning the rebels came out of a large piece of woods in very fine order in line of battle - The Cavalry in advance and Infantry some eighty rods in rear - Their line appeared to be from 3/4 to 1 mile long - Our Cavalry pickets saw them and began to fire upon them at 6 1/2 o'clock A.M. - Our Regiment the 160th and in fact the whole 19th Army Corps here were ordered under arms to be ready at a minute's notice to march - I climbed a tree standing by my tent (after I had my horse saddled and teams harnessed ready to move with Regt) so that I could see the entire field with a field glass I bought in N.Y. City - Our Cavalry pickets came flying in under the steady rapid advance of the rebel army which came on rapidly towards one of the Nims Battereys, with the intention of charging on it - The Battery opened with shell in a way that Nims knows of; sending them very nearly in the direction of the rebel Cavalry and Infantry acting very much as though he meant to hit them - About this time there appeared on the field at the other side about 500 Cavalry and 5000 infantry with some of the best heavy field artillery in America, showing a little different standard of colors presenting a beautiful but rather imposing appearance particularly if one stood in front - I admit I preferred the rear of these men - About this time the Cavalry (rebel) made a dash towards a battery and were met by our Cavalry in a manner apparently unexpected by them - For they went kiting back in double quick I can assure you - The artillery then opened on the woods sheltering them and at every cessation of firing, our Cavalry would dash in on them scouring woods and plains as far as the eye could reach - To see the hasty retreat and rapid following up by our Cavalry was really cheering - The 160th was ordered out to support Battery L, U.S. Regulars at about 10 1/2 A.M. I went out and when we arrived at position with battery the fight was ended -

We had two Cavalry men killed and some ten or twelve wounded - some say there were seventy or more rebels killed & many wounded - I have no means of knowing how many I certainly saw several of their horses without riders I have no opportunity of learning the injuries inflicted on the rebels - Their loss must have been severe from the close Cavalry conflict - Our Cavalry brought in a large drove of Cattle and quite a number of horses and mules, about 20, I saw -

I will send the watch of D. Wing by express to James Cannon as soon as I can return to New Orleans - It is in my trunk at Algiers all safe - Dan'l Wings body was never found and recognized at Port Hudson - I have some little hope he may have been sent off a prisoner and still be living yet have no means of knowing -

I would certainly sell the old mare or give her away - I certainly think you will enjoy yourself best at our own house - hire a boy or man, if you need - I would certainly keep Cynthia I think she is as good as you can possibly find -

The girls I am glad to learn are doing well and reading and improving their minds - I like to have them learn to ride too but I want them to be careful not to get hurt by falling off the horse - I have the greatest horse I ever owned - I should feel safe to have the girls ride him anywhere, or even George - he is not skittish, but he is moderate cannon or guns indeed nothing scares him - he will go over a dead horse or ox or anything jump a ditch or fence like a deer - He don't like to have others run by him - I will write to the girls next time - Give my love to all friends - Hiram Congdon, Firm, and John Strong and everybody - Tell Firman to do the best he can for you and he shall not be the loser if I live to see him - Remember me to Elnora *[his sister, Elnora Fordyce, wife of Alvin Seeley, of Scipio. LGC]* I have not yet seen Capt. Corning - think I will soon -

Your husband ever   Benj. A. Fordyce

Oct 18th 1863

My dear husband,

We received and perused with a great deal of pleasure your letter dated Sept. 29 & 30 - written within seventy miles of Texas and glad were we to hear that you are well and enjoying yourself and have time to play chess we are well and enjoying ourselves as well as we can with our dearest one so far from home & exposed to the dangers of war it is quite healthy in this neighborhood Mrs Anson Whitman has been very sick not expected to live from a day or 2 (miscarriage - boy) dr Hewitt attended Mrs Whitman Mrs Tifft is better Your father is doctoring to James Woods Mrs Murdock is some better Wellington [Murdock][6] gone to Elmira to receive drafted men one drafted man from Venice that is young Asaf Whiting Uncle Raymond and Aunt Ruth Warring have been here today uncle is in a good deal of pain I applied the battery with good effect he was well pleased and took the battery home with him Levi Sherman has lost a child I heard it was Rube it was the one that had fits. Cynthia & I take a great deal of comfort doing our chores milking and feeding the cows pumpkins seeing the pigs grow they are most fat enough to butcher the old mare answers my purpose first rate she is as good as ever I most think I shall winter the stock it seems the most like home to have them to take care of we do all the work we can have not needed Firman but a few days since harvesting Alfred Whipple has moved to Auburn I succeeded in getting 76 rails he promised them   I sent for them at three different times & got a load each time and that was all I could get & the old man wants them endorsed on his note.   I have just heard that Elder Ames is very sick   the elections so far have gone Union by a large majority Ohio Pennsylvania Indiana Iowa have given a large Union majority people think that will do a great deal towards closing the war more than fighting   I do not see any better prospect of its closing here than there has been without the elections have something to do with it.   In regard to the Pierce matter   Mr Fish has been to the surrogate and been released from being bail   the surrogate has written to Mrs Pierce that she will have to procure another bail.   John is a going to Auburn this week and I am going to send by him to see what you will have to do to be released if it needs an order from you   I want you to send one   write to the surrogate yourself and see what he says about it   it is now bed time   I must stop writing   Monday eve Firman has been husking corn in the barn today   it has rained all day   he thinks your corn house never was any fuller of corn than it will be this year   I shall have all the new corn left and some old after the pigs are fat   oats are 70 cts bushel wool is 75 cts pound everything else in proportion   all kinds of goods higher than I ever knew them before.   *[In 1855, oats were 31 cents per bu. LGC]* I told George pa was coming home next spring   he says no he ain't   he's coming home this fall and I think you will have to sleep with George   there will be nothing left of me by spring   he kicks me so and rolls over me a dozen times a night   we shall all come to New Orleans if you stay much longer   I do want to see you so bad as George says   I shall send you a box as soon as I can after I find where you are a going to be   I must stop writing and leave room for the girls   I think of you all the time

From your wife   Emeline

———

Venice Oct. 19th 1863

My dear father

Ma told George that you was coming home next Spring and he said no he aint he is coming home this fall   we don't want you to come home until you get homesick enough to stay home.   Mr Babbitt is husking corn in the barn today   it rains like fun here now I can tell you   I played chess with Abbie Saturday   and beat her twice   she wont play with me very often. We live on old pies, old cake and pork and once in a while a little honey and white fish I guess our folks don't bake only once a week. George says tell Pa for him, Abbie buse me and she won't let me play with her doll and my name is George Slocum Fordyce. George is teasing to write a letter to Pa so I must get him some paper or he won't let me write I just kissed him and he said don't bother me so much for I is writing to Pa You would of laughed this morning to of seen him act as he will when Pa comes home he runned and jumped and screamed about as loud as he could yell. Mrs. Congdon is trustee *[of the School District]* now - I espect we will have an elegant teacher. I forgot to tell you I have made a cone frame and it looks very well. After 3 o'clock P.M: it has cleared off beautiful and it really seems beautiful to see the sun again after it has rained so hard. George says tell Pa he has been out to help Cynthia feed the cows pumpkins. I ain't going to Sherwoods Corners to live this winter - I am scolded enough to home without going anywhere to get more, but the scolding generally goes in one ear and out the other. George has come again and says tell Pa he is a nice boy and Abbie pulls his hair because he wants to help her play chess I must stop writing now.

From your daughter   Stelle

Venice [Oct] 19 1863

My dear father

Stell and ma are playing chess while I am writing and Stell has just took back a move. I have been out to Grandma Slocums and stayed over a week and I went to William Howlands and once to the store along with Grandma and to Hattie Pearls *[Mrs. D. R. Pearl]* Grandpa got some thistles in his hand and got out all of them that he could find and I guess he got cold in it for it got all swelled up and it was swelled up when I cam from there. Ma beat Stell playing chess and now they are playing another game Stell thought she was going to beat her all so fast when all at once she found out that she was beat herself This morning George said to Stell "you are big but Abbie is too little." tonight before he went to bed after he was undressed he got some capes and a Shawl and a pillow   he laid down on the floor and covered himself with the shawl   he called me to come and lay down with him So I had to go but pretty soon he got up and called to ma to put him to bed so I had to put up the things he had got out I am so sleepy I have got to go to bed and I will finish it in the morning Stell has gone to bed but now she has come down again

Oct 20 1863 Ma has gone over to John Strongs to have him write on the letter for she is afraid that if she or Stell write on it that it won't go. I asked George what I should tell Pa for him and he said "tell him that I'm a little man." Stell has come in here and is trying to plague me. Stell is sitting on the floor and George is on top of her. now George has come up to me and wants me to "take him" he has got the umbrella and has come up to me and say that he is "an old Shing" - now I must close.

From your daughter   Abbie

[in Emeline's handwriting - same letter. LGC]

Mr. Bateman has sold 50 acres of his farm where the old house is to Uncle David Martins son in law, Snyder   Mrs Murdick[6] is not expected to live. *[Prob. Clarinda, Mrs. Lyman Murdock; she did "live" - died 1871. LGC]* They have called a court martial to try some of the quakers over west who were drafted and refuse to bear arms or pay 200 dollars. Z Powel Mary Fells husband is one. Mary Jones has come home sick with diarrhoea. The President has called for 300,000 more volunteers John says he is going now over the left...

It is very pleasant this morning write often   your letters do us a great deal of good   write to us every mail   come home as soon as you can the people need you very much & we a great deal more the President thinks the war will soon be ended with 300,000 more men the draft raised money not men

Sabbath eve Oct. 25 1863

My dear husband
As I am alone this evening I thought I would commence a letter to you I write every week so as to put a letter in the [Post] office every

---

Tuesdays mail *[BAF did not save all these letters - or, he did not receive them. LGC]* I have received no letters from you in 12 days - it seems a great while and do not know when to look for one from accounts in the Thursday paper you must be at Point Isabel at the mouth of the Rio Grande a great ways from home John thinks it cannot be so We are all well Estella and Abbie have gone to Singing school the first one of the winter term George is abed he won't have it but that you are a coming home this fall every time he does any thing cunning he says are you a going to write that to Pa - he gets up on my back and kisses me he says you must say what a sweet boy I are - he grows his flesh is as hard as can be he looks nice in his pants he threatens what he will do in them occassionally I do not write much about the girls they write for themselves John has got his fence finished and it seems odd enough to go through a gate to go to his house he has moved his barn a little further west and is a going to build on some stables onto the east end of his barn I went down to Mr. Baldwins this afternoon he spoke to me about taking our sugar bush next spring he said he would furnish as many buckets as we had and would draw old wood from his woods provided there was not enough in our woods would not use any good wood he has a large kettle that would make us as much sugar as we ever have write what you think about it old Mr. Whipple asked for a letter from the church today for himself and wife they are going west to live with a son Myron Cranson has made him an offer for his farm - they differ fifty dollars Firman talks of renting Mr. Batemans house the one where Mr. Valentine live. Bateman asks 2 dollars a month for the house Firm thinks it is most too much   The older part of community prophesy a very cold winter   they say the muskrats are double walling their houses & that is a sure sign Your father was here last week and took dinner with us he is doctoring all along the Cannon ridge *[Indian Field Rd. along the "ridge" west of Venice Center. LGC]* - he inquired your prices for a visit he seems anxious to please your employers Mrs Murdock is better Mrs Andrews has had one of her bad spells - your Father called and relieved her - Sister Maria was down here last week and staid all night. Mrs John Snider was here and spent the day. Phebe Wright was here Carrie was here and staid all night - she has concluded to go to Rushvill to teach a family school and take music lessons so you see our friends do not mean I should get lonesome singing school is out and I shall have to stop writing - it is all hurly-burly now Mon. eve: I have just heard today of Frederic

Allen's wife - she only lived three weeks after he was brought home I heard her disease was diptheria   Alexander Meads wife was buried last week   Old Levy Shermans wife is dead and so is Rube [Sherman]   Wellington Murdock[6] is home yet, he wishes he was in any other part of the army but the Potomac   he says there was twelve able to do duty in his company when he left and there has been five wounded since George Robison   Arza son was severely wounded in the leg   Benny Arnold is quite sick, is at home yet   Mary Jones has come home sick   it is quite cold today   freezes so that the mud bore me up around the barn   I have cleaned out the pig pen and put some straw in the pen   pulled the beets today   the children and myself are alone   Cynthia has gone home to stay a day or two It seems quite lonesome   we miss you more and more as winter approaches   the little fixing you used to do   preparing for winter Firman don't fix a thing only as I tell him   a poor care taker   I dare not and everyone tells me not to send a box to you until I know more certain where you are   I wish you had your drawers - be sure and get up a pair if you can before I send your box   I have one ready to pack when I think you can get it - shall have to pay $7.50 on a hundred   Mrs. Baily called here last week - I paid the insurance which was $8.20   I must stop writing and leave roon [room] for Abbie   I hope you are enjoying yourself and learning as much as you expected to   hope the war will end this winter   do not see much prospect of it   every body that you ever knew send their love to you I miss you more and more but hope for the best   come home as soon as you can or get an appointment nearer home so that we can get a letter every week (or we shall come where you are)

From your affectionate wife Emeline

.

(PS)   We write so often that our letters cannot be very interesting George Fancher sent us only six of your photographs.

(PS)   Estella thinks I made a good many mistakes in spelling and grammar in my letters.

Tuesday Morning   it froze hard last night   had fried pudding for breakfast   the girls and George had quite a time over it for fear one would eat more than the other.   Simon Ferrigo has just gone from here   he wants our cows   offered me $50 for them   write what you think about it   Emeline

---

Venice Oct 26th 1863

My dear father

I have just got a fire out in the Office and it seems real nice to be away from George where he won't climb on the back of my chair and kiss me five or six times and say now Stelle you write that to Pa and is Pa coming home before long and will he bring that gray poney and kiss me and say he loves me I believe if the house should tumble down Mr. Babbitt never would know it until someone had pointed it out to him. We had a real nice Singing School last night Mr. Conklin said he had always had a very nice school here and he was going to have a better one this winter than he had ever had before. George has just come out here and I won't have any more peace until he goes in the house, he says tell Pa he is a nice boy. Alexander Mead teaches our school this winter. Abbie and I have peeled a bushel of apples today. May has got a large pan and a box full of Everlasting flowers. We had a small pan full of horse chestnuts. Carrie Foote wants us to move to Auburn next spring if you are well - she would like to hire a Piano and take music lessons and give me her lessons. Abbie has gone down to Mr. Baldwins to read a book Carrie has got the title of the book is the Wide Wide World George grows mischeivous every day he lives you would laugh to see him perform with his pants - he think there never was anything so nice as his pants and his new cap as he calls it. You wrote you were playing chess when you got our letters I think you might come home and play chess a while with us. I must stop writing for this time

(From your daughter, Stelle to her father, Benj. A. Fordyce.

Venice Oct 26 1863

my dear father

Cinthia has gone away somewhere and I am going to sleep with Ma tonight and Stell has gone upstairs to bed along with George. ma is doing up a paper to send to you for you know you wrote to us to send you papers often Stell and I core and quarter apples most every day. We had a Singing school last night and Stell and I went to it. I saw Wellington Murdock at Singing school[6]. George is as mischievous as he can be and has to comb my hair every once in a while but he pulls more than he combs. He says "Pa has gone to Texas." George says that M is for Emeline. I went out under the walnut trees today and found a few on the ground and then I got a stick about 3 ft long and knocked of quite a good many. I gave George some of them, when I got in the house and had to get him the hammer and they came to pieces pretty quick after he got hold of them.

From your daughter, Abbie

Vermillion Ville La Nov 3rd 1863

My dear wife

By the last mail I did not receive any letters from home - the mail before I rec'd two one from Estella and Abbie and one from Carrie - I am disappointed when a mail comes and I do not get any letters. I hope you will not forget to be sure and have a letter or Newspaper come to me by every steamer from NY - I have received only one newspaper yet from home - I would like to have you send me the County paper *[published weekly]* as often as every two weeks and be sure and send me a daily Tribune *[NY]* every two or three days - I want the Election returns - Today is election day in New York and I thought rather than go to election I would write to you -

We have returned about forty miles from where I dated my last letter to the girls We marched the distance in two days - The men bearing the march quite well - We have some sick with Fever and Ague and some from Diarrhoea - Our monthly report for October does not report a single death in the Regt - So you can judge the diseases are not very fatal - No other Regiment that I am acquainted with here that has no deaths to report for a month - We had a little evidence that we were not surrounded wholly by friends the other night - or indeed in the day time - Our regiment sent out a four mule team with 10 men to get sweet potatoes on the 31st Oct - They went out from Camp about five miles and just as they arrived at the potato field they were surprised by a Guerilla party and all captured - They burned the wagon and made tracks as fast as possible in some other direction - We should not have known what had become of them if it had not been for an old negro driver of the mules - He is perhaps sixty five or seventy years old and when they were captured he could not walk or march so fast as they required him - They put all the men on the mules and they being Cavalry with their horses, hid in the woods at a short distance from where they captured the wagon - they put our soldiers on behind them - They marched the old negro some distance say half a mile but found he could not keep up they put him on behind one of the men - They could not get off as fast as they desired in this way and let the old man go - The old man made tracks for our camp as soon as the rebels were out of sight - I asked him if he could walk better this way than with the rebels - "O yes" he says "a heap better - I could come right smart dis way" The 75th regt are turned into Cavalry now - the boys call them the sore-a__s Cavalry because they had no saddles and probably got somewhat chafed in fact some of them could hardly ride - Well they were sent after the rebels but of course could not find them for the rebels had some 4 hours the start and were well mounted -

Capt. Corning has returned he arrived at his regiment on the 30th Oct - I had recd letters from you of later date than the time of his leaving - He very kindly brought the package you sent by him (as far as he could) to New Iberia which is about twenty miles from where I am now - I think I shall get it all safe but cannot tell - Yesterday we marched about eighteen miles - the work is very hard on a Surgeon when marching particularly when there is but one for a Regiment as with me - No man is excused without my written pass - I am required to see that no man falls out from any cause and to require every man to march who is able - The duty becomes very disagreeable sometimes as some of the men feel discouraged not so much with their hardships (which be assured are great) as with the miserable copperhead peace sentiment at home - This is enough to discourage any good soldier to seek every contemptible means resorted to for political ascendancy when they are exposing their lives and health for the substantial permanancy of our government and institutions - I can assure you they feel greatly humiliated and indignant to think that their awful sacrifice is not appreciated - You would be astonished to hear them express the sentiments of true patriot even with their severest exposures - Nothing intimidates them in the least and such generous promises as they are wont to give these false friends at home who are putting obstacles in the way of our progress I really hope I may never live to see fulfilled - Men who have braved battle of the most sanguinary character who have braved the malaria of the swamps of a southern climate who have seen thousands of their comrades bodies left to molder and decay in a soil far distant from home and kinder, the actual and real victims of the Copperhead sentiment now seeking to become dominant at the north and which, only, is responsible for this dreadful war that is so devastating our land - Mark me a retribution awaits them to which the riot in New York may be compared to a friendly peace gathering - It will be visited too upon the rising generations as the old stain of Tory clings to the degenerate grand children of the Revolutionary copperheads of '76

Tell me that the negro slaves do not have a just appreciation of liberty and human rights! The idea is as false as the D——l could invent and misrepresent a truth - Their whole age of oppression has only proved a school to educate them on this particular subject - It is now and always has been the prayer by day and the dream by night that their rights as human beings shall sometime be respected - The day has truly dawned sooner than the most sanguine anticipated - It has certainly come when slavery must soon pass into history in the United States - One of the ambulance drivers was asked in my presence (the interrogator pointing to some fine negro quarters, some 40 buildings, on the plantation on which we are encamped owned and worked by Gov. Mouton of La) if he had not rather live in one of those nice houses than to be following the army - I shall never forget his answer - There were four colored persons at the table eating at the time - This man is always very still and quiet seldom or never speaks unless he is spoken to - He deliberately looked up and answered - "Yes I had rather live there only remove the yoke but not with that on me - I am willing to follow the army as long as I live and even die if my children or my grandchildren may be free - I fully believe the time is near at hand I may not live to see it - But the promise is that all men shall gain their bread by the sweat of the brow and "I" said he, "believe it is about to be fulfilled" - There was a calmness and assuring resignation about the man that was truly impressive to observe -

His confidence with all the colored population is unwavering that the final result will be the end of slavery - When I notice such unlimited confidence in the result with so much evident capacity for taking care of themselves as is manifested daily here I think perhaps the great sacrifice of life treasure home comforts and all the casualties of our frightful war is well made for the inestimable boon then will be conferred on four millions of human beings - A question comes up with northern men like this will the negroes fight - This is settled here now in the affirmative and with such an affirmation as already makes the welkin ring - More of this some other time -

I am not quite as well as usual for two days past - but am feeling better tonight - I have had some Diarrhoea. But I think I have fully controlled it - We shall stay here several days probably and then go to Texas - have had no battles lately - In fact there is no enemy here worthy of the name - Remember me to all friends - Send your and George's photographs - Lewis Close is at the Hospital in New Orleans is improving - Hiram Galusha is in this reg't - is related to our folks - Send his respects to Uncle John, &c *[John Fordyce, brother of BAF's father; relationship goes back to BAF's grandmother, Rebecca (Horton) Fordyce, and her sister, Susan, who married Robert McCollum. A McCollum daughter married a Galusha, in the Lockport area; Hiram is a McCollum grandson, as BAF is a grandson, of the Scipio pioneer generation. LGC]*

Yrs affectionately, B. A. Fordyce

(PS) My love to Jn Snyder and wife, Jonas Wood and family, Jn Strong & Nelson and Lovina - I should like to have them all write to me - Tell Firm, I send my compliments and place great dependence on him to help you - Remember me to Cynthia and the little ones particularly -

Yrs. - Shall write to Carrie tonight.

My dear husband

Sabbath morning after Meeting, Nov 8

It was with a great deal of pleasure that we perused your last letter dated Oct 10 written near Opolusas to learn that you are well and in excellent spirits - we are well and getting along very well - it is cold and quite snowy. Elnora was down here when we got your letter in which you wrote you wanted me to send you some clothes, shirt pants and vest - we were agoing to pack a box - I have got to wait now until I can go to Auburn again before I can pack it - I went last week to see about your sash, will go and get your clothing as soon as I can - the roads are very muddy and I have no way to go on my own. Firman is so slow with his corn - is about 2/3 done husking - he has hired Mr. Bateman's horse, is agoing to move this week - he does not take care of things well enough to suit me to have him live in my house - had rather fasten it up and come back occasionally and see to things myself. I believe they have concluded to have Elder Glenville come here to preach - is talks of buying Mrs. Hammond's farm - he is a very smart preacher. Mr. Conklin was here to dinner today - his brother, the tailor, lost his wife last week - they live in Groton village - it is very sickly there and around Moravia - think it is caused by the flood *[July 21, 1863]* - New York state has given 35,000 majority for the union, every state except New Jersey has gone union - the soldiers around here got home just in time to vote - were too late in the west part of the state - they thought the railroad men were bribed. Col. Welling of the 138 Reg't gave them so many minutes to start the cars at a certain place - New York City - he told them that if they did not start them in that time he would take possession of the cars himself have them all arrested - in that way they were just in time to vote - Amos Jones is quite sick - Charley Corlies, Vanliew, Shorkley are home. Charley Corlies has sold his farm to John Morse and the english man that has worked for Mr. Murdock[6] - James Wood had to send for Dr. Hurd before they got well. Tim Tehan's wife says if you come home next spring it will do her - she says she cannot have any other doctor. Jos. Mitchell's wife is dead - has been dead for some time - I did not hear the particulars of her death. John Strong goes to Auburn tomorrow meet with the supervisors. Mr. Murdock[6] has gained his suit with Mr. Akin in regard to interest on railroad bonds - I believe it cannot be carried to any other court. Amos Jones called here this morning on his way back to Washington - he said he wished you were in his reg !- they have a new surgeon there now - I do wish you were near home so that we could advise with you and get letters oftener - as long as I hear that you are well, I feel as contented as any one could - if you are sick be sure and come home - Cap. Corning's wife feels very uneasy about him - she has not heard from him since he left home which was about the middle of Sept. *[Andrew Yates Corning of Scipio, discharged 1864; ill health LGC]* - I sent you a towel full of dried fruit and maple sugar by him - write if you get it - you probably will get your sash before you get this letter - let me know if you receive it - George grows smart every day he lives - he wishes pa would come home a dozen times every day - we all count the weeks, days to see how quick the first of April will come - he is an uncommon boy - today when I try to have him mind, when he don't want to, he gets up in his high chair and says I will ball [bawl] - I laugh at him and he soon stops balling - Estella takes things as cool as ever - and Abbie sputters as usual - she is fixing for bed now and sputters all the time. Estella and I think we shan't have her write in our letters without she stops blotting them - Henry has paid me his account, which enables me to get your clothing without taking money out of the bank. I got the children nearly riged [rigged] for winter. Isaac Morse making us some shoes. Cynthia paid. Firman nearly paid - that is all we owe, then if there is any thing left for me without collecting notes or taking money out of the bank shall get me some things - there are a good many unsettled accounts yet. Father has sold an acre of our farm - he calls it - for $70, is agoing to give me half, when I see him, so Maria says - has paid her election day, quite a present. I shall put mine in the bank until you come home - Cynthia talks some of going to Sherwoods - when we go, direct to Sherwood after this until you hear to the contrary - shall go there about the first of Dec to stay a while - your friends are very anxious for you to come home, as it begins to grow more sickly, as winter approaches - they think you have learned and seen enough by this time - have heard nothing more from those doctors - be sure and take good care of yourself and my earnest prayer is that you will live to come home to your family again - it begins to seem as though this cruel war is drawing to a close - give my respects to George Robinson when you see him - excuse bad Spelling and grammar etc. from your affectionate wife E. Fordyce

Venice Nov 8th 1863

My dear Father

Mother has gone to meeting tonight and Abbie is reading Ledgers and George is abed asleep and I think now is the time for me to write to you. Addie Jump came down here yesterday and stayed all night and went to meeting today Elder Glenvill preached today and after Elder Glenvill had said Peace and Harmony long enough Mr Alward had to get up and say that the sermon was most exclent I have got a new winter hat and so has Addie.

Nov. 9th

Secretary Chase's daughter is going to be married to Gov Sprague the 12th of this month. George has said more than a dozen times today I wish Pa would come home and see me. Mr Congdon is coming here tomorrow morning to fix a place to go upstairs out of the kitchen. Abbie and George blotted the paper on the other side so it showed through on my side but I did not get it on Carrie says she dont see how we can help loving him almost to death, he is so affectionate Carrie is going to Rushville to be a Governess in a family and take music lessons. They think to Sherwoods Corners they are going to have an exelent school Mr Briggs is going to teach there he has taught in New York eight or ten years I must stop writing for this time.

From your affectionate daughter   Stelle

Venice Nov 9th 1863

my dear father

ma is spinning and Stell and George are out to the office Amos Jones came here this morning and said that he wished you were in his regiment doctors were not very smart there he didn't think We have had two or three snowstorms the first one we have had was last Saturday toward evening it has not snowed so very [much] though any of the time. We had a Singing School yesterday it began at 3 o'clock the next one we have will not [be] until next week Tuesday evening. George tells us that he shall "holler and howl if we don't mind." George is telling Ma that she "eats flour" and now he has come up to me and has said "Abbie you write [.....] Ma says what a boy you are." Ma spatted George a little and then he said, "I shall go out to the office and tell Stell bout dat" and he is telling ma to fix his overcoat on good. I asked him what that I should tell Pa for him and at first he said "I shan't tell you" then I said dont you want me to write anything to Pa for you and then he said "tell him I'm a naughty boy" I have come out to the office now to get away from George. Ma has just called Stell for something and she has gone in the house John Strong and Mr Summerton have just gone through the yard. Addie Jump came down here Saturday and stayed all night and went to meeting and Singing School yesterday and Uncle Theodore came down after her it had been snowing in little fine flakes when all at once it began to hale it haled a minute then it stopped and then it began again and it is haling now. Cinthia went to Auburn this morning along with Mr Jones folks George is to bed asleep So he will not be here to pull my paper away from me and make me blot. Ma is sprinkling and Stell is reading letters I did not know that I was so near the bottom of the page so I must close my letter

from your daughter Abbie

Camp in the fields near
Vermillion Villa La Nov 9th 1863

My dear wife and children

I recd your letter of Oct 13th on the 8th inst - I was most happy to hear from you and that you were all well - Your letters came by Cairo and did not come so quick as usual - That route is now more uncertain than by Ocean mail steamer and takes several days more time - Capt Corning was twenty two days getting from Cairo to New Orleans - He arrived here all safe and brought your most acceptable package to New Iberia - I obtained it yesterday and will now open it and let you know how it is - I sent for it (as I have opportunity every day) by one of our Ambulance - I have just got choked with some Molasses candy of which we have abundance every day - Jo brought me some not quite hard enough - The choking is not dangerous and

Chapter IV - Teche Country

I can see to write now - I find things all right and nice too - They will prove a great luxury to me - They only cost me fifty cents the way they came - You ask if I have an overcoat - to be sure I have and am writing in it now - I have just come in from a horse race - The officers (some of them) when in camp and no fighting likely to go off spoil for fun so they will go out and have a race sometimes betting something at other times running for the fun only. This is the second race I have seen here but I presume there have been twenty or thirty since we commenced marching - I was visiting Col Geo. Robinson and Dr Lester and they wanted to go up so of course I went along - There are some very fine horses here and fast too - One owned by Col Purlee of the 114th N.Y. Vols is the fastest I have seen - He has always won and is very fast - other officers occasionally think they have a fast horse and so must try him - They do not generally want to try but once

There are little skirmishes every day with the pickets varying in advantages but generally we get the best of the rebels - Our whole Regt with the 116th New York went out to protect a forage train and I went out with them - we went about five miles out some two or more out of the lines - The way a forage train is conducted may be of interest to you - The large army wagons drawn by four mules or horses are sent out protected by Military force sometimes a company at others a regiment or more if danger of capture is anticipated - They go out for corn, fodder, potatoes, wood, &c   The train I went consisted of twenty five wagons - They go till they find what they want sometimes ten or more miles - When they find corn in cribs or potatoes or anything needed in the army they take it without reference to who the proprietor is - The day I went out the teams emptied a large planter's cribs, not leaving him an ear for his family or stock but having a little compassion on him he having two sons in the rebel army they took all his mules and horses fit for use nearly all his pigs and all the sheep they could catch all his chickens all his cattle fit for beef - This merely to save the old man the necessity of looking up fodder for them - Kind was'nt it - I went into the house and talked with the old folks - They talked anything but secession to me - gave me a good dinner of corn bread - they have no flour - and milk I really felt sorry that a portion of our people would put themselves at their age (the man 62, the lady 58) in a situation to make such demands and sacrifices necessary. I gave them a little tea for which they were very thankful.

The results of the elections are most cheering to the army so far as heard from - We have not heard from New York yet - I want you to send me the Auburn Journal *[weekly/County newspaper]* and be sure and send me the election returns -

Emeline rent the place if you think best or rent the office alone or with the house and barn but control the land yourself, unless you sell it - which you may do It is worth $5,000 five thousand dollars with farming tools & sugar aparatus - medicines, Library and instruments - I would not sell it less than ($4500) four thousand five hundred dollars and throw in nothing - You may sell it for this sum and take a mortgage for twenty five hundred - two thousand dols to be paid down and the Mortgage duly executed for purchase money - otherwise, do not sell it - I have paid out too much money on the place and it is too good a house to sell for less money -

Do not let any cattle in to the young orchard & watch it with regard to snow -

Mr Anthony is a very fine man and I think could not fail to do a large business there - Have nothing to do with the quacks in any way they are more dangerous than the enemys bayonets - I would not agree to board anybody or to furnish wood to any one -

Give my love to all - Estella and Abbie must write every opportunity - I have but little time to write - Am still alone Dr Armstrong is still at home quite sick thinks he is not able to return yet - I was never in better health -

I think we shall move in some direction soon I have orders to send all sick to Hospital New Orleans tomorrow - we may go one way or the other - you know as well as we do.

I found a mail was going out in an hour and thought I would write - shall get two months pay soon - Have sent money only once - will write to the girls soon - Write often and send as before - Kiss Geo & the Girls for me.

Your affectionate husband, Benj. A. Fordyce

=======

Camp in the field near Vermillion Ville, La
Nov. 15th 1863

My dear wife

I rec'd your letters with that of the girls dated Oct 18th and 19th day before yesterday - And as always is the case was glad to hear from you -

We continue in camp at Vermillion yet and on Ex Gov Moutons plantation - I send you a copy of his illustrious sons orders relating to the Military operations of this (i.e. the son) rebel General Mouton throughout this country - His mother yesterday came to Genl Weitzels camp asking for food stating that the family were actually in a state of suffering for want of food - She was required to make her request in writing, which she did, bursting into tears - Genl Weitzel with the approval of Genl Franklin sent them a wagon load of provisions of all kinds that would make them comfortable This must have been quite humiliating - I think after such boasting of the ability of the south to do any and everything that pertains to the exercise of power by Military force and civil authority - This part of the country is beautiful and extremely fertile - Immense crops of corn and cane are raised here - I have visited the sugar houses - some of them I think (with the machinery & apparatus) must have cost from 25 to $50,000 Made of brick and put up in fine workmanlike style - The climate is very pleasant and warm - We have had only three frosts yet and we at the north would consider them very light - yet the men suffered considerably with cold - I must stop my description of this country and write you or answer some of your questions of home affairs - I was sorry to learn from your letter of the sickness of many of those who have always been friends to me and highly esteemed in return - Mrs Whitman I wish you would give her my compliments and sympathies and hopes that she will soon recover - Mrs Murdock[6] too do not forget me to her any other of those who are sick whom I have reason to esteem and be assured they are numerous in Venice and vicinity -

You tell me Rube Sherman is dead Tell John that curiosity being gone it will be a serious drawback on fishing excursions at and around the head of Owasco Lake - Rube was a reasonable excuse for many a contract with Levi to fish - May his ashes rest quiet as the incidents are many that will recall him to memory -

You and Cynthia do the work! don't work beyond your strength - I am earning enough so that you can get all necessary outside work done without making slaves of yourselves - Have your wood cut and drawn for the winter - Feed the Old man well and she will do well for you.

The rails were bought of Alfred Whipple with the consent of his Father who was present and wished me to also take enough to pay his demand note - to which I agreed after Alfreds was paid - Keep an account of the rails obtained and when Alfred is out have him present & endorse it on Alfreds note if you do not obtain enough to pay both -

The Pierce affair will be all right I think - I will write to Woodin Surrogate and see what is my liability or get released immediately or in a few days.

[Mark in margin of the paragraph]: Private

I was glad to hear the crops are so good - Tell Firm to be saving and take good care of the fodder - Do not be in haste about selling your grain - I think prices will still advance -

Have John urge settlement of accts and notes - The times are good and you can plead want of money for I may not get pay again in two or three months more - particularly if we go west - Send me a green sash as I wrote before if you can -

Chapter V
Christmas in Louisiana...and in New York State

From New Iberia Dr. Fordyce writes of the hospitality of Dr. Dungan, a Southern gentleman, and his family who by special invitation entertained him for Christmas dinner. He receives a letter from his family telling of their activities; and Father Slocum writes to his son-in-law in quaint Quaker tones. From Franklin, LA, Dr. Fordyce mentions the exchange of 600 prisoners of war and describes military life in tents in freezing weather.

New Iberia, Nov. 19th, 1863

You observe I date from a new place - we moved on the 16th down to Camp Pratt and on the 17th to the present camp below New Iberia - We have a very pleasant situation and a prospect of remaining here some time - We are in easy communications with New Orleans and I shall be able (if we remain here) to receive your letters as regularly as if I was at New Orleans - I have just rec'd your letter of 27th and 29th Oct with that of the girls - I have also rec'd today the Green Sash I wrote to you for - It is a very nice one and I am highly pleased with it - There is not a nicer looking one that I have seen in this Army - I have still some thoughts of changing my position to a colored regiment provided I can pass examination - I think I shall be able to come home just as soon if I make the change as without it - I learn that I can resign better from such a regiment than from this regiment - When Dr Armstrong returns and I learn that he is now in New Orleans I may get detached a short time to some Hospital - I think I would like it for a short time although I like Field service much the best - There is a Captain Underhill in our Regiment who is today notified to come before the Examining board at New Orleans to be examined as to his qualifications for Colonel of a colored regiment - He is a very finely educated man and a relation (distant) of the Underhills in Ledyard - He is very desirous that I should go with him - Many of his officers will be from this Reg't - If he passes - I can not yet fully determine in my own mind what will be best for me - I shall not move in the matter without due consideration. I wrote to you something in regard to selling to Smith Anthony's son - I have since learned that he did not have a first class moral reputation while at Medical Lecture in New York City - This makes me a little cautious about renting any portion of the premises to him if any arrangement is made with him, it should be a sale and that made complete - I have but little favor for drunkeness and other kindred habits - Do not admit anyone to encroach on your rights or privileges - You may if you desire and think it best - I have a kind of notion that if I do not return to Venice to practice medicine, that I shall go with my family to New York City or Philadelphia and spend a year to further educate myself and then locate in some city or go to Oregon provided I can obtain a desirable position and spend the remainder of my days in some such way if practicable and I get home all safe. *[Refer to Dr. F. H. Hamilton's Oct. 26, 1860 letter - Appendix A - Medical. LPH]*

About selling the cows, act your own judgment - the price offered is fair - If we sell the place we certainly do not want them - The fodder they would eat if sold in February or March would make the price good - I have got me a good warm overcoat - and 2 pair of good drawers cotten flannel - I am glad to hear George is so plump and healthy - I should very much like to see the little chub and hug and kiss him (some I guess) - I need some good flannel shirts most of anything - Those I bought in Auburn have shrunk so that it is difficult for me to wear them - I now understand we are going to New Orleans - should we do so with a prospect of remaining long enough I will write and have you buy and send me some if not I will get them here - They will cost me more here it is true but I must have them - I bought me a heavy pair of Military boots yesterday - paid $10 for them - I think they are cheap for this here. Indeed I could not get them in Auburn any less.

Have the house well banked and your wood housed - look to your stove pipes carefully and be very careful of fire - Give my love to all my friends not forgetting to retain your own full share - The 75th are now mounted Infantry and I have this moment just learned that they have brought in today 150 prisoner - One or two Cavalry Regts went out with them - We have some picket skirmishing every day occasionally lose a wagon and two or more men when out foraging - but we capture more - Tell John I am glad to hear of his improvements on his place - let Nelson have sugar bush on the terms proposed.

Your affectionately   Benj. A. Fordyce

Camp in the field near New Iberia La.
Nov 20th 1863

My dear little Abbie,

You cannot think how glad I am to get such nice letters from you and George - I want to say a word to you about writing - do not bear on quite so hard and bring your letters down to the line and not below it - and you will soon write a good hand - I observe you spell all your words right but the letters wiggle round so that it is a little difficult to read - but keep writing and they will all come right.

I must tell you about my Jo. He is the greatest fellow you ever saw he will catch a chicken pig or goose for me or get some sweet potatoes every day if I will let him - Some days he will have five or six different horses - He always rides on a run jumping his horse over ditches and fences stopping here and there to catch a chicken or change horses when he finds one that suits him better - Then he lets the first go and puts his string into the mouth of the second and away he goes again - Sometimes he gets a real ugly one - He had one the other day a real pretty white pony but he was as ugly as a little sack - Every chance he got he would bite Jo or kick him and got so he would bite Jos legs when he was on him - He got afraid of him and had to let him go before night he had two more - One day he had him up showing him to me and he began to bite Jo - Jo says to him, "What you act so for anybody?"

He has been out today with the teams and has just come in bringing me a nice pig and two chickens - He got three chickens a goose and the pig and while he was catching his chickens some of the boys stole his goose - and he says he had to give up one chicken to get somebody

to help him "tote" the others - Jo makes a great deal of fun for me -
He feels very bad when I tell him he does anything wrong he is so
'fraid I will not keep him - He says he wants to come home with me
- If I can I shall let him - The boys got four bushels sweet potatoes
today for us. I wish you had some - From your Father, Benj. A.
Fordyce
(write often, Abbie)

*[Copy of the following letter given to me by Mrs. W. J. Severinghaus, who owns the
original letter and is a descendant of John B. Strong, who lived in Scipio. LGC]*

=========

Estella give this to John

New Iberia, La.
Nov. 27th 63

Cousin Jn B. Strong,

I had expected to receive something from you before this in answer
to my last letter but after having waited this long , I have concluded
to enclose a line in Estella's letter and ask you the reason - I am well
and enjoy myself as well as could be expected - lots of good company
and plenty of fun - We have meetings now every night to improve
ourselves in [.....] matters be assured John, this is in reality the only
real Christianity in the South and is really a sure passport to safety
in any event that may occur - We enjoy these meetings better than
ever before. You will observe by this that we are not wholly destitute
of nice social gatherings of great practical benefit - We have one of
the best instructors from New York who works under New York
Grand Body - precisely according to revised work under Drew. I
never had such an opportunity before and be assured it is worth a
great deal to me. Give my fraternal compliments to Old Cayuga No.
221 and assure them they are often in my thoughts - I hope I shall
be a more worthy member when I return. The war is certainly
progressing toward a favorable termination here - Gen'l Banks
expedition to Texas is a grand success - he has force enough to
maintain his position and Texas does not desire to be disposed of as
Louisiana has been. We have a force in Texas of over 20,000 strong
soldiers, many of them colored - After all, they are the men to fight

- and can and will do it - You would be pleased with the service if you could get a good position. Give my love to Mary and the children and all friends - be sure and write to me.

Yours truly   Benj. A. Fordyce

======

Sherwoods Dec 5th 1863

My dear Father

There is no school today so I thought I would commence a letter to you. I am writing in the chamber above the sitting room on your trunk you always kept your clothes in when you were at home - there is three trunks in this room two beds a stand with two boxes and my basket and my bonnett and Ma's black silk apron in it and two chairs one with the back broken with 2 bedquilts on it and a chest - Ma's basket hangs up above it and hoop skirts dresses saques skirts cloaks are the wall ornaments. Do you remember that morning that you went to Mr Jennings and extracted Carrie's tooth and the girls sang "Rally round the flag boys." Abbie and I can sing that we sung it up to school and the scholars thought it was the prettiest thing they had heard sung lately. It seems real strange living here - it ain't half as pleasant as it is to home. I can hear George down stairs he is playing horse I just asked him what I should write to Pa for him and he had to come up stairs to tell - he said tell you he is a good boy and he is going to write a great long letter to you this time. Uncle Giles has had thirty six scholars this Winter. George has just come up here and he said ask me what you shall write to Pa for me, and I asked him and he says tell him I am a nice good sweet boy and can sing Three rousing cheers for the Union Boys, and tell him he must bite and kiss me Ma has just called me to dinner - she says we have got an awful good dinner I must go down and see if we have

Dec. 6th

Today is grandpa's birthday he is 67 years old. *[For the record: he was 66. LGC]* It snows quite hard now the snow is about three inches deep on the ground Grandpa and grandma and Elihu and Sally Slocum are going to quaker meeting ma wanted me to go but I had rather stay here and play chess with Abbie I can keep still just as well playing chess as I can in a quaker meeting house The black horse is dead it had an awful sore leg and it rotted and they killed it Ma did not want me to write it grandma and grandpa and Uncle Giles would faint if they knew it but I know that you would rather know it now than to have us keep it from you and tell you when you come home I have just beat Abbie playing chess. Ma said we might put on our yellow delaine dresses and read garribaldi's grandma will think it is awful I expect but I don't care a bit. Uncle Elihu said he bet you would come home independly rich you had such a chance to go in to the Rebels houses and get things. He said he would if he had such a chance I would not care if you would get enough to get me a Piano and a pony and a side saddle. Grandpa sends his respects and tell you he hopes he shall see something of you up this way before long. (So do I). Abbie is a bed and I guess she is asleep and so is George you would laugh to see him and Uncle Elihu carry on here he keeps us laughing most all the time if anyone says or does any thing he don't like he will say now you know you lie the only way we can keep him from saying it is to tell him we will write it to Pa and tell you he is a naughty boy and then he will say I know you are mistaken now you must write and tell Pa I am a nice good sweet pretty boy. I must close. I enclose a thousand kisses and good night. Stelle

I will be in bed in less than 3 minutes. Stelle

———————

Dec. 6th 1863

My dear father

I played chess with uncle Giles today and he beat me twice and I beat him once. Estelle and me have been to school every day that there has been any ever since we have been here. Elihu Slocum and his wife came here yesterday afternoon and stayed all night. I can hear him talking to George downstairs. Uncle Giles teaches the school here we have got to Canada in our Geography. Stells and my Grammar are not like the kind they use here so Uncle Giles teaches us at night after school. One day he had us parse with the scholars "Joseph is teaching the scholars" and he asked us "what kind of a verb is teaching" and most of them said active transitive but at last he got everyone of them but me to say active intransitive but he couldn't get me to say so, and then Stell she said it was transitive and at last they all said active transitive and I turned out to be right and I was glad that I stuck to it, to. I have just been playing chess with Uncle Giles and he beat me once and then we played another game and I got both his castles and his queen and both his bishops and one of his knights and all but one of his pawns and he got my queen and too or three of my pawns. and I had one of my pawns so that it lacked only one match of his kings on when he give the game up and said that I would beat him. George sings three rousing cheers for the union boys and the merry merry tambourine. George tells me he is "going down south and is going to get me and Stell some merino dresses and some silk and satin and velvet ones and he is going to get us lots of ponies gray ponies black ponies and bullets and is going to get us some wagons to ride in and he say pa is coming home and he and Pa are going out to get some walnuts and pa is going to give you the basket and he is going to climb the tree and shake it and is going to get off a lot of them for me and Stell and Ma but I must close my letter now from your daughter Abbie

———————

Sherwoods Sabbath afternoon December 6 1863

My dear husband

It is now two weeks since we received a letter from you I presume we will get one to morrow we are well the girls are learning fast they have learned more about grammar for the week past than they did all summer Giles hears them recite evenings. Uncle Elihu Slocum and wife came here yesterday Uncle Elihu says he is going to Washington this winter perhaps farther south he says if he was a young man he should go south and work some of the government land thinks if he was an officer in the army he should steal all he could from the rebels he says it is not stealing he thinks he would divide with the government he says Fordyce will come home with a fortune one of these days says he is glad you have gone into the army. have not had much real news for the past week our dailys come to Venice first and then are sent here so you see they are old when I get them our time is almost up and then father and I are going to take them together for a quarter it seems quite pleasant living here more company not so much time to think I think the winter will pass away quicker I am going to Augustus Howlands to a sewing society Tuesday afternoon   Giles is not going to take Howlands farm next year What do you think about his coming to New Orleans to get into business to take gov't land George is just as keen as he can be Grandpa makes a great deal of him more than he ever did of his own children Uncle Elihu and George have had lots of fun   he is enough for any of them   he is the smartest boy I ever see of his age   have the diptheria some south of here   two children died at John Searings with it Dr. Pearl attended them the third was taken with it sent for Hoxie and it is getting better they think it is quite a feather in his cap   I can't think of near as much news to write to you here that will interest you, as I could at home all strangers to you William Howland says there are a good many Cayuga people at New Orleans this winter   I wish you were permanent somewhere so that we could come and see you it seems as if you had been gone a great while I find that any body can get used to most anything I did not once think I could get along half so well the children pass away a great many lonesome hours in fact I cannot be lonesome when they are all with me   Estella has written about our loss the black horse it seemed next to one of the family Giles come and got her after we had got our wheat ground ploughed he worked her half a day put her in the stable at night she was lame in the morning the gambrel joint. there was not a mark or a scratch upon her she grew lamer he had Thorn Brill see her three times he talked discouraging the first time he saw her I fixed some of your linament Giles done everything he could for her I think no one was to blame he said he notice the joint was a little larger when he got her thought it was natural She kicked over the tongue of the wagon twice one afternoon just before Giles got her   they all done everything they could for her the bone was diseased he kept her a long time   thought I had better not write anything to you about her Estelle thought you ought to know it be sure and write often

From your affectionate wife   Emeline

(PS) Monday morning I dreamed last night that you had got home I thought you put your hands on your pockets and said you had $90 in one and one hundred ninety in the other I told it before breakfast so that it would come to pass your coming home I wanted to come to pass You believe in signs.

(PS) Mr. Woodruff in Auburn has a son in New Orleans overseeing government land or lands worked by the government. We can send letter here every day. *[daily stage route through Sherwood. LGC]* I heard today that Dr. Powers had sent for his wife and she was going to New Orleans. (I wish it was me - get settled somewhere if you can and send for us.)

========

New Orleans La. Dec, 14th 1863

My dear wife and children,

I am just about to return to New Iberia and thought I could not go without sending you a few more lines - The box I have obtained from the express office - and it is so perfect and your letter gives me a list of the articles in it - I have not opened it. If Lotte *[Fordyce, BAF's youngest sister]* put anything in, tell her I will remember her in a letter and will anyway - I thought of sending something and will as soon as possible - I have sent you $220 in money - I want you to buy any comforts or luxuries you may be pleased with - I am very sorry to hear that Diphtheria is prevailing in Venice - You cannot think how I tremble once in a while when I think that you or the children may be attacked with it - and I so far away - On the whole, I am pleased that you go to Sherwoods - I would give the key of the house to Mr. Congdon or Babbit and let them occasionally build a fire in it. I have had some severe cases of Diptheria here all have resulted favorably in the Reg't - I give Quinine about 2 to 5 gr. doses every 4 hours Muriated Tincture of Iron (Ferri Chlor Tinc) to adults 20 drops every 4 hours or 6 hours and Chlorate Potash, 5 gr. 3 or 4 times daily - not combining the medicines but giving them an hour or so apart.

Watch yourself and the little ones for this is of more consequence to me than money - I am obliged to write in haste as I must take the cars at 10 o'clock and it is now nearly 8 AM - I have some little purchases to make, too - must go over the river before I can start - I am feeling first rate - I put up with the Chaplain to our Reg't - He is a very fine man - I went to meeting last night - Methodist Meeting - Attend to collections as much as you can - it is an excellent time to collect now - there will never be better - You can urge it with good excuse - Remember the county contract I presume you have rec'd the order already, it will pay half your taxes - Write if you hear anything from Freeman's heirs if they want any funds; yet they cannot be paid till the end of the year & 1/2 which will be about 1st April '64.

I will try & come home then - If I can get leave of absence - They will not let me resign I apprehend as soon as that - I find I bear this as well thus far as the natives and can do double the work. Must close, or I shall be late - I look often at the likenesses and can see little mischievous cross-eyed George as natural as life and the rest Give my love to all,

your husband,   Benj. A. Fordyce

(PS) 8 A.M. on the ferry crossing to Post Office - You see I have written up to the last minute, so good bye - Kiss little George for me - tell Abbie to kiss him - I would send Estella a kiss, if I could but you will all have to take the will for the deed. Yrs. as ever most affectionately. We are landing, 8 o'clock. B.A.F.

New Iberia La. Dec 18th 1863

My dear wife and children,

I recd a letter from you dated Dec 1st last evening and one from Estella dated Nov 20th on the 10th inst - I have usually written 2 or more letters for every one I have received - I think I have now received all the letters you have addressed to me except such as may be on the way at this time of writing. I recd all the photographs in due time - Thought I had acknowledged the receipt of them in my former letters but presume I neglected to mention it - The girls are extremely well taken and look first rate - George looks as natural as a kitten and as roguish and cunning as a monkey - Yours is not quite as good as I wish it was - Yet they are all a great source of daily gratification to me - It is a good pleasure to me to look upon the pictures of those I am so much interested in at home - I find the mail will leave in a few moments and rather and let it go without sending you a line to let you know I am well so I am under the necessity of being brief - I have found the box everything and even more than I desired - I have turned the eatables over to our Mess of 3 of us at $25.00 which will pay my board for nearly three months and give me an opportunity of enjoying them all the same - Col. George

Robinson & Regiment started for Texas next day after I returned from New Orleans - So, I shall not be able to invite them at present to join in the enjoyment of eating according to your wish - But I showed your request to them for which they send their thanks and wish to be remembered to you and the children -

If you can have Firm open the blind Ditches should the ground not be too much frozen and tread down the snow around the little fruit trees - Watch the bees &c - It may save some things that would otherwise be lost - I am pleased that you are at Sherwoods giving so fine an opportunity for the girls at school to Giles - This is much better than I expected and is far better for them than any other school in my knowledge - *[This is, I think, the private school, supported by Quakers in Sherwood area, already in existence for many years by 1860's. LGC]* I really hope you will not prove a burthen to your parents who have been so kind to you and the children - I fear George will be more trouble to them than I should like - but if he is good they will enjoy his little company some - I think I could -

We have moved a little nearer New Iberia and are very finely situated - I am very comfortable and as happy as one could be away from family and friends - We have many very intelligent highly educated men here who call on me very often - I visit just about as much as when at home - This you know is not a great deal - I select my own company when I visit and receive all kindly and politely who visit me - I am glad you did not let anyone in the house - You will want it in the Spring - I have concluded not to accept promotion in a Col'd Reg't - I find I can obtain it if I wish at almost any time - I think I can get it among my own color if I will accept -

Dr. Powers is in feeble health - yet does considerable in the hospital - I staid with him nearly all the time while in New Orleans and had an excellent visit with him -

Dr. Armstrong is with me and is a good working man and loves the work - so I do not have half as much to do as before he returned-

Give my love to all - Kiss George ninety-nine times for me and the girls fifty - don't forget your dear Father and Mother brothers and sisters who are all so dear to me.

Remember me to my relations when you see them - I have written to all but Lotte & will write to her soon - shall direct to Scipio for her I must close

Yours most truly & affectionately   Benj. A. Fordyce.

Sherwoods Dec 26th 1863

My dear father,

We have just received your letter of the 14th inst and I am very glad to learn you have received the box we sent to you. Ma Uncle Giles and Grandma have gone to Auburn today Ma has gone to get that money you sent. I went to the Christmas tree - you don't know how nice it looked after they lit the wax candles - there was most everything you could think of on the tree. George got a little flatiron on the tree and he got a sugar horse in his stocking Grandpa got a red leather heart on the tree. Ma got a pin cushion and Abbie got a sugar cent in her stocking a sugar bird and sugar heart and a scarf and a shawl pin and a pin cushion on the Christmas tree. I got a sugar bird in my stocking. And five sugar hearts and a scarf and a shawl pin and a real nice book bound in red on the Christmas tree. George says tell you that he likes you and wants you to come home and tell Joe to catch you a pony. Uncle Theodore and Aunt Maria and Addie came here yesterday Addie got an apron in her stocking, Grandpa has been to the store six or seven times today. Uncle Giles had Abbie and I parse for Aunt Maria Addie parsed with us and Uncle Giles said we understand Grammar as well as she does Uncle Giles said if Abbie and I would write a sentence that he picked out and write it right he would get us a New Years present and we wrote it right and he said he would get us each a present today and Ma said she would get me a net and Abbie a box of paints and a china doll. I must tell you what that sentence was that we wrote in a diagram   it was "Fly praise, the orphans tears and widows sighs embalm."

========

Sherwoods Dec. 27th 1863

Ma brought me home from Auburn a new pair of balmoral shoes and a real pretty net and a hoop skirt and a balmoral skirt and Uncle Giles got Ma a photographic Album it cost $2 and he got me a new book the title of my book is Rollo in London it cost six shillings *[75cents]*. I have been to quaker meeting today. Well, I must stop writing for this time.

From your daughter, Stelle

========

Sherwoods Dec 27th 1863

my dear father,

Uncle Giles and I have been playing chess today and he beat me too or three times and I beat him once last week one night we played chess and we played two games. we began about six o'clock and played till about nine or half past nine and didn't play but two games and I beat him both times. they was pretty hard games I can tell you. We went to the Christmas tree up to the school house and Stelle got five candy harts and a scarf with a shawl pin on it (and Stelle got a book to) I got a scarf with a shawl pin on it and a candy hart and the handsomest pin cushion it was red silk and light blue and dark blue silk with little fringes at the corners of it. and I got a candy bird. that was all I got Ma got a pin cushion and what do you guess George got. he got the cunningest little flatiron I ever saw. Grandpa got a little red morocco hart and Uncle Giles got a bird cage with a woman in it and a candy dog. yesterday Ma and Uncle Giles Grandpa and Grandma went to Auburn and Ma got me a hoopskirt some rubbers and a piece of red velvet and Uncle Giles got Ma a photographic Album and he got me a book about Rollo in Switzerland I like it first rate I hung up my stocking Christmas eve and got some peanuts and a pretty little sugar kitten and Stelle got some peanuts and a sugar bird and George got some peanuts and a sugar pony. Addie and Aunt Maria and Uncle Theodore came over here Christmas and Grandma gave her a sugar man. I must close my letter now for Ma wants to write some.

from your daughter Elida *[Abbie Elida]*

December 27th Sabbath even

My dear husband

I rec'd your letter as you were leaving New Orleans yesterday I hardly know how to be thankful enough to learn from your letters of your excellent health we are well and enjoying ourselves first rate under the circumstances with one of our family so far from home it seemed as though you were most home when you were in New Orleans I think I have been highly favored in every thing I have sent you your box just in time for you to get it I feel anxious to hear how you found things in it. I went to Auburn yesterday found the money in the express office took $20 to use Had to give from $1 to 18 shillings [$2.25] for shoes - everything is very high the cheapest sugar is 15 cts pound *[up from 4 cents. LGC]* factory 40 cts calico 24 cts with what money you have sent home, I have got about four hundred dollars in the bank and S Howlands hands have got all the grain yet which I think will sell for two hundred more at present prices wheat is the cheapest of anything in this country 12 shillings bushel *[$1.50]*, I think I shall make our maple sugar last until spring have not bought a pound of brown sugar but few of white I am going to buy a quarter of beef if I can get it I have used a good deal of money the best I could do it seems so to me I am in debt to no one the girls are learning very fast Giles thinks Abbie is very smart to learn Estella had a beaux home from the Christmas tree Leon Searings son he goes to Aurora to school Estella and I went to Quaker meeting today you will have to come home next spring or I fear you will not know your children they grow so fast come home if you can by the middle of March so you can get our affairs arranged for us if you have to go back again Firman wants to take a farm if he can get one Monday afternoon This week is quarterly meeting we are going to have roast turkey one day come and take dinner with us George has just climbed up on the table where I am writing and spilt all my ink he is the biggest piece of mischief I ever see I have just asked him what I should write to Pa he says tell him I spilt the ink it seems as though something happened to all our letters the girls write all the news so there is not much left for me to write it rains today and freezes as fast as it falls some go in cutters we have had no sleighing yet but cold weather enough. Capt. Fitch has resigned is going back to take cotton plantation they say Benj. Howland *[brother of Emily]* is out from Auburn again to see Giles about going south Giles I guess has not courage enough to start he made me a present of a photographic Album Christmas Wheaton and Maria *[Fordyce, brother of BAF]* have moved to your father's this winter your friends are all well do you think there is any prospect of the war ending it seems by the papers that the south are making every effort to carry on the war the draft is postponed to the 25 of this month think the $300 law will be repealed I am most glad you are in a warmer country this winter if you are only well and comfortable we miss you very much we talk about you every hour in the day All of my love to you from your affectionate wife,

Emeline Fordyce

(PS) Mr. Searing called here last evening he is a smart boy studies Latin Giles is going to have the girls begin Latin at home

(PS) Estella says tell Pa we are waiting anxiously for something he is going to send us what does Jo say to the books the girls sent him

---

[now Emeline's father]:

Sherwood, 27th 1863

Emeline wanted me to write a few lines to help fill up the sheet There is not any news but I thought thee would like to have a few lines from thy Father we are all well Emeline has received $220 and I have let S.H. *[probably Slocum Howland - LGC]* it till the first of April at five per cent. I Suppose thee will want to know how George and I gets along we get along first rate I have got him so that he will wait till I get ready to go to the table he will get in a hurry sometimes and say Grandpa dinner is ready he and I have some good times, Second day morning and very dark George and I begun our days work he got up in my lap and looking at the wrinkles in my forehead he wanted to know what made it twisted up so I told him it was old age he is round me while I am a writing and wants to know if I am a writing to Pa. Farewell with my best wishes

George Slocum

Camp in the fields near New Iberia La.

Dec 30th 1863

My dear wife and children

I received your letter dated the 5th and 6th inst and mailed at Sherwoods the 12th inst last night being 24 days from the time of writing till I recd it - You will observe the advertisements in the New York daily Tribune the time when a mail steamer leaves N.Y. City for New Orleans every week - By having your letters arrive in New York a little before the Steamer starts I shall get them a week sooner than if they get there just after she is gone - I was pleased to learn that you are all so pleasantly situated and enjoying yourselves so well - I am glad the girls are improving so fast in their education - I think they will do much better there than in school at Venice - You need not reproach yourselves for the loss of the horse - such events occur to all persons who have horses to lose - Of course I regret the loss but this will not profit anything - Careful attention to collections will perhaps save more than the value of two horses in a few months - Be careful of your health and that of the children - If you all keep well this will be worth more than the lives of all our horses - I have excellent health here as yet - I am very careful in every particular regarding my health - We have moved about a mile since I last wrote to you when I was in New Orleans - I have recd in all three months pay and out of the last two months sent you $220. I shall have two months more due me tomorrow may not receive it till February - I shall not be able I think to send but little if any of it home as I shall pay for my horse out of it - Will send what I can and not incommode myself Tell Giles there is the finest opportunity to make money on the Government plantations here that any man ever saw - A man needs to obtain some favor from head quarters at Washington to get started right and then he is right - Adj. Genl Thomas is the man that can recommend you more highly than anyone else - Yet you can start here by advancing $1000. I learn today that any man with good recommendations can start at once here There is some difficulty now in obtaining good field hands so many have enlisted in the Army - Yet the plantations have been well worked and to enormous profit - some operators clearing $10,000 in one season - The greatest drawback is the Miasmatic condition of the climate - Great care is necessary to insure good health - And what is equally important to keep the hands in good health a knowledge of the use of a few important medicines is indispensably necessary - This I could probably acquaint one with in a short time - Physicians are almost impossible to obtain on plantations and then only at enormous expense - We have had no snow here - The weather is very fine and most of the time pleasant -

You think or Uncle Elihu thinks I ought to get rich here - Well I suppose I might make something more than my wages but I never have nor do I think I can bring my mind to feel satisfied with myself to go into other people's houses and appropriate their property to my use no matter what have been their faults or how unjustly in my mind they may have obtained it - I choose to gain slowly - If I could speculate (which is not allowed officers) I could make a sweeping profit here - I know one man that commenced poor last year, who is now undoubtedly worth $100,000 -

I by special invitation spent Christmas at Dr. Dungans of whom I have formerly written you - We had a very fine visit and excellent dinner - Turkey, mutton, and Tongue - vegetables and desert &wine after - I showed the Drs Daughters the photographs of my family - They were very much pleased with them - He has four young daughters very fine young ladies - They had to see the girls' pictures two or three times each and wished me many good wishes for them - Their mother is deceased - They are living with their grandmother a remarkably fine old lady aged about sixty two years. She gave me as much attention as though she had been a relative - They were deprived of all mail facilities and I gave them some papers and pamphlets - Today the girls have sent us a basket of candy now on the table which is very nice made of Louisianna Sugar some with peanuts in it I wish I could send you some for little George would not he laugh though - They act as kind as relations could but are a little rebellious all of them - It is a great pleasure to meet occasionally with persons well bred even though they differ on vital questions to the Country - These girls actually send their compliments to my daughters - Dinner is ready, I must close - Emeline caution Firm to keep watch of the barn house & fences - You know rails may make good wood for some and while I am absent they will take every advantage - Remember the little fruit trees tread snow around them - Be careful of your health - don't try to write too long letters write short and oftener - I will write to the girls in a few days - I will wish you all a Happy New Year fearing I may not have time to write New Years day - Give my love to all.

I am as ever most truly your husband   Benj. A. Fordyce.

Sherwoods Jan 3 1864

My dear Husband,

In order to keep my arrangements good, that of commencing a letter to you every Sabbath I must write tonight we are all well we are all anxious to hear from you have not heard since you left New Orleans it is very cold weather now thermometer 6 degrees below zero it seems to me yesterday was the coldest weather I ever saw - it was so windy, no sleighing yet. Father and Estella are reading the Bible they are reading about Joseph I think the girls are learning very fast this winter you will see by Abbie writing that she is improving in writing & what is better when they get to school they have a warm house to sit in come home every day to get their dinners Giles takes a good deal of pains with them he was out last evening he saw a young man told him that little one was very smart the large girl was too but she was so full of fun she did not study so hard. It is very healthy around here has been three deaths in Aurora the passed week Maria Richmond, she died very sudden without a moment's warning, James Avery married Cornelia Brownel died of consumption John Shaw of consumption also Owen Eddy of Scipio very sudden. I have heard that brother Seymour *[Fordyce, of Scipio, brother of BAF]* has been very sick, stuck a hog hook in his ancle and came very near having lock jaw Philip Strong *[of Scipio]* recruited one soldier when home, almost large enough to enter the army, it weighed 11 3/4 pounds Dr. Pearl attended her I went to the sewing circle last week with Giles had a very pleasant time have two a week one for the contrabands one for the soldiers I have been to both of them they are very pleasant a change makes time pass away faster meet at George Merritts this week Mrs. Merritt invited me to come there The teacher of Springport school took dinner here last week he appeared like a very fine man I saw one of the lady teachers at the sewing circle [..... .....] she is very anxious I should send the girls to their school I shall not let them go anywhere to school without I go with them and keep house I cannot spare them I saw Mr. Tifft a few days ago he had a letter from his brother south he was in Castle thunder prison Richmond he lives in Jackson Mississippi he expressed union sentiments too freely when the union army approached and the rebels took him and put him in prison took all of his property they could get he sent to Mr. Tifft to draw money for him thru his banker in New York it is now bedtime I must stop writing it seems as though we could not write as much to interest you here as we could over home

────────────

Sherwoods, Jan 4th 1864

My dear father.

It is so very cold today that Abbie and I are not going to school we have got our Geography lesson to home. If they did not have such a nice school here, I should not like to stay here at all. The ladies of Scipio had a New Years Arch at the Baptist church last Friday evening some of the scholars went they said they had a very nice time. Grandma and Abbie are trying to draw a box on the slate. George says tell you he is a nice boy and he likes you the best of any body in the world. We have got a turkey and we are going Ma has just come in and wants to know what I have written on this page for she says I ain't left her room to finish her letter. George has been sitting in a chair by me as still as a mouse I asked him what made him so still and he said he was trying to think of something for me to write to pa for him he says tell you to come home and bring him that pony. George has got so he will sit down to the table and fold up his hand and sit still quite a while and then he will say meeting is out and then he will begin to eat as fast as he can. Uncle Giles has sold his corn for nine shillings per bushel. [$1.12-1/2] You would laugh to hear George sing he sings "We will welcome to our numbers the loyal true and brave. And although he may be poor, he shall never be a slave. Shouting the battle cry of Freemen." I have got to go to school this afternoon and won't have time to write any more. From your daughter Stelle

Monday: it is as cold as ever this morning I am going over home this if it is not to cold then will write how I find things have got 4 or 5 bushels of dried apples been offered 8 cts pound come home in the spring if you can if you think it will be too cold to come in March come as soon as you can and help us get started I have not sold any grain yet think it will be higher towards spring write often and about yourself

Emeline

(PS) I had a letter from Carrie last week she wrote she received a letter from you while you were in New Orleans Mother and father send their love to you take good care of yourself and I think you will come home again

═══════════

Franklin La Jan 10th 1864

My dear wife

I have just received your and the childrens letters dated the 12th 14th & 15th December by same mail I am very glad to hear that you are all comfortable well and happy - I know you are as comfortable as you possibly can be situated as you are at your fathers - I hope you will not be felt to be a burthen to them - You tell me little George grows and is a good boy - I should like to be there and hug and kiss him and eat some apples with him I guess - You tell him to eat an Apple for Pa occasionally - I see he remembers the Bow Apple I wrote him to eat for me - I should like to see him in pants - You say Cynthia stays with you - I am very glad of that - I think she is a good girl and will do as well as anybody can for you - I am pleased to hear that the girls learn so fast - I am really anxious that they should get a good education for each - You write of collections what of outstanding accounts that cannot be collected now will never be collected. The times are such that any man can pay that will pay. Those that you think mean to be heedless about sue and collect by law I have been very lenient about all such matters - It will not do now a pinch will and must come when the war closes, which I think will be during the present year - Every thing looks like - The rebels here who had the 600 prisoners that I wrote of in Carrie's letter exchanged them Christmas day - Their prisoners were carried down the Bayou by us within 8 rods of our tent and ours carried up the same - I could have been present at the exchange, but it was muddy and some fifteen mi. to go and back and I had been invited to dinner at Dr. Dungans thought I would go there - We have just arrived in this camp and have not got fixed up much yet - Arrived here yesterday after three days march on frozen ground in the morning and mud toward noon & till night making a hard time for the men - We had a severe snow storm for this climate on the night of the 5th inst rain first then snow and froze a hard crust and ice over little water holes an inch thick - Although it has not snowed any since there is some ice and snow under trees yet - I am told by the inhabitants that it has not been so cold here in forty years before - I am sure of one thing it was rather cool sleeping in houses made of one thickness of cloth - New Years eve was rather cool - we set up late to keep warm - Our fire place smoked some that night if I recollect right - I could not see the ridge pole of the tent for the smoke - Tonight having no chimney my fire is built before the tent door on the ground and feels very comfortable when on the windward side - The smoke is just as likely to come in the tent as it is to go outdoors when fires are built this way - So am writing with my overcoat on my face and hands all soot and smoke but feeling quite well - We had for supper sweet potatoes (our boys got two bushels today) Beef roasted down nice Soda crackers - some of your butter good coffee (no cream) and of course we feel well -

There is the greatest opportunity for a sharp careful man to make money here in speculation or by honest labor that was ever presented in my opinion in the United States - The plantations are worked to enormous profit - Yet there are more losers on them than are reported in the papers - California offered gold freely to all but only the industrious and saving obtained (except the speculator who was sharp) just so it is here - Immense fortunes are quickly made here and as quickly lost sometimes - I think if I was free from the Army restraint (no speculation is allowed in any officer or private in the Army) with what little means I could command, I could in a year or so come home comfortably off A man must learn to lay round apparently easy and suffer some inconveniences till an opportunity presents for something then walk in according to law and sometimes one purchase here of cotton alone is sold to the next speculator at an advance of $20,000 One man here by the name of Hunt formerly a Capt in this Regiment bought a quantity of cotton on our plantation was taken sick & for a few days was confined to his room - While so confined sold his bill of sale at an advance of $5,000

The people here begin to concede the point that they are whipped Everything wears a very different aspect here from what it did when I came here - Things are more quiet and the fire seems to be coming out of the rebels a little - They begin to know more the common classes than they did - Even when I came here, they thought the north nearly exhausted but when they learn that the last call of the President is being responded to for 300,000 new men they feel now more like yielding gracefully than dying like martyrs - I shall not accept a promotion in a colored Regiment now - The Regiments are not as healthy as the first raised

My Joe has never seen any snow before the morning of the 6th when he got up and saw a white streak of snow under the edge of the tent - He "hollered who trow all dat salt down dare" -

You may say to Slocum Howland that there is money to be made here, if that is the thing desirable and piles of it too - The best and most successful speculators must be bold adventurous men who will follow the Army and take their chances & risks with it - They have to be in favor with quartermasters and wagon masters & often greasing the Wheels themselves

Yours truly   Benj. A. Fordyce

(PS) I shall write to Estella on her birthday if I can - and Abbie too,

---

Franklin, La. Jan 23 1864

My dear wife and family,

I rec'd your letter of 26th and 28th & 29th Dec on the 20th inst together with a part written be Father Slocum for which I am truly grateful - I had often thought you might almost any of these long winter evenings write me among so many of you a letter every few days; but I have given this up and so only expect one in three of four weeks - I recd a letter from Elnora - a first rate one a few days since - I forget whether I have answered it or not - *[His sister could really write "first rate" letters! LGC]* - I am glad you got the money all right - I shall probably receive two months more pay in a short time - I sent every dollar I recd last pay day except enough to pay express charges to you I have enough to get along well I think - I shall pay for my horse next pay day - This will be $100.. I may not send much home particularly if I should conclude to apply to come home this spring - I have not yet fully determined on this yet - There may be some opening here that I shall try to avail myself of, and conclude not to come -

I have sone very strong friends here who assure me they will take great pleasure in doing anything possible in their power for my benefit - The prospect is that openings may occur that will be desirable to me - In that case, I may make some effort to obtain it - I have had four distinct offers for promotion in colored Regiments and chosen not to accept - If something should come about - if I can I shall change my straps in a white Regt before I come home - I shall write you often but cannot of course communicate on the subject -

If I merit the promotion I may obtain it - Our Regiment is quite small now numbering a little over 500 - The regiment may be consolidated with some other in that case I shall be mustered out of the service being the junior assistant in rank - Should this occur I shall come immediately home unless I see an opportunity for and can obtain immediate promotion and I shall not accept I think for a longer term than my first enlistment - The war will in all probabilities be closed in that time -

I enjoy the contents of that box "hugely" - I can tell you it is first rate - The butter is really nice the best I've seen in the State - & so of all the rest of the fixings -

I must tell you a little how I have spent a few days past - Dr Coventry and Assistant Surgeon in the General Hospital here at Franklin had leave of absence to visit New Orleans and requested me to prescribe for his ward in his absence - The Hospital is about three fourths of a mile from our Camp - I accepted his invitation - so for several days past I have assisted at our Regimental sick call and afterwards have been to the Hospital from 10 AM til 4-1/2 PM each day prescribing for between sixty and seventy patients daily at the hospital get my dinner there and am sent out to visit some patients in regiments to examine them and admit them to Hospital if thought best - Yesterday I was sent to see one who I found finely broke out with

Varioloid - I sent him to the small pox ward where there are some fifteen cases of small pox about one mile from the Genl Hospital - I shall revaccinate myself, believing fully in its protective influence -

Thus you see I am quite actively employed all the time and only get time to write or read late in the evening - Dr Armstrong has a pass to New Orleans to go tomorrow for a week - then I shall have charge of Regt. and ward too which will give me work enough I think for a few days - Today we sent from hospital 52 men to Brashear where another Hospital will be established - Dr Coventry will be back in a few days and I shall be relieved -

It is getting late and I must stop writing soon it now lacks 20 min. of 12 o'clock at night but I thought I must write something home - I intended to write some particulars about collections and will if I have time in the morning - I have been offered $200 for my pony I think I shall sell him - he is very gay and strong - Horses are high here good ones - One thing to Giles I think there is going to be quite a scramble here for plantations and the chances to get desirable ones not so good as last year particularly near New Orleans - There is no doubt money in the business and piles of it if well managed - I think I should engage in it if I was out of the Military service - several Surgeons have resigned and taken plantations or shares in them - It requires some capital to start but it is sure the first season to make a good return as anything can be -

Sunday morn: The prospect is that everything is working for the best to close the war - This state has certainly got its quota for re-enlistment in the Union - Election 22nd February & will result favorably - I am in excellent health - This is a beautiful morning warm and nice, birds singing and everything looking happy here. I must dress up & go to the Hospital - Thank Father Slocum for his letter write again - Kiss George for me - Genl Weitzel is now north the 75th are on the way - Genl Weitzel it is thought will be sent to North Carolina.

Yrs affectionately, Benj. A. Fordyce

Franklin La Jan 23rd 1864

My dear Daughter Abbie

I thought I must write a few lines to you even if it is late

I am very much pleased with your letter - I notice you improve very much in writing

You want to be a little more careful about putting in capital letters when they belong and your letter will look and read first rate - Oh! Abbie I had a first rate dinner today - I had fried Oysters - Chicken nice potatoes bread and butter nice apple pie - good coffee & milk in it - I thought this would do for the Army -

Sometimes I have pretty good times; we always live well enough - These oysters were cooked nicest of any I ever ate - The chicken was first rate too I have got Joe so that he can read a little in three letters He feels quite proud of those books you sent him - I hope he will learn & know something -

Your Ma writes she thinks you learn very fast - I am very glad of it - I want you to be careful not to get your feet wet and catch cold in going to school so that you can go all the time -

I show your & Estellas likeness once in a while and folks think I have some pretty fair girls

George plays with Grandpa does he? Well I am glad if he can help Grandpa enjoy himself some - I shall think he is good for a little something now - Tell George he must help Grandpa catch rats & eat apples for Pa but keep in the house and keep his feet dry and I will like him - *[Wet feet "caused" consumption, that "fell destroyer." People, particularly women and children, wore light weight shoes, often of cloth, which soaked up snow and rain underfoot. In the mid '50's, "India rubber" boots and shoes were advertised; people could wear them and ward off tuberculosis. LGC]*

Tell him Joe will catch him a pile of ponies and get him some peanuts and Oranges and lots of pretty things -

Your Christmas tree must have been a fine thing - I should like to have seen you & Stella about that time I think would not we have had our time! I don't see any little folks to talk and play with and I am sometimes afraid I shall forget how - Then I think you will be grown so large when I get home you won't want to be seen playing with Pa you and Stell - But there is George won't I give him some though - We will have great fun I tell you -

You cannot think how warm it is here today is as pleasant as May - The roads are smooth and dry - It has been muddy but is very fine traveling now - Negro boys go barefoot some of them - I wish you could be here a few days to see how nice it is - It is now 12 1/2 o'clock I must stop -   Your Father Benj. A. Fordyce

(PS) Abbie you must hug and kiss George for me 75 times Tell Estella I will write to her in a few days - Maybe tomorrow - both write when you can

=========

Jan 21st 1864

My dear father

Stell and I have been playing chess today and I beat her once and she beat me once Night before last Uncle Henry [Slocum] came here and last night he came here too and I played one game of chess with him and he beat me and then he played with Uncle Giles and after they had played two or three hands uncle Giles beat Uncle Henry and they didn't play but one game and that took them ever so long. Stell and I played three or four games of chess this week and I beat her every time. I and Stell study Latin and I like it first rate. Uncle Giles says that by next spring Stelle and I would be in the first class in grammar. Uncle Giles and I have just been playing a game of chess and he beat me, and Stell and I have bee playing a game of chess and I beat her. It is past eight and I must go to bed now.

Jan 22nd 1864

George is just as cunning as he can be and he says that "when this cruel war is over then Pa will come home." He has heard us sing the piece like that and so he sings it. At school in Geography we are to

"South America" and I think we will be through Geography by next spring. Ma and Grandpa went over home last Friday. Grandpa and Ma and Cynthia Uncle Giles and Stell have gone to quaker meeting. I just asked George what I should write to pa for him and at first he said "tell him I've got a sugar horse", and then he said "tell him i'm going to sleep with Cynthia and Stell tonight." George has got into bed with Cynthia and Stell and is carrying on like everything and he says he "has been to the Store and has bought five or six guns to keep the rats off from Cynthia and Stell. Cynthia is telling George stories now and he manages to keep still so as to hear it. Cynthia and Grandma saw another rat today we have not seen any before today for a good while. I must close my letter now from your daughter,

Abbie

Chapter VI
The Army is Moving

From Franklin, LA Dr. Fordyce reports that his regiment may be transferred into the cavalry and the possibility of his being mustered out, or his resignation from the service. Letters from home keep Dr. Fordyce acquainted with conditions in the North. He sends home tobacco seeds with instructions for starting its culture on the family farm. The doctor receives orders to prescribe for three batteries at some distance from his base of operation and requiring travel on horseback. He is detached from his regiment and put in charge of the three batteries of artillery in the 19th Army Corps 1st Division. He mentions the value to him of his affiliation with the Masonic Order. He tenders his resignation only to have it disapproved as he is too valuable an officer to be spared from the department. Recommendations for a leave of absence are made, but when presented are denied. The army is moving.... hundreds of men are transferred to Brashear, LA. Dr. Fordyce supervises a hospital of two hundred thirty patients and accounts for thousands of dollars of hospital property. Wife Emeline and daughter Stella keep the doctor informed of happenings at home.

Sherwoods Jan 24 Sabbath afternoon

My very dear husband

The girls rec'd a letter from you Friday the 22 dated Jan 3 and mailed the 11 in which we learned that you were in good health and ordered to move I hope towards New Orleans - We are all well the weather fine today with a prospect of a thaw the first weather we have had warm enough to thaw any for six weeks - we have not had snow enough for sleighing at Sherwoods this winter I went over home Friday it was good sleighing on our road found things well taken

care of the mice were playing around some I put arsenic in some
meal I guess that will quiet them some - the old mare is dead Firm
said she would not winter he gave her meal and hay she died of good
old age so we are destitute of a horse. I found out about the taxes
they were $33.15 - your County order was $24.80 - you were allowed
for your small pox business $24 making $48.80 in all left a balance
of $15.65 I have let S. Howland have $20 more at 5 per cent making
in all $240 $150 in the bank $35 father has given me making $425
at interest at 5 per cent father thinks he can let it out on mortgage
by spring my hand trembles so I can hardly write my nerves or heart
seems to be all of a flutter for a few days Jarvis Alward has traded
his house, land around it, with Sara Green for the John Strong farm
over east where Robert Stewart lives he thinks the corners are so
run down that the quicker he can get away the better he is going to
Canada I believe   David Fish is just alive *[died Jan 26, 1864]* I took
your books over to John for him to collect some for you he was not
at home gone to Albany whether he will collect any is uncertain
write whether you can come home in the spring or not I hope so and
to stay it seems as though we could not spare you any longer I think
Giles will go home with us in the spring for a short time when his
school is out as he is out of employment then if you do not come
home and get us started right and collect some for us We were
invited to Dr Pearls yesterday to tea had a very pleasant visit the
Dr is very busy this winter gets some of your practice Mrs. Austin
Wood is raving crazy he says Mr Dabell is very sick Our congres-
sional district has got more than its quota of volunteers it is the
banner district the report is that the 75 reg are all coming home on
furlough Do you think the war will ever close it looks dark to me.
The winter is passing away very quick and pleasant under the
circumstances I expect N [Nelson] Baldwin will have the sugar bush
write what you think I had better do about farming let out the land
whether we had better plough all the pasture this side the woods
provided I can let it out I shall have to buy a horse if I go back which
I think I had better do I would like to live alone with the children
if I could and save the expense of hiring a girl but it will be so
lonesome I do not know as I can do it I shall keep the cows this
summer Mother wants we should stay here I think we had better
go back I have not sold the grain yet prices are about the same they
have been I think it would be a good time to plough the pasture
grain is high with a prospect of its remaining so it is not seeded very

good. I can't help but mention again how fortunate I was in sending the box when I did did the pears keep good - do not fail to send for any thing you want that I can get for you spring will soon come and we hope you will come with it be sure and write often

- from your affectionate wife E Fordyce

(PS) I do not know but I shall have to send this letter without Estella writing any more I have to urge her of late to get her to write to you she is getting slack about it just as she is about everything else it is now bed time I want to send it tomorrow

(PS) I think our folks enjoy our being here Mother says father does not have to go to the store near as much George is as smart as he can be tells stories as Abbie used to by hearing them repeated a few times excuse mistakes

———

Sherwoods, Jan 24th

My dear father

We have just got home from meeting Mrs. Howland was the only one that spoke today. We received a letter from you last Friday what has become of Joe You have not wrote any thing about him lately. every letter we get from you, George says what did Pa say about this cross eyed boy it pleases him very much to have you write you think he is a nice boy George says tell you he has been shooting rats.

25th: Abbie and I are going to school this morning I am in Complex Fractions in my arithmetic I like to go to school here a great deal better than I thought I should. Grandma said she dreamed you were at home last night George and Abbie are going to Uncle Henry's today uncle Henry is going to take them to Grandpa Fordyce' *[Scipio Center]* and aunt Maria's *[Seymour's wife]* and all around up to the Centre. It is now school time and I must stop writing and get ready.

from your affectionate daughter Stella Fordyce

Head Quarters 160th in the field near Franklin La

Feb 7th 1864

My dear wife,

It is Sunday as you say in your letter so having a little more leisure time than usual I determined to stay at home from meeting and write a few lines to you - Meeting is out and it is now 2 o'clock and I have just commenced - so many called on me that I have had no very good opportunity till now - Yours and the childrens letter mailed the 11th & 15th Jan have all been duly received - As it happened I wrote a letter to Estella on the same night she wrote to me being our Contemporaneous annual birthday - I am very well pleased with the coincidence as well as the good home letter I recd The letter of the 8th and 9th was from Abbie Estella & yourself and I am glad to have you all write - You may be assured that it is very gratifying to have real social letters from home - especially when one has so few that they ever had any acquaintance with to converse with - I have been quite well since I last wrote except one or two days - I had a slight attack of Dysentry lasting but a short time that made me feel out of sorts for two or three days I am quite well now - You express a wish that I may come home this spring - I can hardly tell yet whether I can come or not circumstances may very much modify my position here - There is a strong effort now being made to transfer this reg't into Cavalry - A petition has been signed by most of the officers and forwarded to that effect to officers competent to obtain the change - Should this change be effected I may be mustered out as a supernumanary officer. If not I shall resign as I shall not be able to endure Cavalry service. I cannot ride on horse as constantly as would be necessarily required - What the result of the petition will be I cannot tell - It is my opinion however it will not effect the change sought -

If I come home this spring I think I shall resign - But if the prospect of an early campaign is reduced to anything like certainty I shall remain for a time at least to witness the result - There is not much sickness here now - You may tell Uncle Johns [Fordyce] folks that I got a furlough of sixty days for Hiram Galusha He has gone home - He is something like a 3rd or 4th or 5th cousin to our folks -

We had another grand review yesterday a beautiful day for it and a most splendid display was made of the troops - Major Genl Franklin with staff reviewed the force - I went to Franklin last evening to Masonic meeting and had a very pleasant time I can assure you

I have now between three and four months pay due me The pay master will probably be here in some three or four weeks at most - I get Cayuga Co. papers every few days from Dr Powers - the Drs wife is with him I have not seen her yet - I am a hundred and more miles from New Orleans and of course cannot go there often -

You write to know my opinion of having the pasture ploughed up - If I think best or if I should stay here I will write you what in my opinion will be best in regard to it in time for you to have any crop put in that will be most profitable - Should I come home I should have part of it plowed for common shares I think - and use the little meadow southeast of the barn for pasture so as to connect with the wood land - for pasture -

In regard to the Freeman estate your Father or Giles can settle that before the surrogate I think You want to take the Acct from my acct book and remember the recpt given by Deryl Hunter for the personal property and also the notes taken up by me - The Money in the bank is deposited at my risk and no part of the interest is allowable to the heirs as it would be if let out on real estate - The surrogate will show you how much fees I am entitled to - Do not forget the taxes - school tax and road tax I have been obliged to pay if they are not down in the Acct -

Col Dwight is now here - He calls on me almost every day is very social - I have called on him several times He sends his compliments to all his friends and mentioned particularly John B. Strong - please remember it to John -

Remember me to all our neighbors & particularly Nelson B. & John & their families - I regret to hear of Nelsons little boys sickness - Tell them to use cold water on his throat for croup & many times it stops it entirely. I am glad to hear my little George is well and Rather smart too and that Abbie and Estella are improving so fast in their studies - This suits me exactly - I am so glad they are comfortably situated this winter - Abbie writes an excellent letter now - She has improved very much - I wish you show here a little about using capital letters. If she could use them properly she could write as good a letter as any one of her age I think - Joe is very sick with fever but I am in hopes he will recover - He is quite delirious part of the time - Is better tonight - Feb 8th Joe is decidedly better today will recover I think - I have just rec'd Giles and Abbie's letter with the note from you   am glad to hear you are well and enjoying yourselves - Giles letter was mailed the 19th Jan and recd this AM being only twenty days coming in fact all your letters are coming along now every mail-

You speak of having the accts collected by J. B. Strong be sure and do it - The accounts ought & must be collected - Everything is on the New Ledger but all the books should be given to John including the three last blotters - You must keep a list or schedule of the notes, dates, names & principal & endorsements - You can say that I expect to invest some money here - which is true and urge payment - shall write to Giles today -   F. Wheat should pay something - collect Mosher Judgment - Urge John on this.

Your husband, Benj. A. Fordyce

(PS) I was intending to send a list of accts but have written to John today

---

Head Quarters 160th N.Y. Vols
Near Franklin La Feb 15th 1864

My dear wife

Yesterday I partly commenced trying to write you an interesting letter and got so far as to enclose a package of Tobacco seed of my own gathering which of course would be the most entertaining part of my letter & was then interrupted by friends calling to see us - This morning I concluded to go on with program laid out yesterday - I thought I would send the Tobacco seed in time for having it sowed and grown in time for use when I should get home as Tobacco is very high now -   What I really think is if you can get the plants started early and let out one or two acres of land having it well enriched with manure on shares for raising Tobacco you can realize five or six times the gain from it that can possibly be realized from any other crop - If you do not conclude to try it let your father try it - This is said to be the best quality of Cuba Tobacco

I have not received any letters from you since I wrote last - We shall have a mail in a day or two & then I think I shall get some letters - I really wish I could get the county papers - I get very little news of county matters except an occasional paper from Dr Powers who obtains them regularly -

I am as well as I ever was in my life at present - It is very pleasant here now birds singing of which the number and variety is almost immemorable - The Mocking bird[7] can be heard at all times of the day and many nights at any time in the night - Grass is green - trees budding - yet they call the season back ward here - Really there is no place I was ever in so pleasant in all respects so far as climate soil and productions (except snakes and alligators) are concerned as the State of Louisiana -

I certainly think I should spend the remainder of my days in the Southern States if it were not for the unsettled state of affairs which must continue at best for quite a number of years - Eventually it will be the garden of the world - Yet one is surprised to see how limited the culture of fruit & the various luxuries so natural to this climate - Indeed none are cultivated extensively except Tobacco - Oranges might be produced in the greatest abundance and - Yet the natural indolence produced by the institutions of the Southern State has permitted millions of miles square of beautiful land to lay at waste - Giving all their attention to raising the sugar & cotton which are so profitable that everything else is purchased from the profits - The wealthy have every luxury heart could wish while the poor are awfully destitute of the common necessaries of life - Even though they have a few acres of good land the same indolence in regard to cultivation is actually epidemic and exercises its deleterious influence on all that comes in contact with it -

In regard to our Regiment I cannot come to any conclusion what we will do - Our Regiment is small and must become consolidated or changed into some other form either Cavalry or Artillery in either case part of the officers must be mustered out - In that case I am one of the supernumeraries officers and unless our regiment is recruited which some effort is being made to effect - The prospect is poor for our recruiting & in my opinion I shall of necessity be out of the service in three months or sooner unless I obtain some other position in this department or am assigned some duty in some other Reg't, Battery, or Hospt which I am in hopes to be excused from - Just as I was writing the word prospect above an orderly called for me to go and prescribe for three Batteries - [8] One about two miles from here & below Franklin 3/4 mile the other two half a mile above us -

Well I shall have these to attend to for a few days and then be back again to my old quarters - I have just discovered a bowl of cotton that I gathered at Carion Crow Bayou and I thought I would send part of it to you with this letter some of the seeds are in it - I will also send you rattle of one of the largest Rattlesnakes I every saw. The one I promised Estella last summer -

I shall from time to time send such articles of curiosity to me as I come across them for your amusement & that of the children - Dr Armstrong and I were invited to dine with the family of a citizen today - We are just informed that part of the company cannot be present & dinner will be deferred till tomorrow when we will be expected to be present

The cotton I send is a variety that grows here and is used extensively mixed with the white which is as white as snow for clothing for the confederate army - Warp white and filling brown making the strongest and most durable kind of cloth - The inhabitants are manufacturing it in the domestic circle - In this respect the war is certainly going to prove an inestimable blessing to this people - You know you have my love for yourself and the babies so I won't say any thing about it - Give my love to all friends - Write often -

Yrs &c &c Benj. A. Fordyce

Camp in the field near
Franklin La Feb 18th 1864

My dear wife and children

I rec'd your united letters mailed Sherwoods 25th Jan yesterday and was really pleased to learn that you are all so happy and so comfortable - I see that the girls are improving finely; they both write much better and I think I can see a shade of improvement in their knowledge of Grammar - Use all the care you can for keeping their health good - I have no fears that they can not learn some if they have good health -

I am in first rate health but feel the cold a little today - It is some colder than it has been for a few days past - Once in a while today we see a very fine flake of snow in the air but it is not freezing cold by any means - It has been so warm that the men have lain in the shade with coats off - The peach and plum trees are in blossom - roads hard and dry - grass green trees green - and everything looks as it does with us in N.Y. an early spring on the 1st day of May - So you can judge whether the climate is pleasant or not - There is a little fine round snow falling now as I am writing. The inhabitants think it awful cold - I do not mind it at all - Some of the soldiers who wintered here last winter looked pinched a little - When we have rain at this time of year it is apt to be cold after I am told

I have become acquainted with a good many citizens by meeting in the Mas___L____ and I can assure you it worth every thing to me I am invited to more places than I can possibly find time to visit - I occasionally call on some of them who treat me only with the utmost respect and friendship which I have every reason to believe is as true as I could find in my own native State - They have invited us to be instructed in additional progress in the institution and have given us as much confidence as though we were natural brothers but of course differ on the question of the national policy in this awful devastating civil war

I have lately become acquainted with a rebel, Captain Jumel - Who gave himself up as a hostage for one of the mean rebels violating a flag of truce - This fellow is a daring reckless sort of man name Bailey

---

Vincent who fired on our men who went out met their own flag of truce and did it in the presence of this Captain who immediately surrendered himself as a hostage for the delivery of Vincent to us - This was done last week - so you see we have little skirmishes occasionally - This Captain is a fine appearing man and is honorable and means to be in the mode of warfare that ought to characterize civilized Nations - I was with him half an hour or more and had a very social visit with him - But he talks all rebel I think however wishes himself well out of it -

I am detached at present from the Regiment and am put in charge of three Batteries of Artillery - 1st Indiana 6th Mass and Battery L, U.S.A. being all the Batteries of this Division -[8] How long I shall remain I do not know - The batteries are near our Regt and I lodge here as yet. My address will be the same as before till I advise you further in regard to it - The batteries one of them is two and a half miles from the other so you see I have something of a ride yet as we say of Doctors - It makes it quite hard for me when stormy - Col D [Dwight] thought I ought to be relieved from one - He told me he could congratulate the Batteries - I considered it quite complimentary - This if continued may take me from the Regt some distance at some times but then I shall have a chance to see something

Does my little George eat an apple once in a while for Pa? I rather guess I would like to eat one with him occasionally - would we not have a time George - I guess we will when I get home - George must be a nice boy and be good to Grandpa and Grandma - and I will bring him something pretty I guess when I come home - I am glad you keep Cynthia with you and hope she will stay next summer

Hear but little about Cavalry now but some change will be effected without doubt in the Regiment in one or two months -

I have recd no pay yet & my money is getting somewhat short but I have enough for the present -

Write often as you hear anything or see anything new and sometimes when you don't -

Yrs affectionately, Benj. A. Fordyce

Camp in the field near
Franklin La Feb 22nd 1864

Major Wickham Hoffman
Adjt Genl 19th A.C.

I have the honor to tender through you to the Commanding Genl of the 19th Army Corps my resignation -

For reasons hereunto adjoining I do hereby resign the office of Asst. Surgeon of the 160th N.Y. Vols -

I am Your Most Obt. Servt. -
Benj. A. Fordyce Asst.Surg.
160th N.Y. Vols -

The following causes have induced me to tender my resignation

1st A sense of honor to the Government; my services not being needed - The 160th Regt has less than 400 enlisted men present, and they in good health generally - The aggregate of officers and enlisted men present and absent 514. There are a competent Surgeon and Senior Assistant Surgeon officers of the Regt besides myself -

2nd Importance of personal attention to my own private business- It became necessary on the promulgation of the proclamation of the President of July 1862, that a town bounty should be offered to induce men to volunteer - I became responsible for the entire sum paid by the town of Venice N.Y. (my residence) with one other signer - The amount so raised is two thousand five hundred dollars ($2500) which is due on the first day of April next

In addition to the last I am sole executor for the last will and testament of Lewis C. Freeman (deceased soldier) by which I am empowered to covey his real estate - the statue limitations for settlement expires on the 11th of April next - The value of the estate is about one thousand five hundred dollars ($1500)

My own interest and that of my family require that I should attend to this business in person - To do so, acting justly to the Government as well as to myself I have tendered my resignation -

Respectfully your Most Obt Servt
Benj. A. Fordyce Ast.Surg. 160th N.Y.Vols

[5 superiors approved or disapproved - final outcome]:

Camp in the field near Franklin, La, Feb. 27, 1864

B. A. Fordyce requested leave for 60 days to go to Venice to attend to business: 1, as surety became responsible for bounty paid to soldiers, by proclamation of the Pres. in July 1862, and the amount raised in Venice is $2500 which is due on Apr 1; and 2, as sole executor of will of Lewis C. Freeman, he is empowered to convey his real estate and statue of limitations runs out in Apr. 11, 1864. *[On fold of the paper are signatures, with approval and "disappred" of superior officers.]*

Hospital of Batteries
1st Division 19th A Corps
Franklin La Feb 25th 1864

My dear wife and children -

I recd your letters of Feb. 1st and 6th also one from Mr Lawson of the 9th on the 21st inst they having come quicker than any I have received from home since I started on the expedition As is always the case I was glad to learn that you are all well and enjoying yourselves this winter so much better than you even anticipated - I am in excellent health and spirits - The medical Deptment always furnish me plenty of business so I have no time for ennui - I believe I have written to you that I am detached in charge of the Batteries of the 1st Division 19th Army Corps - Our Regiment is in this Division and I am not very far from them at any time - I have been attending an additional Battery the 1st Indiana - Heaviest guns in the army corps - They are the Reserve artillery - was relieved today from this but given another about same size in place of it - I have had the above, the 6th Mass and Battery L. U.States Regulars - I now have in place of the 1st Indiana - the 25th New York and shall have in a few days Battery A, U.S. and 4th Mass -

They have got a notion I believe that I had best not be idle - I am not certain but it is a good idea for idleness is apt to produce discontent and might lead to vice in young persons like me -

I should have answered your letters before but I had sent in my resignation and I thought I would wait and learn the result and perhaps be able to bring the letter myself. My resignation was based on the ground that my services were not required in the 160th N.Y. Vols the Regt being only, or little less than, 400 in the field and the necessity of my personal attention to important private affairs settling Town Bounty and Freeman Estate - Well, I rec'd my very nice document back again with the following endorsements on the back, which I will copy to let you know how curiously things work sometimes. The 1st was obtained by arrangement on my part - The others were of course beyond my private influence or favor

1st Hd.Qrs 160th N.Y.Vols. Franklin La Feb 23rd 1864
    Respectfully forwarded approved, W. H. Sentell, Major Comd'g

2nd Hd.Qrs 2nd Brigade 1st Div.19th A.C. Franklin La Feb 23 64
    Respectfully forwarded disapproved as none of the reasons
    given are regarded good - Jas. W. McMillan Brig. Genl. Comdg.

3rd Hd.Qrs 1st Div. Feb. 23rd 1864.
    Respectfully forwarded disapproved as Dr. Fordyce is too
    valuable an officer to be spared from the department if it can
    possibly be avoided.
                    C. B. Hitchins Chief Surgeon 1st Division

4th Headquarters 1st Division 19th Army Corps
    Respectfully returned disapproved with permission to apply
    for leave of absence.
        By Comd Brig.Genl Emery - also signed by Adjtd Genl &c &c

Thus, you observe I am an appendage of this Dept, not (of my own ability) so easily dispensed with - I really thought they would be glad to let me go but you see I will have to be content with asking for a leave of Absence - This I shall do within a few days and if it is granted I will start for home on or about the 10th of March so as to arrive there before the first of April - I have been in no place yet since I have been in this deptment where they really acted anxious to get rid of me - But people dissemble so much that it is many times quite difficult to form just appreciations of human actions -

Well I am really glad the children learn so fast - They write me excellent letters and when the mail comes I as much expect to get a letter as I do to get my dinner and I am gratified to say I am not often disappointed -

Then there is that little George wont we have a time when Pa gets home - The girls say he is a nice boy - I guess I will squeeze and kiss him some if he is a nice boy - Tell George I want him to save some apples so he and I can have some when I come home to see him. 26th: I recd a paper today - Daily Tribune - Feb. 9th but no letter - It is so warm here today that it is very uncomfortable riding in the sun with my thin Navy Flannel clothes on, Everyone likes the shade today - some of the boys are playing Ball some pitching Quoits all sorts of Sports - We are having large Regiments arrive here almost every day - The force here will soon be near 20,000 - Something is certainly going to be done and soon too - Louisiana elected her Free State Candidates by overwhelming majorities - The feeling here is as different as can be possibly imagined from what it was when I came here even - The residents begin to concede that the rebellion is about played to the end - The wonderful gigantic preparations the government is making really astonishes the most loyal and the effect upon the disloyal is beginning to be perceptibly felt and realized The regiment of Genl Banks that all the plantations must be worked or considered abandoned is causing a great amount of sensation among the rich or those who were rich in niggers - Niggers are very slippery property here now - I think a man could not sell even a choice lot for eighteen pence each -

I subscribe myself most affectionately yrs Benj. A. Fordyce
(Closed in haste on acct of mail)

Genl Hospital Franklin La March 10th 1864

My dear wife and children -

I recd your letters of 15th Feb also one from Jn B. Strong of 20th and one from Elnora of the 20th Feb - I was heartily glad to hear that you are all well - I have just recd an order putting me in charge of this Genl Hospital ⁽⁹⁾ - This does not look like my getting home this spring - I have not yet heard a word from my application for a leave of absence - I must hasten to write you a few lines as I am called on every few minutes for something and am now engaged in making out an immense invoice of Hospt property that I am obliged to recpt for - The army will move in a very few days - I shall probably be left here - how long I do not know perhaps half this summer - will write again as soon as I am in any way settled -

Be sure and have my notes taken up given for Town bounty See Mr Tifft and have him get the money of the Supervisor &ct you take my name from the notes there is one at Azras [King] and one at Alvin Fitchs the large $1250 notes inquired after particularly & let me know what become of them - See that my name is erased - Mr Tifft will do it at once when you wish it as soon as all is straight -

The Freeman estate I wish you to have your Father and John B. Strong settle the receipts and papers are all in the desk and a perfect acct of the whole except: Town Tax, Buggy Tax, School Tax, Road Tax, and my fees, &c. There is a receipt from Hunter and wife to apply on their share of one hundred and some twenty or more dollars - don't forget to take this out of their share - The time for settlement is about 11th April - Be sure & have receipts in full from each one paid - & if it can be so done have it settled before the Surrogate so that it shall certainly be all right - Let the Surrogate make out my bill of fees for a settlement. & if it cannot be arranged then send a bill of the whole to me and I will swear here before a commissioner of Deeds - this will be considerable expense however -

I am still hoping I shall be able to come home this spring - This position came to me, not by any effort of mine - But as a matter of necessity to the Service - Someone must be left here supposed to be competent to take charge of two three or four hundred sick &

wounded men at once - I knew nothing of it till I was relieved from charge of the Artillery - The Artillery officers swear some I can tell you because they take me away from them - I am entirely out of money, not but 10 cents left - had no pay for last 4 months - I am well. Address me Benj. A. Fordyce, Asst. Surg. in Charge Gen'l Hospital Franklin La via New Orleans - Don't put on 160th Regt or it will not come right. My love to you all, George, Abbie Estelle, yourself and all friends. Benj. in haste write soon

———————

General Hospital Franklin La Sunday night & Mon Morn
about one o'clock, 13 & 14th March 1864
Estella and Abbie, my dear Daughters

I thought I would not close this letter without writing a few lines to you - I have just made up my bed and thought I would smoke and pencil a few lines to you acknowledging your excellent letters to me every time one is sent - You do not know how glad I am to receive your letters and hear all about home and your progress at school - And then you write too that my little George is a nice boy and grows finely and is good too - I am really glad to hear this -

Joe has been very sick - There were a good many days I did not think he would live - But he is getting well He is not with me now - But I have more than a dozen now that I have set at work and twice as many white men

I have about 150 patients and they have good care - and good food - and it requires some help & I have to receipt for all this property - some 300 beds & quilts & everything else here -

What nice weather we have here - the Orange trees are blossoming now - the ground hard and dry - Birds wake me in the morning particularly the mocking bird - to bed - 5 1/2 o'clock up at work and have to work all the time now day and night - for a few days - Excuse me this time - will write soon again
Your father, B. A. Fordyce

(PS I put on my new pants yesterday for the first time - I done well with the old navy flannel -

Genl Hospital Franklin La March 13, 1864
My Dear wife and Children

I am still here in Franklin - I wrote to you a few days since that I might remain here some time - But I am informed by the Medical Director tonight that I will be sent with the entire hospital to Brashear in some two or three days; there to await further orders - I think I shall be able to receive letters from you at Brashear directed as before advised in my last or one or two days sooner directed to Brashear - Leave off the 160th as before directed and direct to Hospital - My application for leave of absence has returned and about as I expected all properly Disapproved by Genl Banks So you will not see me this spring probably unless I can get a sick leave which I am altogether too well to see any prospect of - They seem to have just found that I can stand an immense amount of work and what looks more unfavorable for my getting home soon The superior officers appear satisfied with my work

So you must do the very best you can to get along comfortably - Let out the land as you and your Father shall think best - Be sure and see to the notes given for bounties and have your Father & John help you about the Freeman estate - Other matters settle and arrange as you think best - I would have a transcript of the Mosher judgement recorded tell John to see to it before Uncle Amos gets any more ahead of me - get pay on it if possible.

The army are moving tonight - it is now midnight and I have just been interrupted to admit 8 men into Hospital I expect to send off a hundred men tomorrow (to B) from this Hospital and must of course be very busy - they go to Brashear - You would be astonished to hear the clatter of Cavalry horses feet and the rumble of the Artillery in passing in the night - The force moving tonight is more than 6000 Cavalry and artillery - The army here is very large probably over 40,000 men - and they really act as though they would do something if they had a chance - probably Texas is meant in earnest this time - I shall go and the way things are shaping now I shall be in charge of Hospital all the march if I can possibly endure the labor & fatigue - I thought I must write you a few lines tonight although it is late - I shall not have time again in several days - I could not get away now any way I could work, because every Surgeon that is anybody is in good demand - But I will come as soon as they will allow me to - probably not in some months as the campaign promises to be a long one - I shall if I have my health have an excellent opportunity of seeing the country and will write of everything I think will interest you and the children - I should have been really glad to see you all this spring but it cannot be - I am highly pleased with the respect shown for my views of late by all that are acquainted and I enjoy Military as well as any man of my age - You have my love for you all - Yrs as ever

Benj. A. Fordyce

PS) I saw Dr Lester and Mr Boughton today - they are well though Mr Boughton is acclimating a little but I think will enjoy good health here - I must retire - it is so late, now 12 1/2 o'clock..

Brashear La. Mar. 20th 1864

My dear wife

I have written about all I could think of to Stella and Abbie but I thought I would enclose a few lines more for you and George - We have now left in this Hospital about 230 patients left not many of them very sick - I have passed from the Hospital at Franklin to this Hospital between 5 and 600 sick soldiers - and I have been almost alone so far as medical help is concerned to do it - I had to receipt for an immense amount of Hospital property some 3 or $4,000 dollars worth yet I believe I have as yet lost nothing -

I shall turn it all over to Dr Powers on his receipt tomorrow or next day then I shall feel free & easy I have not yet received any pay for the last four or five months and of course am getting very short of funds still I can get along for a time to come - I think I can get my pay when I get to New Orleans if so I will send you all I can spare -

Be sure and get every settled safe and right about the bounties and the Freeman Estate - One of the Surgeons told me he thought I would get leave of absence before long - I have little confidence in it however - I shall come home for a few weeks if I can - If not do the best you can watch the children in regard to their health and be careful about fires at night

You had better keep Cynthia I think and perhaps hire Firman or let out the land just as you think will be best & most saving and comfortable for you - Have some one see to the fences - Buy you a good gentle horse so you can go and come when you please and enjoy yourself and also for the benefit of the girls & George I want you to have just as many comforts in my absence as when I was there and more if reasonable - I can hardly form an opinion when I shall be able to come perhaps not till expiration of the war or of my term of Service - I shall try and get a better paying position if I am obliged to stay without coming home - Be very careful of George and try keep him in robust health - Be careful to teach him to truthful in everything - Abbie must not read and study too much or first we know her health will give way - Have her walk ride and play whenever the weather is suitable - She is so slender I feel uneasy about her unless she becomes stronger in bodily health - Estella is usually well and strong and will continue to get along some way I think - But she ought to learn to work a little as well as some other things

Joe has just brought me in some peach and plum blossoms - I will send you a few leaves of them in this and I guess you will receive them before you have any there - I have a long inventory to make out and must stop

You must try & make the best of things as they are and I shall come home to help you some time if I live

I am as ever most truly &c &c   Benj. A. Fordyce

(PS) Direct as you used to - 160th NY Vols &c

[Envelope]: Dr. Benj. A. Fordyce, Asst Surgeon,
   in Charge General Hospital, Franklin, La
   via New Orleans

[Forwarded to]: Mansfield, La.

[Note on side of envelope]: Will Major Long please forward, after
   Examination to Dr. Fordyce who is in charge of wounded at
   Mansfield.

[Signature illegible]: Examined. Major W. Long

[Envelope marked]: Venice, NY Mar 24 -

[Letter marked in pencil]: Recd May 2nd 64.

Venice Mar 23rd [1864]

My dear husband

You can hardly imagine our disappointment when J Strong received
a letter from you that you were not coming home at present we were
looking for you that very day our letter having gone to Sherwood I
presume I cannot see why they could give you permission to ask for
a leave of absence and then not grant it. it may come in the future
I am glad you are not going with the regiment if you are agoing to
be permanently, or in charge of hospital any length of time or till
winter perhaps George and I can come and see you if you cant us
We delayed writing to you part of a week I am afraid we shall not
send this in time for the next steamer I do not feel well this spring
my stomach or just below it upper part of my bowels are so sore I
can hardly walk and a good deal of pain has been so two weeks grows
worse instead of better I have fixed me a syrup taken some British
oil some thought that would be good I do not know but I had better
take some blue pills my heart beats very fast at times I do not know
but it is (Hysterick) every thing I eat distresses me very bad write
what I had better do it hurts me to fetch a long breath across me.
I have a good large wood pile since I came back enough to last all

summer no thanks to Firman either Summerton Rob Steward Congdon Tibbetts Denis helped Firman when he found I was going to have some wood cut then offered his services We have made no sugar since I last wrote you it has been very cold since I cam back and it has settled across me. We postponed putting up notices for collecting when we thought you were coming home John will help settle the Freeman estate he will appoint a day right away I shall go to Auburn with them if I am well enough Mr. Tifft told me the town bond matter was settled your name off of the notes I thought I had written you before about it I beat Giles selling wheat I got 12 shillings *[$1.50]*, he $1.45. I let Firman have 4 bushels he took to Moravia a little over 19 bushels oats are 70 cts at the lake the corn I have got to have shelled if I take it to Moravia I can do as I please about it if I can sell it in the ear at Genoa I think I shall and not bother to have it shelled I have $40 by me now lack only $10 paying for my horse I have got my help pretty much paid Have got $455 for Giles besides the C. Corlie interest and money due on the mortgage I do not know what Mosher is going to do I rested quite easy about matters when I supposed you were coming home I will do the best I can to settle up accounts and every thing else farming &c George had the croup last week very severe I used cold water and vomited him with Antimony he is well now is on the hearth cracking walnuts Dennis is splitting wood at the door Cynthia sweeping the girls have a fire in the office they have been a regulating [cleaning] two or three days so as to have it look nice when you come home I am writing at the kitchen table I have got tomatoes up cotton also I shall not be able to get anyone to take land for raising tobacco it has been a very hard winter for wheat I as much expected to see you this week as could be Bill Babcock had a letter from a Lieu Carpenter wrote you was going to start the 10 of March so you see we felt pretty sure I think you will come in the course of the summer do not fail to take good care of yourself, as warm weather approaches I think you will come home yet all safe and sound It is quite sickly around more people miss you very much Mr Merithew little boy is very sick with inflamation of lungs John Moshier is very sick typhoid fever Morgan Jones is very low with consumption I must stop writing it is almost mail time

Your affectionate wife Emeline

Ma has left a little room and I can tell you we were a little disappointed when we heard that you did not know as you should come home this Spring Abbie and I had a fire in the office and cleaned it all out and we have got a fire in there today but it wont do any good to clean it out because you are not coming home (Stelle)

Chapter VII
The Red River Campaign

Aboard the Laurel Hill, anchored at New Orleans, and awaiting transport to the front to participate in the Red River Campaign, Dr. Fordyce describes the city and tells of his attendance at a theater, his first experience of the kind. Alexandria, LA finds Dr. Fordyce aboard the John Warner. They pass Port Hudson and Baton Rouge and enter the Red River. But, the heavily-armored ships of the Union Navy and the massive movement of men and materiel by General Nathaniel P. Banks is routed by the smaller forces of the Confedereate Army. Disaster overtakes the mission and we read Dr. Fordyce'Parole of Honor and learn of his capture at the disastrous Battle of Pleasant Grove and his internment at Mansfield, LA.

New Orleans La Mar 30th 1864
On board Laurel Hill (Steamer)

My dear daughter

I thought I would write a few lines to you so you should feel sure I had not forgotten you I am now on board the steamer Laurel Hill in the Mississippi river oppositc thc foot of Lafayette St City of New Orleans - The view of the city is beautiful beyond any description I can give you - The beautiful blocks of buildings bordering on the bend of the river are almost numberless - They form part of a circle in the bend and from this shape the city is named the Crescent City - Indeed the whole map of the city proper is about the shape of the moon at the end of the 1st quarter and the most beautiful part of the city is that fronting the river and in its vicinity although the city extends some two miles back or more from the river and is very dense - It is some six miles long - The river here is about three fourths of a mile wide and runs rapidly. Algiers (where I have staid at Madame

DeGears St Peter St. and left my trunk and clothing) is directly across the river from the foot of Canal St and is the terminus of the Brashear and New Orleans Rail Road -

I visited yesterday Jackson Square one of the most inviting resorts of New Orleans - It is a square as large the little lot north of our house only it is square - It surrounded with an Iron fence about seven feet high and of beautiful workmanship - The walks are all made of shells drawn from the Lake (Pontchartrain) - They are bordered with evergreen and laid out very much as our flower yard used to be - The corners square and inside circular, then different shapes inside - The outside beds filled with beautiful evergreen shrubbery and at the roots the nicest kind of flowers - The center was a small circle about forty feet in diameter and a monument of granite in the center upon which was placed a bronze statue of General Jackson sitting upon a very large bronze horse all armed and caparisoned in the style of military dress he used to wear - The bronze was very dark nearly black as all such Statues are - There were about fifty kinds of roses in blossom & numberless other flowers - Thurs morning 31st The Steamer is still here and I am on board. I think she will certainly go today - I can wait patiently although it is very expensive living here - a good common meal costs 6/- at least - Would you believe it Abbie I went to the Theater last night for the first time in my life - It is what is called the Varieties Theatre - The best in the city - and really it was one of the finest acted pieces I ever read of - They have some excellent performers here I am told - The principal piece was the crime ignominy and trial of Effie Dean, who was discovered to have murdered and secreted the body of her child - To see the anguish of her old Father and her sister Jeannie was really thrilling Then when Jeannie was positively assured that her sister could be saved if she could swear in court that Effie had told her about it - To witness her great trial of mind before and when she was brot on the stand to be sworn When her consciousness that she should swear false came before her and was exhibited to the public it was so simple and so clearly portrayed that hundreds shed tears she could not swear false even to save her sister Though she was persuaded and even her life threatened yet she would not lie - So her sister was condemned to be executed and Jennie went clear to London from Edinburgh on foot and at last obtained a pardon for her sister and returned just in time to save her from the gallows - The other was a man Taking the census - was very good - I am in excellent health - shall write you often - shall go to Alexandria and perhaps to Texas - Had no letters yet from you for more than a month but will find them when I get to the Regt. I really hope you are all well. Give my love to all..

Benj. A. Fordyce

(PS) The view is alive with Steamers - News came yesterday that our folks had taken Shreveport if so that is all the stronghold that was left in Louisianna -

On board John Warner
April 2nd 1864
near the mouth Red River, La

My dear wife

We are just meeting a Gunboat and I have barely time to write that I am well and going forward to the front - I really hope you are all well - I was obliged to leave the Laurel Hill & take passage on this boat - Will write particulars next time - Remember me to all - My love for you & the children -

Yrs &c   Benj. A. Fordyce

Alexandria La April 3rd 1864

My dear wife and children

It being Sunday and the boat having stopped for a short time I thought I would write you a few lines I arrived here in the John Warner at 1 1/2 PM. today and we have had a very pleasant trip thus far a very pleasant crew and intelligent passengers among them the Chaplain of the 77th Illinois - I find the Reg't have gone on to Shreveport in the south west corner of the State This Steamer is going on and I with her - We shall probably be off in some three or four hours - I could not I thought do better than write you a few lines partly describing our trip - We started as I wrote to you in my last on the 31st March at about midnight - I was obliged to leave the Laurel Hill in consequence of some misunderstanding about transportation - I had my transportation all regularly printed and signed on my pass by the Transportation Quartermaster & went on board at 8 o'clock A.M. 30th It appeared the Chief Quartermaster Col Hollibird concluded to change the boat to a Hospital boat and was going upon her himself and sent an order to the Captain of the boat to have all soldiers sent off - The Captain did so and informed me of the order - I went to the Transportation office immediately to obtain transportation on some other boat but he told me my papers were all right to remain where I was - I did so - Col. H. came or sent first a Lieutenant who examined all passes and said mine was all right - The Col came on and began to examine papers - I politely showed him mine he immediately ordered me off the boat under arrest (as he stated to the Lt for disobedience of this orders) to go before Maj. Genl. Reynolds who received very kindly and politely and when I made my statement precisely corresponding with the foregoing he told me I ought to be with my Regt as soon as practicable, and to go and take the first boat that was going up I got on this boat and everything has been very pleasant since - I attribute this all to bad whisky, which sometimes works wonders in the army as elsewhere -

The remarkably level country bordering the Mississippi so far as I have traveled over it first impresses the mind - One monotony of level swampy country for hundreds of miles yet fine plantations on either side - We passed Port Hudson in the night consequently I did not see it although I got up to try The bank is very high above the river some 150 feet and no doubt the place was naturally very formidable for military - We passed Baton Rouge in the night also We entered the Red River in the day time I thought the Mississippi was dirty and riley but I concluded I had been misled in my ideas of the great father of waters when I saw the Red River - Of all Red muddy streams this is at the upper part of the list - Its banks are muddy and covered with small trees and Alligators & snakes in great abundance - There are but few inhabitants along the river - Not more in population I think from the Mississippi to Alexandria than 1000 all told niggers & all a distance of one hundred and fifty miles - Alexandria is a pretty little village - The rebels are deserting & coming in daily since I came here about 50 came in with horses - It is said a thousand more will come as soon as thy can get in - Well, good bye I must stop - will write again soon when get up further.

Yrs. B. A. Fordyce

[Then, six days later]:

Mansfield April 9th 1864

I, the undersigned, Benj. A. Fordyce, Asst. Surg 160th New York Inf do swear and give my parole of honor that I will not in any way assist any force employed against the Confederate States of America until regularly exchanged, and that I will not leave this town until ordered so to do

Benj. A. Fordyce Asst Surg. 160th N.Y. Vols
Subscribed before me this 9th April 1864
   s/ J. K. Gourvain
   Capt Comdg Post

[On outside fold of this, is written]:
Mansfield La June 9/64   The bearer will pass the Guards at this place. [signed] J. P. Montgomery, Capt. Comdg Post

[The above explains the envelope of Dr. Fordyce' letter of Mar. 23, 1864, postmarked May 31 64 New Orleans La, marked Examined - Willm M Ley, A.A.___. *with a notation* pr Flag of Truce, Mansfield, La

Also included, and in Dr. Fordyce' handwriting, was a "List of Wounded U.S. troops prisoners at Mansfield La in Hospital Ward C". The detailed list numbered eighty-two prisoners, with a tabulation by Name, Rank, Regiment, Wound or Disability and Remarks & Result. - LPH]

Mansfield La May 3rd 1864

My dear wife

I am pleased to acknowledge the receipt of your letter dated Mar 24th and forwarded by Col. C.C. Dwight, our Commissioner for exchange of Prisoners in & for this Department and very kindly transmitted by Major Levy Commissioner for Confederate Army to whom I am under great obligation for the favor - I regret very much to learn of your ill health and hope it may not prove as serious as your description has led me to apprehend - In your letter previous to the last you have mentioned the same difficulty I notice but supposing I should have been at home before this I have neglected to write anything in regard to it I will suggest a few remedies which I hope may prove beneficial until I can be relieved and come home which I trust will be in a few weeks at longest

Rx Fluid Ext Valerian zz i
"   "   Rhiv   zz i
Soda Super Carb. zz ii
M

Take 1/2 teaspoonful at any time when the distress faintness and palpitation come on (in water)

Rx Potassae Iod   zz i
Aqua   zz ip *[or iss?]*
M

Take 1/2 teaspoonful three times daily - If the stomach becomes initable from effects take it alternately for three days and omit for three - Using some stimulating local application over chest as Mustard or even a blister if the pain increases -

I am in excellent health, but have all I can conveniently do in helping to care for our wounded who are prisoners - As soon as my services will not be required for them I have the assurance that I will be permitted to return immediately to our lines - I think I will be permitted to come home on leave of absence at that time & will make an effort so to do -

I can assure you that I have been treated in every respect gentlemanly by Confederate Officers and Soldiers since I have been in this place - In many instances they have done more for us than we could reasonably expect -

It would be highly gratifying to be able to reciprocate for some of the favors shown me personally and I earnestly hope the time will soon come when I can do it in Peace and not be obliged to witness the awful devastation of war to develop nobleness of human character -

I am glad to hear that the children are well - Do not allow yourself to be too much annoyed with business matters put it all into some ones hands and be as quiet as possible

I think you will enjoy yourself better at our own house than to undertake to live elsewhere Keep all the help you may require so as not to be annoyed with household duties - Send the girls to school - You can write to me here but must necessarily enclose your letter in two envelopes - the inside one unsealed that it may be examined at the lines where the inner will be permitted to pass under flag of truce

Yours truly   Benj. A. Fordyce

Chapter VIII
Prisoner of War

Dr. Fordyce, in prisoner exchange, is returned to the lines of the 19th Army Corps at Morganza, LA. He details for his family some of his prison experiences and the conditions existing in the Mansfield, LA area. Then, to allay the fears of his children, the doctor describes the bird life in the area. From Algiers, LA he writes to his wife that an expedition is planned for the regiment. He is concerned for her ill health. He is considering resignation due to her health and his responsibilities at home, as well as his own poor health.

The May 7, 1864 issue of a local Auburn NY newspaper listed the killed and missing of the 160th NY Volunteers, including the name of Benjamin A. Fordyce among the missing. Only three days later John B. Strong, the Fordyce Family friend, penned a letter to Col. Charles C. Dwight inquiring for Dr. Fordyce. Col. Dwight's reply of June 4, 1864 replying to John B. Strong's inquiry had been preserved and is quoted below as it reassures Emeline of her husband's safety and welfare.

Office of Inspector General,
Headquarters, 19th Army Corps,
New Orleans La June 4 1864.

John B. Strong Esq.
My dear sir:

Upon my return to New Orleans today I find your letter of May 10th inquiring for Dr. Fordyce in behalf of his wife. I trust that long before this time Mrs. F. has received a letter from the Dr. written at Mansfield La, which I forwarded to her several weeks since. It gave a full account of his capture and assured her of his good health and comfort in every respect. I have heard verbally from him since that time: that he continues well and in good spirits.

As Commissioner of Exchange on the part of Maj Gen Banks I have just completed arrangements with General Taylor's Commissioner, by which they are to deliver our wounded to us immediately. The Surgeons who were captured, and those who remained in charge of the wounded will all be returned with them. I hope to receive them (at the mouth of the Red River) within a little more than one week from this time. Dr. Fordyce will be one of them. I shall be very glad to see him again, and his wife will no doubt hear from him by the first Steamer after his arrival within our lines.

There is no news here. No movement since the close of the great Red River Campaign.

I am your very truly   Charles C. Dwight

Mansfield La June 12th 1864

Capt Montgomery
     Provost Marshall & Comdt post Mansfield
Sir

I have the honor to communicate to you that a robbery was committed in my ward of the Federal Hospital for wounded prisoners in this place at about 3 o'clock A.M. today by armed men in the dress of confederate soldiers - Clothing of the feeblest wounded and other articles were taken.

Your Obt. Servt -
Benj. A. Fordyce, Asst. Surg. 160th N.Y.V.

Morganzi La. June 19th/64

My dear wife:

Really I do not know how to express my feelings on first coming into the Lines of the 19th Army Corps and particularly the 160th Regiment after a captivity among the rebels of two months and eight days - I was captured the 9th April and placed on board of a U.S. Transport on the afternoon of the 17th June and I did not hardly dare take a full breath fearing it might prove a dream - Today I realize that I am free again and may express my thoughts without being subject to the surveilance of a guard - No person except those who have been subjected to captivity can form an adequate idea of the restraint exercised over Military prisoners although my condition was of the mildest character of captivity - Others did not get along so easily - The country around Mansfield is not as rich for agriculture pursuits as it is on the Teche - Yet they raise some very good wheat though yield small - from 5 to 8 bushels to the acre corn is a good crop When I left, some pieces were 10 feet high - The profitable productions have been formerly cotton & slaves - The slaves have been sent on to the sugar plantations further south - The treatment of captured negroes is cruel in the extreme in many cases - Some I am satisfied were shot, who were as innocent as living beings could be of any wrong or crime except that of loving to be free -

Monday 20th June - sunrise - I should have finished this letter yesterday but the Paymaster came around yesterday and made the payments of the Regiment at our tent - I will send you some money by express I think about $200 - I shall also send you my watch It does not run although I had it cleaned - It needs some little repair which if you desire you can get done - If I am taken prisoner again I do not want so much property with me - I do not see any prospect of my getting home very soon however much I desire to come - Dr Armstrong is quite sick (nothing dangerous however) He is anxious to get home and means to succeed - I have learned that Dr Powers has gone home a little sick I suppose - He was looking quite ill when I saw him last - So you see the chances for me are quite limited - When I come however I shall not return to the Army in my present capacity of Asst Surgeon If your health continues poor I shall offer my resignation as soon as I hear from you -

I did not lose my horse or any of my clothing - Indeed I did not lose one pennys worth of anything - All the other Surgeons lost more or less - Dr Armstrong lost his Rubber coat and instruments - I save all of mine - They were with me too I brought away considerable money (belonging to others), although many were robbed of all their valuables - My Masonic pin was worth you cannot tell how much - Men were very friendly who were of the order - I had a pin presented by a young friend - Dr O. E. Ross of the 8th Vt a very few days before I left or was captured - I send you his photograph - He had heard me speak of my cousin Carrie *[related via his Mother's side: Clark. LGC]* -

he gave me one to send to her. I enclose it with yours and will write her soon - I am quite well though not strong - Will write to Stelle & Abbie

Yr. affectionately Benj. A. Fordyce

(PS) It is reported here that Tortugas is captured by the rebels - I do not believe it - I recd the letter stating Aunt Ruth's death - give my sympathy to the family. *[Ruth (Sandford), wife of Raymond Warring, d. Mar 7, 1864 in 68th yr, Scipio. LGC]*

_____

Morganzi La June 20/64

My dear Daughters,

I have at last got out of captivity and feel mightily relieved - I found quite a pile of letters here for me - You can hardly judge how glad I am to learn that you are well and that little George is well - I have seen a great deal and experience a great deal to tell you about when I am able to see you - When I was at Mansfield the beautiful Magnolia was in blossom - also the Catalpa and China tree - with abundance of wild flowers - some flower gardens were beautiful indeed - O, how devastated and poor the country looks - This awful war has ruined thousands & thousands here many good Union families are suffering worst of all There is a noisy mocking bird right over on some bushes put up to shade us - He is about ten feet from me and yells every thing he hears loud to make your ears ring - He comes every morning about 3 o'clock and begins to sing and such lovely bird singing I never heard before - I would give $10 in a minute if I could send to you all well as he is now - He stays with us all day & sings more than half the night - I dont think he ever shuts his eyes for sleep - They are a brown bird with white feathers in the tail not handsome or beautiful to look at but such singers I never heard before - [7]

The 75th N.Y. have got back - I saw Jo Wood - Austin Woods son and inquired for you all He said you were all well when he was at home - He is well and healthy - I send a likeness of a fine young Asst. Surg. of my acquaintance to Cousin Carrie - He is a very fine young man - I saw Dr [Elias] Lester yesterday - He is not very well - His brother

[Solon] died here a few weeks ago of Typhoid Fever - The Dr is really homesick and discouraged since his brother's death He now advises me not to go in a Colored Regt - I had concluded this way before - *[Although the "very fine young" Asst Surgeon's photograph was sent to Carrie Foote, Dr. Elias Lester married her Dec. 23, 1864. LGC]*

I shall be obliged to stay here some little time I suppose unless something occurs to relieve me - I performed a good many operations at Mansfield and am gratified to say that my operations resulted very satisfactory under the circumstances - The first operation I performed of any consequence I amputated Col John Connell 28th Iowas arm above elbow when I parted with him he was perfectly well and the tears run down his cheeks - He is one of the best men I have become acquainted with - I had all the ranking officers 2 Cols and one Lt Col under my care while at Mansfield with over sixty others -

How glad I am you are well - Try and learn all you can that is good - Be particular about the associations - Don't forget to kiss George for me - and Abbie must and will go to the little grove to read I suppose - You do not know how much I want to see you all but probably cannot immediately - I will as soon as practicable come and see you all - I shall write again in a few days - be sure and give my love to all - Remember me to all friend - Tell Ma to remember me to all relations - Your father I really hope Mr. Whitman is better give him & his family my compliments & kind regards -

Benj. A. Fordyce

(PS) Get John to do best he can for me in collecting - Dr Armstrong proposes to stay with Regt as soon as able & let me come home on leave - I will make application immediately but keep this still as I may be disappointed

Morganzi June 21st 1864

My dear wife

I wrote to you yesterday and sent the letter in an express package containing ($200) Two hundred dollars and my watch - I thought I would send the watch it does not run; probably needs some little repairs. I have just had it cleaned - I concluded that I preferred expressing it home to expressing it again through rebel lines if any accident should again require it - I have paid all charges - I had hopes to be able to come immediately home on my release but Dr Armstrong thinks he is quite sick and must go to New Orleans for a few days - this will prevent my making application for leave of absence with any prospects of obtaining it or even of resigning which I intend to do as soon as things look favorable for getting it through - You may rely on it I shall come home this season - If you write to me more particularly of your palpitation of heart and faintness of which you wrote in March last - I can base an application for leave on it or resign - I am feeling quite well though weak - have lost 20lbs in Rebel dom but do not know how to play off I have never lost an hour from duty yet - I have been in every position of danger with the Regt till I was captured - The battle of the 9th April was very severe on our Regt we lost two Captains killed 1 Lt died soon after 1 Capt wounded 1 Lt wounded and 8 privates killed - In all we had 36 killed & wounded and 14 taken prisoners making our loss 50 -

You can hardly realize how much I should like to come home but I am not naturally babyish much and can go on if necessary to the end - I fear Dr Armstrong intends to resign he feels that he has not been well treated by Dr Powers - I know how it is in my own case - Dr. Powers I suppose is at home on Leave of Absence - He is always sick-

The mail is coming - I must close.

Kiss the little ones for me. I send Dr. Ross photographs one for Carrie Foote and one for me.

I will write to her soon - My love to all friends - Write often

Benj. A. Fordyce

Morganzi La June 26th 1864

My dear Little Abbie,

I have written to all the rest except you & George I could not pass you by - I hope you and George are well and happy - You know I depend on you to watch George when Ma is busy and not let him get hurt and also to learn him his Letters and make him a good boy so you see how much I depend on you my little dear - Estelle I expect will help Ma now Cynthia is gone (so I understood Mas letter) and you and George will have to do the reading and playing and having the fun - I really hope you won't forget me entirely nor let George forget me - I shall write you as often as possible - Our tent is on the bank of the Mississippi river only about 40 feet from the water - We use the water for cooking and drinking and swimming and everything else - The boys catch very fine fish from the river some weighing 10 or 15 lbs - I have been in swimming in the river- yes to be sure - The river is about 3/4 of a mile wide here and is very deep - We have a beautiful prospect of the river - Great Steam boats are running on the river and may be seen every hour and indeed all the time - My mocking bird comes almost every day - but does not sing as much as he did -

I hope he will continue to sing for me I would like to bring him to you - You must kiss George for me - Remember me to Ma & all the little boys & girls around there

Yours affectionately Benj. A. Fordyce

Algiers La July 5th 64

My dear wife and children

You observe I date my letter Algiers - we arrived here on the night of the 3rd and we are now waiting transportation for somewhere some expedition is intended the direction or object has not yet transpired Conjecture says Mobile! Fortress Monroe, Charleston, and several other places - I am expecting to go along, although I am quite unwell - I have had considerable Fever for several days feeling very bad - I am now while writing suffering from one of the spasmodic attacks that I used to have with my stomach sometimes I am obliged to stop writing and wait for pain - I have just received the letter from you sent to Mr. Akin for me - being the first news I have received direct from you since I had returned to the Regiment from Dixie - I am now the most unwell I have been since I came into the service - Yet I hope it is only temporary - I intended to have made immediately an application for leave of absence but an expedition being just ready to depart such application would not be received with favor - If I am well I would like to be with the expedition provided you are well - I shall resign, if you do not get decidedly better - I sent you $200 in Government 20 bearing 5 prct interest - so if you cannot do better you will be sure of 6 prct on it - I sent my watch also I paid all charges I have left my clothing trunk and Valise at Madame DeGears Peter St. Algiers - As soon as this expedition closes I shall come home I think in some way cannot tell -   Dr Armstrong is over in the City and has been there nearly 2 weeks - Dr. Powers has gone home of course very sick on leave of absence - I am feeling a little unpleasant about the manner I have been treated - I have never been relieved from duty for a single hour since I came into the service Dr Powers never has been with the Regiment since I came here D Armstrong went home and staid three months last year - is now anxious to get a sick leave during the hot months -

To see the planning is really ludicrous some times - I am feeling better now been taking some Ext. Ginger and sodae I am really glad Estella has gone to your fathers she will be so much better surrounded socially - I am pleased that the girls are improving in their minds and you are in good health - They have both written me some excellent letters - I have always recd Georges letters inside of Abbies - I hope the girls will continue to improve - I shall write to John B. Strong a complete history of Mansfield battle and also affairs in Dixie - I should have finished it yesterday but I was too sick to sit up long enough to write - Will finish it soon -

The people are having Green Corn, plums, Banannas, blackberries, new potatoes, Tomatoes, Green Apples - Beans, peas, Cabbages, beets & radishes are gone long ago - probably many other things also - I have not been over to the City since we came here not feeling well enough to go - You wrote to me in one of your letters some time since that you thought of going to your Fathers to stay this summer

- I fear this will be too much burthen for them - If I can get away this summer I should like to remain at our own house as long as I stay. except visiting some &c

I got a letter from Seymour and Wheaton *[2 of his brothers]* some who appeared to have Idea of adventure as expressed in their letters - My opinion is they will enjoy themselves best to remain near their homes & in reality be just as well off in the end - I recd Elnoras letter too but have had no time to answer - Also one from Lotte - I shall answer them all soon if I get around all right - nearly all of the 19th A.C. are ready to move on the expedition Some have already gone others are at this moment embarking - everything moves as still and quiet as clockwork - every little while a boat moves off with its freight of human and animal life, bound upon a warlike expedition - I hope really that we shall be successful without the awful loss of life which has sometimes attended our advances - and if we have to fall back I will get back fast enough so as not to get captured again. I enclose few daguerreotypes or photographs of some of the friends in the Regiment I would like to preserve them - How happy it must be all around you with no confusion and din of war - you can only judge of it by the absence of many yet I suppose they are not so much missed out of the aggregate -

I shall have many little particulars to tell you that I cannot have patience to write - Remember me to your Father & Mother and all our friends You wrote that mothers health is poor *[Alpha, his mother]* - Please write and let me know how all the friends are

Yours most affectionately Benj. A. Fordyce
(my belly aches) and will stop writing.

─────────

Algiers La July 8^th64
My dear wife,

I have an opportunity of sending a note to the Post Office so I avail myself of it to send you a few lines - We have not started yet as you well know by this - We have orders to go on board at 5 o'clock we go north somewhere - My disease has increased since I last wrote I do not sit up but little - I have Dysentry - although I feel better this

P.M. Yet one of the Surgeons tell me I must not attempt to do duty but lay still and be perfectly quiet - I have all my baggage with me and if not better soon shall certainly be relieved to come north - My flesh is wasting rapidly - Dr Armstrong with some four companies of the Regiment went off day before yesterday although he knew I was hardly able to sit up - Of course I have been on duty all the time but in camp - I shall endeavor to get a good stateroom and keep quiet and full of hopes I shall certainly be better -

I am in good spirits though weak and quite spare in flesh

I have been in hopes to hear from you direct before I left - I hear there is mail down the river but it may not arrive before we leave I am anxious to get away from here - I have not been able to visit the city since I have been here - indeed I have hardly been out of camp - I am very careful in my diet - feel quite certain of ultimate recovery-

Remember me to all I shall write every opportunity - and inform you of my whereabouts and health - I am heartily glad that you and the children are well - I shall go on board the boat as soon as it arrives and select me a state room which will be I suppose in an hour or two

My love to all who may inquire after me

I am as ever most affectionately yrs   Benj. A. Fordyce

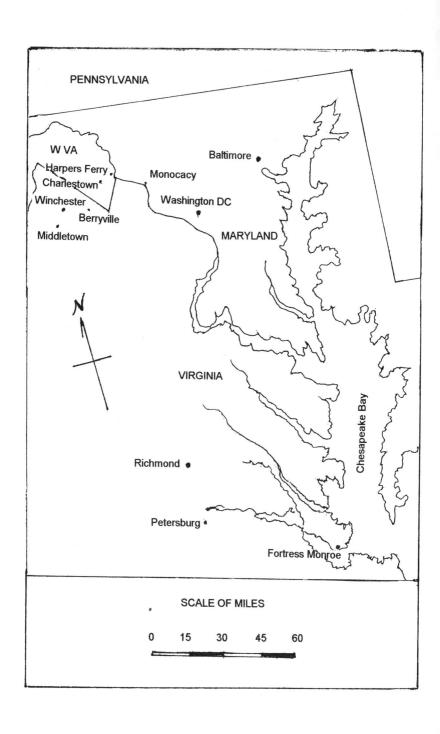

PENNSYLVANIA

W VA

Harpers Ferry
Charlestown
Winchester
Berryville
Middletown

Monocacy

Baltimore

Washington DC

MARYLAND

N

VIRGINIA

Chesapeake Bay

Richmond

Petersburg

Fortress Monroe

SCALE OF MILES

0   15   30   45   60

Chapter IX
Transfer to the Shenandoah Valley

Arriving at Fortress Monroe after a sea voyage, Dr. Fordyce learns of the unsuccessful Southern raid on Washington and the optimistic turn of events under the guidance of General Grant. He relates the experiences of the sea voyage and gives an eyewitness detail of the battle as the Second Army Corps crossed the Potomac River. He receives a letter from home telling of the death of his mother, Alpha Clark Fordyce. The regiment is ordered to move to Harpers Ferry, W VA, with the change in assignment of his group and the subsequent association with the 165th. He admires the natural beauty of the Blue Ridge country through which he travels. He tells of conditions near Winchester, VA and describes the skirmishes that occur as the skillful General Sheridan leads the Northern forces in its push southward.

Fortress Monroe
Courtesy of the Casemate Museum, Fort Monroe, VA.

Postmarked OLD POINT COMFORT VA

Fortress Monroe Va. July 19th 1864

My dear wife

We arrived here last evening after a very unusual tempestuous Voyage - A detachment of our Regiment came on the C.C. Leary, Steam Propeller - I was very sick (for me) when I came on board with Dysentry but by great care on my and laying in bed nearly all the time I am now considerably better - What our destination is I do not with certainty know but suppose from appearances that it is James River Richmond &c I hope I shall be favored with good health for this will open a field of observation such as I have never seen before - I shall ask for leave of absence if I do not as I anticipate - I am very weak yet. My horse has not come yet and what success they will have bringing him I do not know - may possibly lose him - I have just seen a paper - it is full of news in regard to a raid on Washington unsuccessful - a portion of the 19th A.C. arrived in time to assist in the defence - There is a great amount of excitement with regard to all these matters but the greatest confidence is felt in Genl Grant - His coil is winding tighter and tighter around Richmond - We have news that the Rebel Steamer Alabama has been captured and sunk - We can cheer for this - Our boat is ordered to City Point - we start immediately - it is now 8 o'clock A.M. - I really hope you are all well - The great effort is now being made for the perpetuity of the Govrnt - or its overthrow - The result must soon transpire before the civilized world and History be the only herald of what is now so exciting to the American People -

You must write to me as often as you can you know it is almost impossible for me to come home now if I can stand erect - at all - Every man that can do anything in the field is needed now if ever - I am really glad I am nearer home than in Louisianna - indeed I have no fancy for anything there except the climate - This is delightful - but excuse me from snakes, alligators, swamps and especially captivity - among the enemies of the country in Louisianna - it is a little too far from home - I am writing surrounded by lots of officers, writing & in all sorts of confusion - so I will not write much more now I have just learned that the horses have arrived - whether mine is safe or not I have not heard - Hope he is -

I am quite short of funds just now but hope to receive pay soon and will be all right then - I shall write every few days & will try and give you more particulars of events &c that have transpired of late - I will write Estelle and Abbie soon I have not received any letters direct from you since my return to our lines now more than a month. I sent you $200 of my last pay and my watch - all paid.

Have the girls write and tell me about everybody I know - direct as before to Asst. Surg. 160th Reg, N.Y.V 1st Div. 19th A.C. Washington D.C. and it will come all right.

Yrs &c Benj. A. Fordyce

Postmarked OLD POINT COMFORT

Bermuda Hundred Va
July 20th 1864

My dear wife and children

I thought I would not let an opportunity slip of writing, whenever I had time, so I write again today - I am very much better than I was yesterday although I still have this old relic of my disease remaining but not to such an extent as to be alarming in any respect - I am now on full duty and feel able to perform it - We arrived here this morning about 8 o'clock A.M. - This place is directly across the river from City Point, where Genl Grant HdQuarters are - We are about 1 1/2 mi. from his HdQrs - I sometimes think I have got near the seat of war now - You may rest assured I am well pleased with the change - I feel that I am almost home for one thing that if any accident should happen to me or I should be severely ill I am within two or three days of home at most - The country here is delightful - Hilly and rolling like our own Cayuga Co and abundantly supplied with excellent water (A luxury you know nothing about comparatively) There is a beautiful spring within forty rods of our tent - is not this really good after using Alligator slime soakage of Dead mules old horse offal and filth of all kinds that accumulates in a hot climate and is thrown into the rivers Bayous & pools of water all over the country and this the only water accessible to an army - Then to feel

---

that I am removed Military Control of Political Aspirants incapable of exercising Military Command or of executing an important Military movement however carefully concocted and planned -

Really I should have become sick or homesick if I had been obliged to stay in Louisiana much longer -

Well I was going to describe my sea voyage but really have run so far off the track that it will require quite an effort to get started again - Well as I wrote you before we embarked on the evening of the 8th and started from Algiers on the morning of the 9th and arrived here this morning the 20th not having been off the vessel crowded to its utmost capacity with soldiers and officers being more than 800 in all for 12 days - going on board sick and not fit to move at all - Yet feeling so desirous to come a little North that I felt able to take any risk for this object - So I came on - For the first five or six days I did not sit up but very little - Then a storm came on with North East wind lasting three days and part of the time very violent - We were about opposite Charleston when the storm commenced and I do not think we made more than 100 miles in three days although the boat was a propeller and new - No casualties occurred during the Storm although such a seasick lot I guess you hardly ever read of and permit me to say your humble servant was not among the least of them - Of one thing I am certain that everything taken into my stomach in the way of food or drink had such a remark able tendency to seek external atmospheric air that I really got discouraged ever trying to eat or drink - and gave it up entirely for two or three days except occasionally taking a little drink and if I recollect the tea water and even Whisky (which latter I do not use much of) all had a very brackish sea water taste - After this I began to feel better and really I have improved rapidly since and hope to be able to fulfill all the Govt have a right to expect of me - I shall not ask leave to come home if I feel safe in regard to my health to stay or unless you some of you are dangerously sick - Well so much for myself on the Sea Voyage - Well a Sea Voyage about all I can say of it is that which relates to myself except that there is awful sight of water around and seems to be nothing else except an occasional porpoise or shark running up in sight and once in while particularly when the wind blows has a practice of raising up in ridges many miles long with foamy white looking tops Some of these ridges appeared to be fifty feet high and when the Vessel went over them it shook about amazingly sometimes seeming to stand on the bow throwing water all over those in front then the bow would raise and the other end would be down so the ends of the Vessel would raise and fall 30 or 40 feet - Then when she got between ridges she would roll the other way and sometimes she would seem to be going over and over sidewise and you may judge it was quite difficult to walk even for experienced seamen and I with the others felt very much as though the vessel had got awful drunk and that we might help her a little by holding tight to any part in our reach that we could cling to, at any rate this was a practice quite universal among the passengers who dare venture out of their berths - And really laughable too it was to see strong men clinging to the railing endeavoring to lighten the Vessel and relieve her by throwing the contents of their stomachs overboard - All to no avail she would roll and act drunk till the wind abated when strange and how quiet it all was but those who strove most to relieve the vessel looked very white for several days after -

We had but one man die at sea - he was mortally sick when taken on board and died 3rd day out was buried at sundown in the Gulf of Mexico nearly opposite Tortugas - I thought it strange and singular burial - to see a [man] wrapped in his blanket snugly sewed up and a weight of stone attached to his feet by cords - Then after the brief funeral sea service slid off from the plank into the Green waves of the Gulf, sinking! sinking!! sinking!!! until the equilibrium of the water shall equal that of the weight and body - There to remain with no monument to mark his resting place till the great Resurrection Trumpet shall call him before the bar of the Supreme judge of all quick and Dead.

I must close - they are waiting for my letter good bye my loves all - write soon - Yours truly, Benj. A. Fordyce
Direct to Washington D.C.

Washington D.C. July 29th 1864

My dear wife

You observe I keep dating my letters from different places - We have just arrived in this City on our way to join the remainder of our

Command We had some sharp fighting before we left Deep Bottoms our Brigade which was only half present lost 78 killed wounded & prisoners. On the morning of the 27th Genl Hancock &Genl Sheridan crossed James River at the point we had been holding with the 2nd and 6th Army Corps enroute for some grand move the full particulars of which have not yet transpired We were ordered to Washington on the 27th and arrived today enroute as I learn to Harper's Ferry to join 19th Corps - There is another raid up the Shenandoah & it must be suppressed - We had quite a number of important operations at Deep Bottoms - I am improved somewhat in health although quite weak yet - Have not received any letters from you yet but shall as soon as I join the Regiment - The great fight is now in progress every day - I have great confidence in our ultimate success - I earnestly hope you and the children are well - Keep them assured of my anxiety and love for them - Teach them to do right & I believe they will be happy - I had hoped to come home before long but you see at once any man that can do any thing can not be spared from the Army now - If I am comfortably well I do not wish to come just now

When the 2nd Army Corps crossed the river near us and advanced on the Enemy I was in plain sight of the whole - The Rebs during the night before had planted seven cannon so as to rake every foot of ground on which our little camp was placed - At the same time our forces covered the bridge with dirt and flags and crossed in the latter part of the night - In the morning they marched up to the Reb guns & captured them before they fired more than ten shots - one of the shell went over my hospital tent - They captured in all 10 pieces of artillery & 300 prisoners - made a fine thing of it

Our Cavalry about 30,000 strong then advanced probably to Malvern Hill - I hope they have been successful - Give my respects and love to all my friends and all who may inquire after me - I must close - Good bye. Direct your letters to 160th Regt Washington D.C. as you have done before

Benj. A. Fordyce

PS - I sent my trunk to you as I could not be annoyed with it when moving so often I did not pay express chgs give my love to Father & Mother Slocum my Father & Mother & all the brothers & sisters & dont forget my own little ones -

Yours affectionately   Benj. A. Fordyce

Monocacy Md. Aug 2nd 1864

My dear daughter Abbie

I have not written to you in some time but have written to all the rest I believe - I thought I would write to you and see if I could not get an answer & some news from home - I have not recd any letters yet from home since I was a prisoner - you may judge I begin to feel somewhat anxious to hear from you - I do not know whether you are well or sick - Since I commenced writing this, we have an order to move a short distance and must stop a little while I am writing on the battle field where John Tifft Lt 9th Artillery was wounded - *[John Tifft, of Venice; the 9th Heavy Artillery began as 138th NYSV, Co. E. of Cayuga Co. LGC]* It is a lovely romantic place surrounded with hills and mountains - the Monocacy river running only a few rods from our tent - I was in swimming in it today and the way the little fishes would bite my toes and legs I guess you would laugh - They would come around so thick you could hardly see the bottom though the water was perfectly clear - Nice smooth little fish as you ever saw, not the least bit afraid - The Regiment is in line, I must stop - About as soon as we were in line we had orders to go into camp again on the same ground - I just now learned that the rest of the Reg't were coming to join us here - We had not seen them since leaving New Orleans till just now 2 P.M. They are in sight - One of the boys immediately brought me the first letter I had received from home in months - One written by Ma on the 26th July - Judge of my Grief and surprise to learn that my dear old mother was dead and buried some time before - *[Alpha (Clark) Fordyce, wife of Dr. Benjamin Fordyce, died July 14, 1864, age 68 yrs. LGC]* This was the first intimation I had had of her sickness except in one of Mas letters in April, she mentioned that she was not very well - I suppose I must have some letters somewhere on the way to me describing her sickness & notifying me of her death as there is no date given of her death or burial - Only that Uncle Horton *[Nathaniel Horton Fordyce, brother of Dr. Benjamin. LGC]*

---

staid a few days after mothers funeral and was at our house - *[The cobblestone house at Scipio Center, which was built by Dr. Benjamin Fordyce, in 1841. LGC]* I could hardly contain myself for a little time - I would like to have the particulars - O how I sympathize with my Dear Father brothers and sisters in our great bereavement

I had anxiously looked forward to the time when I should come home and greet you all again when peace should make our land happy once more but one ever dear and kind to me must be forever absent from our circle - I will write to Father in a day or two

Ma wrote to me that you are not very well - you must not read too steady - go down to the brook or up in the woods where I used to go with you - And my little George I hope he is a nice boy & hope I can come home and see him before long as well as all the rest - Dr Armstrong is said to be very sick - was sent to Hospital yesterday - I have not seen him - I shall go and see him today - He is at Frederic City three miles from here - I have been there and inquired for Johnny Tifft but he was sent to Baltimore I suppose - I have a hundred other things to write you all but I feel oppressed this morning - I am now quite well to what I was when last wrote - I have seen our sharp fight - helped operate on quite a number with credit - I hope to myself - My love to you all - Ma write Estella write & Abbie write to me all about George

Yours, Benj. A. Fordyce

(PS) Emeline - I will write to you in a few days when more composed
Yours   Benj -

Monocacy Junction Va Aug 5th 1864

My dear wife

I recd your letter describing my mothers illness and decease day before yesterday - I am really glad that you could be with my dear old mother in her last hours - I regret to learn that she was so long insensible previous to her decease - I know she would have left some kind word for me - But Mother had lived to a good age being nearly seventy years of age and was of a temperament that gave no reason to suppose here decease might be sudden and perhaps come unexpectedly as all changes of this kind do come - To me it was really sudden and quite unexpected yet I must try soldier like philosophic calmness - But I really grieve for my poor old Father in his loneliness - My brothers and sisters are younger and can wear out their grief sooner and in the active duties of life realize a partial forgetfulness of their loss but to Father it is irreparable - I am improving in health every day and now feel quite equal to my duties - I am always pleased to be able to fulfill my required duties and I am told that I gain some credit to myself perhaps too much to get easily relieved for absence or resignation - Dr Armstrong being sick and at Hospital and Dr Powers absent prevented my being able to accept the appointment of Medical Purveyor of the 19th A.C. - a very nice responsibility and desirable position that would have given me many advantages that I cannot obtain from service in the Regt - This is two or three times something might have been obtained but always defeated from same causes -

We had orders to move to Harpers Ferry yesterday and were under Arms from 2 P.M. till 9 1/2 P.M. crossed by fording the Monocacy the boys wading the river where it was 2 ft deep - Then we bivouacked on the Bank till morning - then we were detailed to guard the train and at last came back to same camp we started from and are now in charge of train - The train is here yet - The forces are gone that we are connected with - so we are left with 165th here yet - this gives me time to write - There is nothing going on among the rebels that we know of - Although camp rumor has them everywhere - We see none of them about here - Perhaps our Corps may be kept along the river for a time to guard the crossings - You write that Col Morse is dead and Bishop Ames, Lewis DeLap - The old must die but these young men it seems sudden as healthy as they used to be -

Lucian keeps a good store you write - I am glad for him - He is a very deserving young man - Give him my compliments - Remember me to all the neighbors - I have not heard from Anson Whitman for some time past and when last heard from him he was dangerously ill - please write me how he is - Give Jonas Woods folks my compliments I tried to go to Joe Gregorys but could not get away long enough -

Remember me to all my friends and relations particularly your Father and Mother - The boy is waiting to carry this to mail & must stop - My love to you all - Kiss George for me - will write to Stell soon.

Benj. A. Fordyce

(PS) I send Col (Lt) VanPetten photograph

———————

Halltown Va Aug 8th 1864
Valley Shannendoah 4 miles west & so - Harpers Ferry
My dear wife

I received yours and Abbies letters of Aug 2nd yesterday and really glad was I to hear from you - Your letters come regularly now, and I can assure you I feel greatly relieved - I am pleased that you are improving in health - I am improving somewhat - Indeed I feel almost well again though on duty all the time - You are very anxious for me to come home - Yours cannot exceed mine to come yet at the present time it would be impossible for me to obtain leave of Absence if I can stand up - Regiments are so short of competent Surgeons that nothing but immediate danger of dying from disease will relieve a Medical Officer - Not one is obtaining leave now - You can imagine only how much I want to see you and the children - I will come home just as soon as it is possible for me to do so and I hope to stay - as I shall hope not to be obliged to ever go from home again - If I came home on leave it would be a greater trial for me to leave again than it was at first - In all probability we are about to start or very soon on an important expedition no doubt attended with some of the serious casualties of War - I can fully appreciate how discouraging every thing looks to you in regard to the final result of war - I sometimes feel very desponding and then when I reflect that in the All seeing eye of God our cause is just that in our success the people of the whole nation must be benefitted the condition of fallen man ameliorated I believe God will favor our efforts & who he favors will succeed - I take heart again and am ready to go on - My heart bleeds for our poor Country - I see no way but to fight it through yet I would be willing to see the struggle close by almost any conciliatory process - Slavery must end, even if the war closes by recognizing the South the great majority of the people south would hail the day with acclamations of joy - I know this Yet Politicians win pullers money gamblers and villains cannot see the propriety of closing the war quite yet - There has not been bloodshed enough houses enough burned widows and orphans enough made The grave has not been often enough used to cover the remains of our noble soldiers who have so cheerfully and manfully sacrificed their lives for our suffering country - There are not yet enough maimed to greet us for life who may live to see the end to satisfy them - O how heart sick it makes many of our good noble, gallant soldiers to think their sufferings if at all are only sympathized with in mockery by the political managers of the war - Sometimes they become discouraged with hard marching fall out sometimes die on the road - Yet the survivors when the strife comes go in with undaunted courage only to have the enemy slip away again from them to some more inaccessible part of this extensive country - But I must stop - the end will come sometime, and I hope to live to see and cherish a happy free & prosperous nation of my own native land -

Abbie writes a good letter - I wish she would take a little more pains in using capital letters and punctuating keeping lines straight &c Then her letters would be as pretty as any child of her age I ever knew - I have not had any letter from Stelle in a good while - Tell my dear child, she must not forget Pa write as often as she can conveniently and have Grandma and Grandpa write too with her -

I came through the great gap in the Blue Ridge at Harpers Ferry yesterday where the Potomac & Shenandoah unite and break through the great Rocky mountain 700 feet high on the way to the Atlantic - The rocks extend from the river bed to the extreme top of the mountain - I saw the rock on which Jefferson sat when he wrote the lines describing this passage of these rivers - It is situated about 400 feet from the bed of the river on the Virginia side and 300 below the top of the mountain - The rocks are almost perpendicular here and in many places overhanging road railroad and canal that run at the bottom of the Valley - This place Harpers Ferry is a great curiosity in nature and presents scenery as impressive as any I ever saw in my life - As a military point it would be impregnable with a true genuine and determined force to defend it - The surrender by Col Miles was one of the most disgraceful affairs that it ever became the duty of the historian to record -

I want you to write every opportunity and as you say if it is only a few lines and Abbie tell George to be a nice boy and kiss him for Pa - Tell him to eat one good apple for me - I will fetch the pony home with me tell him - Give my love to all friends - I don't believe you can read this I have scrawled so

                    Yours affectionately   Benj. A. Fordyce

(PS) I am glad the trunk watch and money got home safe - I hope to come sometime write often - good bye   BAF

(PS) Does Firm keep up the fences & things neat? Dr Armstrong is very sick with Fever; improving a little - I believe I would stay on the place till crops are secure but act on your own judgement

<hr />

                         Aug. 14th 1864, Near Middletown, Va.
My dear Estella

I thought I had a little time and would write to you if only a few lines - I learn that you are at school at Sherwoods and living at your Grandpa Slocums and that you are well pleased with your school and with the arrangement generally - I am really glad that you are so well provided - I hope you will be greatly benefitted by your efforts to acquire a good education - You certainly have the advantage of excellent society *[some of the "best" families lived in Sherwood! LGC]* which will prove of great value to you - particularly in improving your conversational powers - There is nothing more entertaining than interesting conversational powers - Such persons always draw around them a circle of friends and if good choice selections are made no source of improvement is greater - While no acquaintances should be cast entirely aside unless vicious or unworthy yet few should be allowed to be our intimate friends and they wisely and cautiously selected and only admitted as intimate friends after couciling parents or relatives upon the subject - Sometimes very worthy young persons are surrounded by influences not well calculated to favor the best kinds of development of character - Now this class require a great amount of discretion in associating and forming intimacies with but I know you will consult your friends and relatives in all your social visits &c and have no fears -

So I will write you a few words in regard to where I am what I have seen &c for the last few days - This camp is west of Middletown about one mile a very pretty little village south of Winchester -This country is beautiful in scenery - Mountains very high on either side of us the Shenandoah running along the base of one of the mountains - These mountains are very rocky some places nothing but rocks for a great number of acres - The land between the mountains is of good quality - raise fine crops - We are following the enemy up the river with a large army - They run well but we get a little fight out of them occasionally - There are so many chances to hide here in ravines woods & mountains that it is impossible to corner them anywhere - We march hard they slip away - We hunt them out they are gone - We catch a few of them and they do likewise of us - On the 11th we had a sharp fight of Cavalry we had some 200 killed & wounded - a good many rebs killed by the graves made on their side of field - Today a rebel spy was hung in sight of our tent - He had yesterday betrayed a portion of our train into the hands of the enemy by which we lost some 50 or more wagons - He overreached the matter a little got caught and a rope was put around his neck to relieve him of such habits & practices - I just recd a letter from home and heard that Ma & all were well - I am hoping to get home in about 4 weeks I think the principal campaigning will be over by 1st Oct - I will tell you so much more than I can write then that I hope you will all be satisfied with half I can tell you - Yours affectionately - may write more before this goes -

B. A. Fordyce

My love to all GrandPa & Ma & all

Aug 20th 1864 Near Charlestown Va

My dear wife -

I should have sent Estellas letter some days ago but we have had no mail till this morning - I am quite comfortable in health Have been on the campaign thru the Susquehanna [Shenandoah] Valley under Gen Sheridan - We are now waiting for them to give us fight if they wish - We went as far as Strassburg & have fallen back slowly to this place - This part of Virginia is very fine indeed - We went through Berryville, Newtown, Middletown & back through Winchester having gone over much old Battleground -

The mail leaves in a few minutes and I must close - Dr Powers has sent in his resignation - Grounded on his poor health - I think it will be accepted - It has already been forwarded - approved here -

Remember me to all friends - Dr Armstrong is sick at Hospital this leaves me entirely alone with the Regt so you see I do all the labor intended for three surgeons by Government -

You think I can come home if I wish to - You are very much mistaken about this - I can come when they will allow me to - I think I shall be able to come in five or six weeks at longest - but of course cannot tell certainly - I received no letter from you last mail - Write as often as you can - I shall do the same

Yours most truly and affectionately, Benj. A. Fordyce

Near Halltown Va Aug 23rd 1864
My dear wife

I recd your letter of Aug 9th just as I had dispatched my last together with Abbie and George letters - I am always glad to hear from you and that your health is comfortably good - I want to receive letters every mail from some of you. You can hardly imagine how cheering it is to get comfortable letters from home situated as we are - We have been moving every day for many days past - First we steadily advanced on the enemy driving them further than any army that has ever gone up the Valley of the Shenandoah without getting licked - Genl Sheridan has managed our movements with great skill and adroitness in my opinion - When the enemy were likely to flank us with heavy reinforcements through the gaps of the mountains we have steadily fallen back into their rear at night so that we have constantly held an advantageous position in which they dare not attack us - We have steadily fallen back to the position we now occupy (the same I addressed you one letter from before) and have it firmly fortified with earthworks and barricades - the enemy have followed us closely and have been skirmishing every day for several days past - We have taken several hundred prisoners and lost some I think on the whole the advantage is with us - Our position now I think cannot be carried with less than three times our force - Our strength is very near 50,000 including Cavalry and artillery and my impression is Lee cannot spare men enough from around Richmond to whip us without losing Richmond and Petersburgh both - Our Army before Richmond is not materially weakened as you will observe by the papers of the last few days - Everything looks to me more favorable than it ever has before

Real genuine success is attending our arms and God grant that it may continue till this awful war shall end in a good and glorious peace for us all - I am in rather better health than when I last wrote to you - Although I do not feel strong yet - The Col promises me that I shall have leave just as soon as this campaign ends I know he will do all that anyone can do for me - Dr Armstrong is still sick at Hospital and will probably [not] be able to resume his duties for some time to come - Dr Powers has tendered his resignation on account of poor health and it is accepted and he has an excellent and honorable discharge from the service - Dr Armstrong will probably receive the commission as Surgeon of the Regiment - He is a hard working good officer and is justly entitled to the promotion and I hope he may receive it - I shall make no effort in that direction, although I can get the best of recommendations - It rained here very hard yesterday and cooled the air wonderfully - This is a lovely country here and delightful climate at this season of year not much warmer than with you - We are sometimes several days without seeing our wagons - Then I carry a rubber blanket and an overcoat on my horse and sleep on the ground as sound as I ever slept in my life - Except when they get to shooting around a little too close or the Regiment is ordered to fall in - Then of course I rouse up have my horse saddled and get ready for what may transpire - On the whole for a younger man, it would be really exciting and entertaining - I am most too old to be disturbed quite so much - Write often - I will come home as soon as I can - Give my love to all

Yours affectionately, Benj. A. Fordyce

(PS) Tell John B. Strong to write to me what the political prospects are and how the people feel in regard to the war - I want to hear from him and indeed all the neighbors Mr Divine & all others - I have very little time to write being alone but will write to Mr Congdon first time I have time I hope Firm will do well for you - Give him my respects   Yrs &c

$$======$$

Near Halltown Va Aug 25th 1864

My dear wife and children

I received your letters of the 14th and 15th yesterday and today and was pleased to hear that you are generally well (except Estella)   I am improving in health slowly -   I wish Estella to be extremely careful about being out in night air or getting her feet wet with dew or rain - Let her exercise out of doors as much as her strength will permit - Let her ride on horseback but not be out in the evening - As to medicines I hope she will not need any - Should she require any Tincture of Guiaci is one of the best remedies I am acquainted with - There is plenty of it in the Office in a quart bottle on the south shelf over the cupboard - Dose 20 drops in a tablespoonful of sweetened milk 3 times a day before eating   Continue about a week then omit for two or three weeks

Tincture of Iron is excellent - marked Ferri Tinct Chloride - 5 drops 3 times a day in sweetened water will answer - Be sure and write me if she does not get better soon - Estella writes she was going to have a good dinner on the 14th and wants to know what I had   We were way down among the rebels at that time near Middletown Va   We had hard tack a kind of cracker so hard you can neither bite break or soak it soft - Some coffee without milk or sugar though we generally have sugar and very good fresh beef - This was our whole bill of fare -   On this we were marching every night more or less - some nights twelve or fifteen miles - You may think this rather hard fare - We do better a great deal of the time but our living costs each at best nearly $5 per week - prices very high - beef 17 1/2 cts pork 25 cts hams 26 1/2 cts potatoes 5 1/2 cts per lb and other things in proportion - And what is bitter I am entirely out of money - I think I must get some pay in three or four days so you need not send me any - You say you have sent me a little package by Lt Edwards - It will come all safe but not in two or three weeks yet - I learn he is exchanged & will come to the Regiment before long - You write that Giles expects to get married you did not state to whom - *[married Mary Grace Taber, Oct. 6, 1864. LGC]* If he desires it and it is possible for me to come home at the time I will be there - But not so much to come to the wedding as to see and visit the rest of you - I shall be very happy I assure you to come home and see my family - Would I not like some of those apples pears and plums George and Abbie are going to eat for me though -

Mrs Signor brought you some berries and wished to be remembered to me - Tell her I often think of all my friends though distant from them and thank her for her kind remembrance of me and all others who think of me away from home earnestly trying to help our poor bleeding country in her great struggle for integrity - God save our country - Those who lie supinely on their backs and see her awful struggle and raise not a hand to help but talk of peace are no better than traitors in arms against us - O how I despise them - shall our country be lost when we have such ample means to save - God forbid! - Remember me to Cousin Carrie Nelsons & Johns folks and indeed all our friends. How I should be pleased if they would write to me - Carrie will if you ask her - Dr Armstrong is better and writes from Annapolis that he will be back with us in eight or ten days Get Abbie a bonnet sure and Estella one if she needs - I think it best they are both good girls -

All my love to you all   write often   Benj. A. Fordyce

Chapter X
The Third Battle of Winchester

The Northern forces engage the enemy as they move on through Charlestown, W VA to Berryville, VA, Halltown, and arrive in Winchester. Doctor Fordyce is charged with the responsible position of Inspector of Hospitals. His work load is heavy as the Third Battle of Winchester on September 19 wreaked havoc in the ranks. His letters do not reveal the fact that he also performed operations demanding the utmost skill in surgery. Military archival medical records, however, reveal outstanding surgical procedures that he performed to save the lives of some of the casualties of the battle of the 19th of September, 1864.

Near Charlestown Va Aug 30th 1864

My dear wife and children

I recd a letter by you all dated the 24th and 25th inst yesterday - I learn with painful interest of Estella's poor health. I have written to you in regard in two letters which I trust you have received before the date of this - I hope she will get better before cold weather begins - Riding on horseback active exercise out of doors good diet and great care about exposure to night air with the remedies I have suggested will be the best of anything I can think of not seeing her -

I recd Abbie's nice posy and am glad to have you raise some flowers from those I sent you from La - The Tobacco you say grows finely but the grasshoppers have commenced chewing Tobacco - I knew they acted very meanly here with my clothing but did not think they would commence chewing my Tobacco - This a degree of meanness I had never even attributed to them -

My navy flannel Blouse and pants are nearly worn out if you could get and have an opportunity of sending me a suit (I do not need a vest) I should be very glad - put in a good inside pocket in the blouse

- If you cannot send by private conveyance you can probably by mail - Be sure and get it at the lowest postage price. Get a pretty good one if you can

I am quite well we have moved since I last wrote up the Shenandoah Valley again and are now above Charlestown Va - This is the place where John Brown was hung - Our bands sometimes play Jn Brown when we go through - The inhabitants look anything but pleasant

We have been expecting a fight every day for several days now - We have found the enemy in force and have offered fight which he has as yet declined We are now in a strong position and if they mean to fight they cannot seek a better opportunity - We are fortified with good breastworks and quite a goodly number of men - Our Regiment worked all night last night on them before us & they are strong - I must stop as the man is going who carries this to mail. My love to all

Yours affectionately Benj. A. Fordyce

(PS) Respects to John B. Strong - tell him save the town from Draft if he can

---

Near Charlestown, Va Sept 1st 1864

My dear wife and children,

Today is the first day of Autumn - I really experienced quite a change from summer - Sleeping on the ground and in the open air is not quite as comfortable as a good Feather bed in a warm house I am sure from actual experience - It is probably about as cool here as with you now - I have plenty of blankets for the present however and do not suffer with cold - Dr. Armstrong has not returned yet to the Regiment although he has been expected for a few days past - Col VanPetten wrote to him to get a sick leave of absence and go home for a time - I do not know but he has succeeded - He is very fortunate if so - We have had no appearance of the enemy in our front since I last wrote to you We have had several quite severe Cavalry fights within the last 10 days in our immediate vicinity - One on the 21st

22nd 23rd 24th and on the 25th the rebs attempted to cross into Maryland - We had a cavalry Division opposite the ford where they made the attempt <u>under</u> <u>Averill</u> - He waited until they got to crossing finely wagon train and all and then he politely invited them to retire with canister shells and carbines - They took the hint in about two hours and hastily fell back with a loss it is reported of 1000 men killed and wounded and 400 wagons with very trifling loss on our side - The 26th we had a sharp fight in our front of Artillery and Infantry considerable loss on both sides - Rebels driven back I saw 74 prisoners brought in in one squad - They looked a little bit long-faced - Some of them had on our soldiers pants - Our boys asked them why they wore our pants one answered that "he could not get any others"- Our Regiment was not engaged in any of these although we were nearby -

On the 27th behold no enemy could be found during the night they all missled - Today I bathed in the Shenandoah - I have bathed since I left home in the Atlantic, Gulf of Mexico, Mississippi River, Red River, Bayou Teche, LaFourche, James River, Monocacy, Potomac, &c &c - Indeed I have been where there was water enough to keep clean but I get occasionally very dirty we have to make a great deal of effort to keep clean - I get washing done as often as I can generally succeed well am hardly ever obliged to wear a shirt more than three weeks If I am I change and put on the last one taken off for a few days while the worn one cools off a little so a body can change occasionally anyway I generally change weekly - Some of the soldiers do not change at all - wear a shirt out without change and some of them without washing -

Well, I had forgotten on the 28th of course we were bound to hunt up the enemy fearing some untoward accident had happened to them and of course we marched as near as we could judge in the direction they had taken - After a while we came to a grave yard of new made graves I feared then they were all dead and of course sympathized with surviving friends - We went on however till I began to be mistrustful we might get into the position of the fellow who went out hunting woodchucks - Getting very tired and almost discouraged still persevered till at last he thought he saw one run into a hole under a stone pile - To make sure he was there before he commenced digging he run his arm into the hole and got his thumb bit off - Said he had one satisfaction he now knew he was there - I would prefer not to get the thumb bitten first -

Well we moved to our present position and found them after a sharp cavalry fight in which as near as I can learn we came out much the best -

Well we are now in a good fortified position Genl McMillan says all H—l could not drive us from it - No fighting since - All very quiet and we are in a pleasant place in the edge of a pine woods -

I am very much pleased to receive your letters so regularly now - I read the one in which Estella and Abbie both wrote a real good letter - *[BAF has not saved family letters since March. LGC]*

I want you to write me about everybody of our neighbors - Alward - Manchester - Ellsworth - Gallup - Bateman *[Stewart's Corners families]* & everything of interest you think of I must close

I wish, if you send me blouse you would get one that is lined and warm - You can send in a box by express - I will write again soon in regard to it probably before you get it & advise what else I would like to have in the box.

I am most affectionately yrs Benj. A. Fordyce

(PS) Send me Cousin Carrie's photograph for a friend of mine - if possible -

---

Near Berryville Va Sept 6th 1864

My dear wife and children

Having but a few moments to write I pencil you a few lines to let you know I am all right side up yet - I have recd no letters from you for several days the mail came to us today and no letter & is going immediately back I will not let it return without a line from me - Yesterday I heard that I had a brother inquiring here at Head Quarters for me was directed to the 75th N.Y. who it was I cannot imagine as I did not see him I staid in my quarters all day hoping someone would turn up that I knew - Well Im as well as usual except I am lame with Rheumatism some - You will recall I used to be troubled with one hip occasionally this I think is the same - Hope it will not prove serious - Dr Armstrong has not returned to the Regiment yet - so I am alone. I think he has gone home on leave of absence but do not know of course - I think the campaign must close before long as the rainy weather has already begun - It seems so to us as we get wet, every time it rains - Last night was one of the worst nights I have ever experienced on acct of rain since I have been in the service -

We could not keep from getting wet roll over as we would - Still I feel quite well today except lameness and contracting a little cold I am in hopes that the fall of Atlanta will be premonitory of speedy peace and a restoration of the Union - I have great confidence in the final result if the devilish scheming politicians will let the Government alone not even to say aid it -

I hope to hear Estella is better in your next - I have written in two letters my advice in her case & told you where in the office you would find it viz: Tinc Guiac and Tinc Ferri Muriatis. Of the first 20 drops at a dose in sweetened milk 3 times per day of the 2nd after using the first one or two weeks then omit give 5 to 8 drops in sweetened water 3 times per day -

The Piano tell the girls to wait till I come for and If I feel that I can I will get a good instrument of some kind - I do not believe I shall be able to get relieved before the first of October - I certainly will come home this fall -

George was 4 yrs old the 4th I believe - I must try and send him something or bring it when I come -

I must close as the man is waiting to carry the mail - my love to you all Write often -
Yours affectionately & in haste B. A. Fordyce

PS We have no severe fighting here & may not - I think not. tell John to work hard for the administration for I am sure Unc Abe is right - Yrs, B.A.F.

Near Berryville, Va. Sept 8th 1864

My dear wife and children

Having an opportunity I send you a few lines - I am in better health than I have been for some time past - not as lame as at the date of my last letter - It is a rainy unpleasant day - The weather indicates that Fall has commenced in real earnest raining every two or three days - The air quite cool and damp - The girls are anxious for a Melodian Now you act your own judgement in regard to purchasing one - I have always intended to purchase for them an instrument - Now if one can be obtained that will suit for $150, I think you had better purchase one and give them an opportunity with Carrie in the office if you think best I am fearful that it will subject you to great inconvenience for wood and other things that you would not otherwise have On Estellas acct I would like to have her where you can be with her most of the time - I feel very uneasy about her since your last letter - I would like to have her get well without taking too much strong medicine and I think she will with good care on her part - I have just received a letter from John Strong & will send a partial answer in this enclosure - We have had no fighting here of late - One small fight about the 3rd principally of the 8th Army Corps - within about a mile of - I obtained most of the particulars from Cousin Barnwell Clark who married Sarah Howland for his first wife - He belongs to the 123rd Ohio He says all the boys now living are in the Army - Is not this noble - Barnwell is Orderly Sgt, has a noble heart I can assure you for his country and he would as soon go into the fire as for McClellan - He is strong I can assure you for the Union - He was in the very front line of the fight the other day and has seen very hard service 2 yrs - *[He is perhaps the "brother", looking for BAF, a few days earlier. LGC]* He tells me that Victor Clark Eri son was in his company - That he became very tired & on the last retreat under Gen'l Hunter when they were licked so - Near Winchester He became so tired although Barnwell kept him by him during the dark night as long as he could - He tried to get a ride for him but could not - At last he missed him and has not heard from him since - He fears that he is dead - He was a good soldier & did well -

The mail is just going and I must stop writing - Eliza Ann Volintine's son - I will try and write about that next time - We had mutton and apple sauce for dinner and hard bread -

I have got no pay yet & only 10 cts in money left and no postage stamps - Send me 8 or 10 in your next Yours most affectionately - I will come home first opportunity

Benj. A. Fordyce

John - the Army is all right - they go strong for Uncle Abe - The change is great in a few days I never saw so great - Can't write any more. my love to sf and wife - B.A.F.

Hd.Qrs.160th N.Y.V. Near Berryville Va Sept 15th 1864
My dear wife

I have waited a few days hoping to receive a letter from you but have not since yours dated Sept 3rd came to hand - We shall receive a mail today and I shall without doubt hear from you - I feel quite anxious about your and Estellas health - Should your health continue to grow more feeble I can with quite a certain prospect of having it accepted base a resignation upon it - I am promised a Leave of Absence so that I can get home by the first of October by Col VanPetten and I am sure he will make every effort to get it through for me - He is willing to do any favor for me within his power. Dr Armstrong has returned to the regiment but in very poor health - He had a chill yesterday is comfortable now playing chess with the Col -

We had quite a sharp battle day before yesterday about five miles in front of us near Winchester - We captured over 300 prisoners - Our entire loss two killed and eight wounded -

Our Regiment was in line last night expecting an attack from the rebels - This morning dawned as quiet as usual with no attack - Everything quiet today - I am improving in health although I lay on the ground and sometimes in the wet - I sometimes wonder at my own powers of endurance -

Tell the girls I have as fine a pony as there is in the 19th A.C. I have purchasers for him every day - Today Col. Purlee of the 114th N.Y. Vols was here to see him and offered me $225 for him - I did not take it for him I must have $300 for him -

If he was in any way suitable for the use of the girls I would not sell He has too much life and strength for any female use although he is perfectly kind and nothing frightens him - But a woman could hardly hold him steady in a bit for common riding - He has a hard mouth and firm will for a pony and the boys say he can outrun anything in the Corps - Of horse, enough! - I have recd no pay yet am getting roofully short of funds - I borrowed some and get along as long as anyone has money to lend - I need some stamps in order to write to you as often as you wish - I wish you would send a few say 10 in a letter - I will use them all for you at home; I reckon -

I hope to be able to tell you all I would write in a few days and will close

I will every two or three days and keep you informed - Capt Cowan of 1st Artillery with whom John Lawson was enlisted was wounded day before yesterday - I think not seriously - did not see him - I hope not serious he is a very fine officer - Our main pleasures are social meetings among the officers as we have no other society - We enjoy ourselves well this way when in camp - I must stop I am as ever most truly

Your husband   Benj. A. Fordyce

I hope I shall get a letter today - good bye

Head Qtrs 19th Vol. Hospitals
Winchester Va Sept 23^d 1864

Dr. B. A. Fordyce
    Doctor

I have just sent out a circular announcing you for Medical Inspector of the Hospitals of this corps - Your duties will be to observe first, the Sanitary Condition of Wards Secondly, The appearance of wounds, whether ___ = Inspections or not - Thirdly - If wounds are well dressed by competent drapers - Fourthly, If the wounded get enough to eat and well cooked victuals, Fifthly Inspect the Kitchens, Sixthly, and Important!!! See if any of the Medical Officers are neglecting any of their wounded - And report to me frequently what you observe -

Very Respectfully
s/ T. K. Bigelow
Surg. in Chg. 19th A.C. Hospitals

Winchester Va Sept 25th 1864

My dear wife

I have just time to write you a line to let you know I am well I was present at the great battle part of the day - 19th - Was in charge of Ambulances and wounded and of course busy every minute am so still -

This is the first moment I have had to write you a line - I am now engaged in inspecting the hospitals for the wounded at this place of the 19th Corps Will probably go to the front in a day or two - I do not see clearly how I can get home on the 1st Oct, will try best I can - Col VanPetten was wounded & is in hospital at Harpers Ferry or has gone home - so my best chance is cut off - we lost our Captain I send you his photograph in this and one Lieut & sixteen others killed from our Regiment - Our forces are now probably fifty miles in advance of us here - I sent from my ward sixty slightly wounded this morning to Harpers Ferry - I have not received any letters from home for several days for obvious reasons - 1 will write particulars as soon as I possibly can - We had an awful battle here but how we whipped them - They fought like Lions but had to run - A host of prisoners were brought in last evening from the front and twenty-two pieces of Artillery - I must close this scrawl but will write as long as I can Dr Armstrong is with the Regiment in comfortable health - I sold my horse next day after I wrote my last letter for $300 - got a good note - Have had no pay yet am entirely out of money no horse clothes wearing out - Aint I in a sad fix - and another thing, I am permitted to work night & day which I am glad to be able to do if it will do good for the soldiers & our bleeding country -

I believe the end is beginning to be visible - The whole Rebel army is scattered from this Valley & I think cannot make another stand - Gen Sheridan is after them at the rate of twenty miles a day with Infantry & pushing them with Cavalry nights - We have a great many prisoners - and many wounded rebels in our hands - Some of their Surgeons are here - I have not had time to look into their hospitals to see how they look - They seem cheerful those I have seen I guess are glad to get into our lines - Many are coming in and giving themselves up

I am glad to learn that Estella is better - I hope you will all have good health I may start for front today we have some wounded at front We had here probably 3000 killed and wounded.

Remember me to all friends. I am yours most affectionately

Benj. A. Fordyce

Chapter XI
Hospitals of Winchester

Dr. Fordyce continues on at the hospital in Winchester. In addition to his responsibilities as Inspector of Hospitals, he is engaged in dressing the wounds of the soldiers and performing surgery. He describes the life he experiences in the City of Winchester and expresses hope that there will soon be an end to the conflict. He describes conditions in the hospital and praises the work of the Sanitary Commission (the forerunner of today's American Red Cross). He prepares to go to the front to join his regiment near Middletown, VA.

Hd.Qrs Post Hospital Winchester Va.
Sept 27th 1864 9.P.M.

My dear wife

You will observe I date my letter from Winchester again - I expected to have been ordered to the front 2 days ago but on the contrary I was ordered to stay here and continue Inspector of Hospitals for 19th A.C. - My duties are quite laborious requiring me to examine everything pertaining to the management condition of wounds to ascertain whether the men obtain supplies of food clothing &c and surgical care or not &c &c - I also assist in Dressing about Thirty Officers wounds daily - and am one of the board to decide on the necessity of all operations now required for the men wounded here of our Corps - We are not operating much now - have had a large number - Lt Col Babcock of the 75th lost his leg above the knee - was a prisoner long enough to be robbed of everything of Value he had - even his Cap was taken from him and an old white hat given him worn out - We have several Confederate Hospitals here I have visited some three or four of them - They are very well conducted and well supplied with delicacies by the sympathizing ladies of this place who do far more for them than they do for us - At present however they begin to come to our Hospitals and do something for our wounded no doubt many were afraid to do anything at first fearing our army would retreat and leave them again to the tender mercies of their friends - But no victory was ever more complete - Our army is still following them at least ninety miles from here - Capturing and routing all who make a stand - I may go forward any day but the Surgeons think I can do more here than at the front for the present - I think I may stay long enough to receive a letter from you after you get this provided you get this in two or three days - I will send you in this the address - I am quite well but very tired actually worn out - but my grit is good yet - I had hoped to be on my way home at this time but you see what has prevented - My papers had been sent in all right but this battle kept every Surgeon at his post - I shall not be able to be at Giles wedding - I regret it much - I should like to be home in the good weather of October if possible will come - No Surgeons were killed & only one wounded and he a poor worthless officer - Asst. Surgeon -

Tell Jn B Strong everything is working right politically here now and further if he wants to do me a favor I think indeed I know he can enlist the influence of a few friends in Auburn and get for me a Commission as Surgeon in one of the One Years Regiments in one week if he can give a little time to it this would enable me to come home for a spell at any rate and my term of service would expire as soon as now - I could be at home part of the time during the organization of the Regiment and my impression is that the war must end soon - All Asst Surgs that have been able to get home have been promoted and it seems that I deserve some notice for if ever a man worked I have - I can forward any number of Recommendations from here if required - and will if desired - I should like to be full Surgeon before I leave the Service - But shall resign if I do not soon get it - I have done more service than any one of nine out of ten of the Surgeons that I am acquainted with -

I am glad to hear you are well or comfortably well - I have recd no letters since the battle here - Had no pay yet - got only 50 cts left - Fruit of all kinds is abundant here but nothing to buy with - My love to the girls & George -

Yours affectionately   Benj. A. Fordyce

My dear wife

Although I do not hear from you often I shall write every time I have time just to let you know you are not wholly forgotten by long absence - We are getting off many of our wounded to Harpers Ferry enroute for Gen Hospitals somewhere and for home on furlough or leave of absence - Our labors are not so arduous as a few days ago I think our Hospital here will be broken up in a few days at longest - Whether I shall be sent front or permitted to remain here for a while yet I am unable to say - I should be pleased to stay here a short time if I could had I any money - As it is I would rather go to the Regiment I should be then quite sure of getting some pay for paymasters have already gone forward to pay the army and I think our Regiment will be paid - I would like to get some pay and then apply for a leave of absence - As you must well know leave of Absence is almost entirely out of the question (unless for the most extreme reasons) when such active campaigning is in progress - If I was sick and in actual danger of dying I could readily get it but I am satisfied the Surgeons here consider my services of some value I may be required to go into Hospital this winter here - The work would be much harder than with the Regiment - Should your health continue poor I shall resign or try to at least and come home to stay - But if you are better I shall only ask leave of Absence although to stay is a great pecuniary and personal sacrifice - I am satisfied my business at home with the same health I have had in the service would have been worth twice as much as I am really saving yet I am considered quite economical here -

Since the battle here I have performed some Surgical Operations that are even here considered a little better than some others - One case in particular of amputation at the shoulder joint I feel a little pride in - My patient is apparently making a fine recovery - The wound is nearly healed and he is able to be about some - *[Refer to Appendix A - Medical -* The Medical & Surgical History of the Civil War, *Ch. IX, p. 616, Case 1590. LPH]* He with the Officers whose wounds and amputations I dress, are quite anxious that I should remain here till they can be removed at least - We have in some of the Hospitals of course cases of erysipelas and gangrene & various kinds of

Mortification - some men have died from apparently slight wounds of hemorrhages after coming on in the night suddenly &c Well we meet with unexpected events here as in other pursuits of life - We have had no such cases in my ward yet - True some have died but none as yet that I did not expect would die when they came in - I am well pleased with the practice of Surgery and I have certainly seen something of it for the last year and had probably my full share of practice - I should be pleased to spend another year in the army as Surgeon in a One Years Regiment but no longer as Asst - although I operate more than half the Surgeons Yet the actual rank would give me a better right to decide cases -

I have not had any time to run round this city yet - It once must have been an active business place but now it has wofully lost its ancient prestige - Many of the finest dwellings are vacant some of the most rabid burned to ruins like Masons and Hunters - All stores closed not a particle of business done except as permitted or done by our own people -

One thing a little singular too the inhabitants tell me no market wagons come to this city while the rebel army occupied it now the streets are full every week day morning - They all refuse to take Confederate money often saying they had rather give away their goods that be annoyed with such poor stuff - This shows to me the want of confidence in their cause and government - They readily sell for our money (when we have any) and at reasonable prices - We buy excellent apples at 10cts a dozen peaches at from 6 to 10cts a dozen potatoes are high 6/- a peck. Cabbage 5 to 10cts a head &c &c Milk 10cts a quart & chickens & turkies &c reasonable - Beef is scarce & high mostly appropriated by rebel army

I see some very nice girls and little boys who often remind me of some others that I should be very happy to see and hope I may be able to see soon - The Campaign will last till after Election I think as active as it now is in all points - The army is now in the best fighting order it ever was - And when a fight comes on led by such Genls as we now have somebody is likely to get hurt before our army will run much - The Conspicuous glorious retreating of the early history of the war seems to be played out When our Army now retreats after a fight I calculate we are licked and not retreating for strategy - Genl Grants last move if truly reported is a grand affair - I have been over part of the ground where the battle was fought - We have gained I think an excellent position which must tell in other movements favorably for us - It does seem this awful war must end soon - The awful devastation of Virginia alone is enough to sicken one however blood thirsty of war. Every movement made of late has certainly strengthened the administration in the minds of the soldiers and the result will tell favorably in the election if no disaster befalls us - This awful rebellion must & will be put down and the great curse of the South - Slavery - gone down with it as certainly as effect follows cause if God is just seems to me

I am really glad the girls are improving in education and that George too is learning his letters & what a nice boy he will be when he can read - The girls inquired after Joe - I left Joe in New Orleans he was quite feeble after having Typhoid fever and not able to come with me - but I have heard from his since he is well and servant of a Surgeon in New Orleans - I must stop - give my kindest regards to all friends - probably the wedding will come off before you hear again from me give my congratulations to bride and groom

B. A. Fordyce

(PS) I should like to hear from Maria & Theodore & Addie and all the other relations - how are they all? Have they sold out again?

[U. S. Sanitary Commission Stationery]

Winchester Va Oct 6th 1864

My dear wife

I shall leave here tomorrow morning to go to the Regiment with a large train and strong escort - We have sent away from here all our wounded that will bear transportation - This relieves me from duty here and of course I must rejoin my regiment - I am in good comfortable health at present except a little lameness in my ankle of my leg that was broken - This is only temporary I think and will not interfere with my going - I am furnished with a horse by Lt Col VanPetton who was slightly wounded on the 19th Sept and has gone home - I have not received a letter from you in some time - some 10

---

or 12 days - I had hoped to hear from you by this train - but no letters came for me - I hope to hear from you soon and think I shall get letters at the Regiment from you - What the army movements will be in front I cannot tell - My impression is they will not advance much further as it is a long route to obtain supplies over and of course more or less exposed to the enemy - We have had no disasters as yet -

Just as soon as the army stops long enough to get a paper through I shall send a resignation forward - I have been acting as Inspector of Hospitals ever since I have been here - I can obtain a good position in front at any time when I am there Dr Armstrong is with the Regiment and I shall not be needed at present with Regt & will be placed on other duty - I hope not however as it is always harder to change about -

8 o'clock P.M. I have just been to get my order to be relieved and go front which was all made out in due form but not yet delivered to me. I have my things all ready to leave at 6 A.M tomorrow - but judge of my surprise when the paper was torn up and I was informed that I must remain some longer and help in one of the wards - So I shall remain a few days more probably at Winchester - probably long enough to hear from you - If you direct your letters right — If you in writing to me will let me know how much you cough and also Estella it may be I can advise something in regard to it, or I can take some more decided action in regard to it here - I am in quite a comfortable room compared with sleeping on the ground - Still I do not complain much either way - I think we must succeed before long in quelling this awful rebellion and the army be reduced and sent home but we have thought so so much that it may all be visionary at best - Our forces are having a fair amount of success at present I think but it certainly is not as great as is sometimes represented - you know it is very near Election time now and something must be done to make a good show for Electioneering purposes - Many times a reverse is represented a success - This awful battle here in my opinion in loss of men was decidedly greater to us than to the enemy - Our loss of killed wounded & prisoners certainly is not less that 4000 - While the enemy did not lose over 3000 on that day but afterwards their loss was far greater than ours -

Lt Col Babcock of 75th NY died this morning -

Little Fish is in the office of the Med Director here as a copying clerk - He is not very well and was detailed from Hospital here - He has not grown much to appearance but his stomach can and does hold every day far more brandy and whisky than mine although I am a full size the largest.

All the boys I have seen from Venice and Scipio are generally well - You would be surprised almost to see the many friends of the killed and wounded here to take care of their friends and carry home their bodies of those that are dead and die here All the Eastern States N.Y. & Pa are largely represented in this way Many are embalmed particularly the Officers also many privates who have friends who can pay the expense.

I suppose that said wedding has transpired ere this and the pair are enjoying the extreme of happiness in conjugal felicity - I really wish them much joy - I believe if I recollect right the 4th was Abbies birthday. I intended to have written a letter to her but was too busy on that day but will write to both the girls soon My love to all - write often.

Yrs truly Benj A Fordyce

It is now 12 o'clock - I must retire -

[U. S. Sanitary Commission stationery]

Winchester Va Hosp 19th.C.
Oct 9th 64 (Sunday 9. P.M.)

My dear wife and children,

Again I write you a few lines although I have not yet received a line from you since sometime in Sept - yet I thought I would keep writing every few days You will observe I am still in Winchester. and working away as usual at bad wounds and for poor suffering soldiers yet they seem glad to see me come round - All the officers who are wounded and have been here or nearly all are sent off to Harpers Ferry and Genl Hospitals further north & east -

You can have no idea of the great advantage the Sanitary and Christian Commissions are now and have been since the battle to our wounded - They were here first with supplies and clothing for the soldiers - Indeed they were here two or three days before the Govmt with some bandages lint and dressings and then the thousand little things they furnish in the way of fruits and luxuries is truly astonishing - hereafter let no one say the sanitary does no good it is absolutely false - Without them our soldiers would have suffered frightfully - The Christian Commission has furnished several female nurses one to each large ward who cook and fix these little niceties for the soldiers and such faithful tireless women I never saw before - They work from daylight till 9 o'clock at night without sitting down a moment - They are looked for by the wounded soldiers with as much anxiety as the Surgeon is - and sometimes I think they do as much good soothing the distress of the wounded or with consoling conversation to the dying

They become in these cases really ministering angels in our cause

Our Army is now slowly falling back towards this place the main body is only 22 miles from here at Strasburgh - I think they will be here in a very few days at most and then we may all fall back to near Harpers Ferry or go somewhere else - I do not know which - At any rate I think I shall get some pay soon now - I borrowed $10 today so I am not dead broke yet -

I think we shall go into winter quarters somewhere before long but where I do not know - The weather is quite cool now for a few days and feel highly favored that I have been permitted to sleep under a roof for the last few weeks - The ground would have made rather a cool bed - But there is nothing like getting used to it - I am in tolerable good health though rather tired -

You must remember me to all the friends and neighbors I shall hope to be able to come home when the army gets here in a few days after - I really hope you are all well - Write as often as you can - My love to you all   Ben. A. Fordyce

[U.S. Sanitary Commission stationery]

Post Hospital Winchester Va. Oct 13th 64

My dear daughter Abbie

I have written to all the rest I believe and have not yet recd a word of reply in several weeks so I thought I would write to you and see if you could not answer my letter so I can hear from you in some way.

The last letter I received from home was dated Sept 18th and contained the little flowers (so very beautiful) you and Estella sent me - I have got them yet in the same letter - They please me as much as ever when I look at them I love flowers as you well used to know when I was at home - How I wish I could go out with you and George and look at the little Diamondshaped beds & pick a few flowers (not too many you know) and just smell of them a little as we go along towards the old Jersey sweet apple tree and get a lot of good apples - Then if we don't find any to suit us look for some good ones on the other trees - Does George like Jersey Sweets? I know Abbie does - I tell you won't we have a good time when I get home - I know you will save a few good apples so we can eat them together - Can't you make a little cider too so we can have some sweet cider - How nice a little sweet cider some fried cakes and cheese would go - O dear me! I have almost forgot about such things - Hard Tack (a kind bread used in the army called Pilot Bread) beef. Pork & beans, no butter no milk no eggs - This Hard bread sometimes needs a hammer & stone to break it Shouldn't you think my old teeth were worn out - Well, they are pretty near - Biscuit butter & honey Bless me - I have heard tell of it and have a kind of recollection that I have seen some sometime; but it is only an aggravation to think of such things now

I really wish you would write to me what you can get up for a change of diet if I come home a spell - really if you cant improve on this I don't know as it would pay to come - I will try and come soon anyway and risk it - I believe I will bring you a few hard tack too - The only trouble would be George might fall down on them and get hurt

---

Who is going to teach your school this winter Abbie? And how did you like the fair? Have you rode out any along with the doctor lately and made him ask you another question so many times that he almost gets tired What has become of Estella - O come to think she wrote a little in that last letter - If you should see anything of her just mention to her that I would like to hear from her again sometime - I tell you I think I shall get relieved from here before long and then I shall make the greatest effort to come a spell or to stay I ever did-

I operated one poor soldier today by cutting off his thigh - I have had a good many such to do since the great battle here - I don't like to hurt anybody yet - I am not quite hard hearted enough for that - Yet some think I can do these things nice -

If you see anything of Ma just tell her I am here at Winchester and should be very much pleased to hear from her sometime - I won't say anything about your writing for I know you will write just as soon as you get this - direct to Benj. A. Fordyce, Asst. Surg. 160th N.Y.Vols Washington D.C. and twill come all right

Your Father

I forgot to say I am quite well except lameness - I don't drink much whisky think I get along just as well

Yours   my love to all.   B.A.F.

Medical Director's Office
Winchester Va
October 14" 1864.

ORDERS:

     In accordance with instructions from the Medical Director of the Middle Military Division Asst. Surg. B. A. Fordyce 160" N.Y. Vols is relieved from further duty in the 19" Army Corps Hospital and will report without delay to the Commanding Officer of his regiment.

s/ Jas. V. Phiney [illegible]
Surg. N.Y.V. Medical Director
Winchester Va

Winchester Va Oct 15th 1864

My dear wife

I am just starting for the Regiment which is in front a distance of fifteen miles and what is most annoying the boy that cares for my horse went off after hay with him this morning and has not yet returned so I shall be obliged to go on foot - I think I shall get along well - There is some prospect of a battle and the Surgeons are needed in front - I go up with the Brigade Surgeon - I am quite well though I am somewhat lame - I trust all will come out for the best

Keep up good courage & write as often as you can - I think the Govmt is determined to end the war this fall - I really hope we shall succeed - The great energy displayed at present promises much - God grant this awful war may end soon.

It is dreadful beyond any description I am capable of giving -

Yours most affectionately   Benj. A. Fordyce

Had no letters from home yet - Think I shall receive some at the Regt -   Yours B.A.F

.

Direct: Asst. Surg.160th N.Y. Vols
         2nd Brig 1st Div. 19th AC
         Washington D.C.

Camp of 160th N.Y.V.
Near Middletown Va Oct 18th 1864

My dear wife and children

I have just received three letters from you of Oct 4th 6th & 11th all came safe and right - Your other letters I have found were sent promptly as Dr Armstrong supposed to me at Winchester by one of the Surgeons whose term of service had expired & was going home but he forgot to deliver them & I never recd them -

---

I arrived here all safe & right although only three days before a Surgeon was shot coming the same route and died next day - I write in haste so as to send you this by return mail - I am quite well except a little Diarrhoea from change of food -

I am promised an opportunity to come home as soon as the enemy leaves our front or we get where we expect to remain a short time I shall make application as soon as it will do basing it on your health

It is now dark and I must stop I cannot see the time Send me some stamps & write often - Yours truly   B. A. Fordyce

(PS) Dr. Armstrong has got his Commission today - I am glad for him Will write Estella next letter B.A.F.

Chapter XII
The Battle of Cedar Creek

Dr. Fordyce has been returned to Winchester where again he had been stationed to care for the wounded. He had been sent to the front prior to the October 19, 1864 Battle of Cedar Creek and describes the horror of the engagement. He describes and praises the service performed by the female nurses and the role of their leader, Dorothy Dix. He applies for leave of absence and makes application to be relieved from duty in the army, but to no avail. He describes the damage to buildings, as they are commandeered for use as hospitals, and tells of the use of a church organ to bring beautiful, soothing music to the patients.

Winchester Va Oct 23rd 1864

My dear wife

I have just time to write a few lines to you the only time since the great battle of the 19th inst - I was at the front in the battle. It was an awful battle. The enemy came directly into our camp within a few rods of where our regiment was stationed routed our forces before sunrise and such a skidaddle I never dreamed of before - The balls came around as Chestnuts fall with a boy shaking the tree after a heavy frost I was unharmed although one brushed the hair on the back of my neck - I have been operating since till day before yesterday night - was sent here again on duty - I am well except quite lame

I have recd all your letters at last - Some containing stamps -

Our Army rallied in P.M. & licked the enemy awfully - this pleases some I guess

The mail boy is here - good bye   write often
                                    Yours affectionately,   B.A. Fordyce

Medical Director's Office, Winchester, Va.
Oct. 26" 1864

ORDERS:

Asst. Surg. B. A. Fordyce will report for assignment to duty
to Surg. L. P. Wagner, in charge of 19" Army Corps Hospitals, until
further orders.

s/ Jas. Phiney [Illegible]
Surgeon N.Y.V Chief Medical Officer

[U. S. Sanitary Commission stationery]

19th Army Corps Hospital   Ward. B.
Winchester, Va.   Oct 29th

My dear wife

I have received several letters from you of late and expect there are
some at the regiment now - I am here in Winchester again
endeavoring to care for those who were wounded on the 19th inst at
Cedar Creek - I was in that battle but am going to reserve all
description of it till I can come home and tell you about it - I am now
in charge of this ward; this is the largest number of any one ward
under care of one Surgeon here - I have now fifty-six sick & wounded
men under my care - have 10 male nurses 2 female - These female
nurses are sent by Mrs Dix [Dorothea] - They are quite old maids
but the best women to work and cook for wounded and sick - They
shrink from no necessary work and the men by their help are kept
clean and neat - Genl Sheridan visited all the hospitals in town
today   Shaking hands with the men and giving them words of
encouragement - permit me to say I was not ashamed of my ward -
My men were looking clean although I have a large number of the
severest wounded in the village - I received four months pay
yesterday and have sent to you $350 (Three hundred and fifty dols)
by one of the pay masters clerks who will express it to you - I would
like to have you acknowledge the receipt of it as soon as you get it -
I have sent my vote to Jn B Strong to be deposited for me in case I
am not able to do it myself - I hope to be able to come home before
long but cannot tell yet - I regret to hear of your poor health - and

shall try and come on your account and that of the children - I have not received any pay yet for my horse but shall probably as soon as I can see the man who bought it - He is abundantly able to pay at any time as he is rich at home but men are often without money here who are quite comfortably off when at home - I have never been so long on borrowed capital for my living that I remember of -

You would be and indeed I am quite astonished at the great change in this since the arrests I wrote you of in Estellas letter - Everything is very quiet - Genl Sheridan means to quiet things if he has to fight for it - He is a small man of very modest quiet ways - except when animated then one would much prefer him for a friend to any other feeling that might stir him up - I really like him for he has got the go ahead in him - together with an immense amount of caution. He is never disconcerted with anything Seems ready with resources for any contingency and has the tact to apply them - Very quick and active in his motions inspires everyone around him with the same energy - He is about 5 ft 7 1/2 inches high weighs about 145 strong built, plain good looking features about 37 years old and on the whole a real General - He is about the height of Genl Grant does not look quite so determined however -

Well I stopped a few minutes suspecting from certainly sensations I had that I might find some lice on my shirt & drawers so I stripped sent a skirmish line over the main body of the garments reserving the main force for the seams and after thoroughly exploring the whole territory with no success brought the artillery of my fine comb to bear on my head and actually caught one alive - I sacrificed him in a short time for the benefit of humanity & armies in general - Well it is 11 o'clock at night Ill stop   good bye - write often.

Yrs.   Benj. A. Fordyce

(PS) Give my love to all who care anything about me.

Yrs Truly   Benj

(PS) Stell must be careful of her health and Abbie must look after George for me Ill come and help you eat the good things one of these days.   love to all   good bye

---

U. S. Post. Hospital Winchester Va Nov. 3rd 1864

My dear wife

Mr. Andrew Race *[of Scipio]* is here in my room now and I can assure you it is gratifying to see anyone from so near home - I am in tolerable good health and am in charge of the largest ward in Winchester under care of one Surgeon - I have 57 sick and wounded and 12 attendants beside myself - Mr. Race will tell you some of the particulars if you have the opportunity of seeing him - I have recd your letters of Oct 23rd mailed 25th today - I am very sorry to learn of your continued ill health - I shall try and come home as soon as possible on your account - I would not if I were in your place attempt to come to Winchester - It is almost impossible for a lady to get here safely -

Do not have very serious apprehensions for me - I shall try and come out all right - I forwarded my vote to Jn B. Strong with power of attorney &c - I am very glad you bought a melodion for the girls - I think you did just right - When I come I shall come the quickest route - probably shall not go to New York but come by Elmira -   I have I hope done some service that is of benefit to the soldiers which perhaps may prove creditable to me - My main object has been to save life and give strength to the army - The Medical Director usually visits ward daily and brings friends and officers with him to show particular cases in my ward - I shall keep a record and hope I can bring home a copy that you may see it -

It would be a source of the greatest pleasure to me to watch my cases to their termination if I could feel unanxious about family at home - But I must come home, and shall, if I can be permitted to come - There are many matters that require my attention there which it seems I cannot postpone much longer - I must come home I see -

I bought me a blouse today paid $20.00 for it It is a very good one however, and warm, well lined worth in Auburn at least $14 or $15-

My best clothing is in Baltimore, i.e. my dress coat and vest - that I brought with me - But I could not get them here - I have not seen them since the last of July - What condition they are in I do not know

- Hope I shall find them all right - We have excellent living here now - The Med Director Messes with us - It costs something to live well here however - something like $5.00 pr week - I do not mind this however - Having so fine an opportunity for improvement in Surgery - I hope and think I have turned every opportunity to advantage - I have seen something of Surgery within the past year and ought to learn something -

I have here a nice cozy little room with a stove in it for my office and lots to do -

Well Estella and Abbie & George what shall I say to you really I don't know - occasionally I notice George puts his autograph on Abbies letters and occasionally obliterates a word of Abbies Without your letters I hardly know what I should do - They are a source of great pleasure to me - Mr. Race says he saw Estella with Addie going to Church at the Center not long since and that Estella is a great big girl - Abbie I hear does nothing but read - I hope she got my letter - I wrote to Estella not long since - I heard that Jn B. Strong was in Martinsburgh today - It seems he ought to have come and seen me but I suppose he wants to get back to Election - I think he will have time it is only 22 miles - He may come - I hope he will I like to see folks from home -

I sent you $350 by a clerk of paymaster to be expressed - I hope you will receive it all safe - I have not got pay for my horse yet - shall probably before long - I will come home with that when I get it - I think that will bear my expense -

Well I must stop I know this is uninteresting - So good bye - All write often   Yours affectionately,   Benj. A. Fordyce

[Envelope reads]: By Favor of Mr. Race

[postmarked Baltimore]

My dear wife

19th A.C. Hospital Ward B
Winchester Va. Nov 7th 1864

I have just received your letter dated Oct 25th and having an opportunity to forward an answer so as to have it mailed soon I avail myself of it - I regret to learn of your prolonged illness and if I can possibly get time to write it will forward my resignation tomorrow and hope on your account, it will be accepted I am in tolerably good health and doing an immense amount of work in my way - I am still at work in hospital here - Have 55 wounded & sick 12 attendants - My patients are generally improving - I believe I have the credit of keeping a good ward and giving general satisfaction to my superior officers - I have made efforts all in my power for the good of the men under my charge - My female nurses are unexpectedly to me ordered by Miss Dix to Washington D.C. and leave tomorrow morning They are two excellent women old maids but the greatest workers I ever saw never leaving till 9 o'clock and then having everything prepared such as milk punch sling &c for the sick &c till next morning - They have prepared all the little dainties and much of the more substantial food for them the sick & wounded since they have been here - I did not know at first what to do but soon found two others where a hospital is to be broken up. Two old ladies who are devoting their time to this business who wish to come to my ward and the Medical Director has promised them to me - I stopped writing last evening at 10 o'clock It is now morning 8th - We had news of a contemplated attach on this place during the night by Imbodens [?] Cavalry 8000 strong I was a little nervous at first but slept good and find myself all safe and sound this morning - This is Election I suppose - Well we do not have much excitement about it here - We are as quiet as lambs in May - I will have but a minute to write longer as Ambulance is coming for my sick man and letter -

I am glad to hear of you all General Health with you - You write of J. McLaughlin's wife's death [of Venice] - this is some five or six in that vicinity by same cause & same person

You write you got some mud for your stomach from that source - what do you think about it now - I say there is no real honor there I must close - My love to you all & remember me to the neighbors

Yours affectionately, Benj. A. Fordyce

Ward B. 19th A.C. Hospt.
Winchester Va. Nov 10th 1864

My dear wife and children

I have this evening recd your letter of Nov 1st and am glad that you have learned of my safety - I am in comfortable health working hard every day - I am still in this Hospital at work hard - I shall send twenty to Martinsburgh tomorrow - I think it really strange John did not come to see me when so near I knew it was near Election time and he might have some doubt about getting home in time; but if any train came up while he was there he could have come just as well as Mr Race - He came and saw me and I had an excellent visit with him - You may rest assured I was glad to see him - He told me your health was very poor & I ought to go home - The Army has fallen back now to this place and I shall have a much better opportunity of getting through than at any time before this - In my opinion this Hospital will be removed or the principal part of it to some other place where I do not precisely know probably to near Harpers Ferry or to Baltimore -

I shall then be temporarily relieved I think and will avail myself of the opportunity to come home if possible - My business affairs seem to require my attention personally at home aside from my anxiety about you and the children in your illness - Deacon Mosher should pay something on that Mortgage and judgment that is certain I cannot depend forever on promises - although promises are good if well kept - About selling the cow & horse fodder &c - I can not advise just yet - I should be pleased to have you keep them till you know the result of my application to be relieved from the Army - It cannot be long before I shall know and will either come and tell you or write immediately - We are having quite a large number of the severely wounded die about this time - This is the time most die who are not killed immediately that do not recover between 14 to 24 days - Those who survive over 24 days usually get well - I have had but few die

---

in my ward - I make and assist in all Post Mortem Examinations that I have an opportunity of seeing - We have made two today - Three yesterday - No person has had more privileges here of this kind than I - And I trust no one will be more benefited - Mr. Race can tell you something about things here that will be interesting to you I think - I have heard enough from Election to satisfy me all is right that Lincoln is elected without doubt - That the policy of the Government will be sustained and is sustained by the people

This is our hope for the future of our country I would have chosen a milder plan but when there are two parties and two sides assured people will not think alike - The Southern States have chosen and acted on their views of the subject and we must meet them or our country is ruined - Some think it is already I am not one of them

Well I must stop it is now late near 11 o'clock P.M. and a hard days work before me for tomorrow - I intended to have written to the girls but hardly have time tonight - Will write to them soon - I am really glad Carrie is at home this winter That the girls may be benefited by her instructions and society - I should have written to her long ago - but have hardly time to write home without encroaching on hours that I should be asleep Dr Ross the young Surgeon to whom I gave the picture often inquires after that cousin of mine - He is making an excellent reputation here and is held in very high esteem - I am really glad Dr Lester has got home all safe *[In about a month, will marry Carrie. LGC]* I wish you to give him my compliments and kindest regards hoping that I may be able to see him soon I think we could talk over some things that would be entertaining to us, if not very interesting to others -

I have seen some things in Virginia too that may prove of some interest - I hope to you and the children if to no one else - I do not know how I should act If I were free from the Army - I am very much pleased with many things connected with the Army as a Surgeon - But continued field service is very fatiguing to me not being used to riding &c

Well I must stop now so good bye till another mail.
                              Yours truly   Benj. A. Fordyce

[U. S. Sanitary Commission stationery]

Winchester Va. Nov 18th 1864 Ward B 19th A.C. Hosp

My dear wife

I have just received Estellas & your letters of Nov 5th and 11th - am sorry to learn of your continued ill health - I hope to come home soon that I may do something for you - I have everything ready to act as soon as an opportunity favorable presents & shall act promptly - I do not know what to think about the money not arriving at the Express office - This annoys me a little too - I sent seven fifty dollar bills bearing 7 3/10% & thought you would receive it before this time - I think it will come all right yet - I am in tolerable good health at present I bought me a pair of pants & boots today - paid $8.00 for both - Am tolerably economical I think - I do not know what to write in regard to Firms case - I think you had better occupy the premises yourself - I am disappointed in the man very much - If you think things will go all right for the future you might try it a spell longer - I have but little confidence after a man has forfeited all right to it once - All I can say is act your own judgement in the matter - Deacon Mosher must pay something on his demands - I must come home I see and soon too -

I am as busy as ever - if I send away a lot of convalescents, enough sick come in to fill me up again so my ward is full all the time - Estella writes me a good letter - It is gratifying to hear good news from home - Situated as I am it is very unpleasant and causes much anxiety to hear that you are sick & the children sick Of course I think of you every hour in the day and cannot get you out of my mind long - Viewing it in this light I shall tender my resignation and if accepted settle up my business with the government and come home

The weather here has been very fine most of the time till within three days past - It has rained and is now quite muddy - Here in the city we have but little mud - The streets are paved and good walks though rough - I am living first rate - We have a good Mess - There are five of us who mess together here a cook and servants and have chickens beef potatoes and almost everything desirable - We have but two meals a day - Breakfast at 10 & Dine at 4 o'clock aint that stylish

---

You might think and perhaps not be entirely mistaken that we consider ourselves belonging to the upper crust - We do not put on airs however - We move on moderately and quietly not assuming to be of the F.F.Vs, although we occupy rooms in an old Bankers house that once was of the said Fs - The said Banker being absent in Dixie somewhere - while his wonderful worthy old spouse keeps things running at home here among the miserable nasty Yankees as she calls them - They have to be a little careful about their talk however -as sometimes their finest houses are taken for hospitals and it does not improve a house and premises much to use it for a Hospital two or three months -

Partitions have to be moved stoves put up in places unusual and many other changes such as making bunks out of fences or using them for fuel all of which does not always beautify the place - Sometimes the sash are taken out and blinds taken off and I have never known them to be particular about returning them - A beautiful Brick Church is occupied across the street from me for one our hospitals - Of course the seats had to be taken out and all extra fixtures and many other important repairs made - such as making the seats into bunks, altering the window casings fixing the curtains so they would all be right and proper for the sick & wounded - Two other churches one brick the other stone have been repaired and are used for hospitals in same way - One has one of the finest organs in it I ever saw - This organ has not been injured - but is used occasionally for the benefit of our wounded when some good player comes in of which there are quite a number in our Army The Germans often play well - Many of the officers have amusements of various kinds but I have very little time to enjoy myself & do not go - I have work or study for every minute of time I have - I dissect evenings when I have an important case to examine - I have had excellent opportunities of this kind lately and of course I enjoy this as it is of great benefit to me

The army has fallen back to within a few miles of here and are camping for winter, I think There will be no danger any longer from the rebels We feel quite easy now - The last letter or the one of the 8th inst we were expecting an attack at this place but day before yesterday Genl Sheridan had occasion to send out a flag of truce with the body of a rebel Major and had to go some forty or fifty miles to get into the rebel lines - So, I think they are not very close now & I may get my matters through all right - I hope so as it is a matter of real necessity - I am glad the girls are learning to play on the Melodeon - I shall certainly be so happy to hear them play -

George too can't he eat an apple for me every day till I come - But don't churn the kittens - I would prefer the cats on one plate and butter on another Tell him we will have some fun when I get there

Yrs affectionately   Benj. A. Fordyce 160th N.Y.Vols

Winchester Va. Ward B. 19th A.C. Hosp.
Nov 27th 1864,

My dear wife

Although I have not heard from you since I last wrote I will write again as this is what I do always as often as I have time - We are having very comfortable weather here now and everything looks as pleasant (except the mud) as the middle of October at home - In your last you mentioned that Mrs Gregory was unexpectedly called to leave for the west on account of the sudden and fatal illness of her son - You did not state which one - I can sympathize with them for their loss You can hardly imagine how often our sympathies are called for here by those bereft of a fond and doted son, who falls a victim to traitors bullets - Yet while we sympathize we have a swelling glow of pride that our country can and will furnish such noble specimens of mankind in her hours of trial and danger to stand and fall between her and her enemies Such noble devotion so self sacrificing must from a just posterity have in the history and memories of the people are ample reward - True the dead will never realize it (would to God they could) but the living will revert to their noble sacrifice with pride and honor - While the Copperhead and his descendants I hope will go down to unhonored graves despised by every true patriot - I hope the taint may not leave them till life is extinct - Then have their bodies excluded from burial except in by places so that the traveler of future times may never be obliged to record the great number who were willing to share our Countrys blessings yet gave countenance and favor to those who sought its destruction - The dawn of peace I hope is breaking and what a glorious Country we shall have when our enemies are again reconciled to our old and time honored (but of late blood stained) flag - Indeed the old stars and stripes will be more precious to the Americans than ever before and when descried afar off a thrill of pure patriotic joy will be felt in every breast - A confidence that there is a banner under whose folds true genuine freedom will always find ample protection - You may rest assured that the noble southern man who fights so earnestly and heroically for what he confidently thinks is right will grasp the hand of the true Union Soldier who has fought against him with the warmth of a true friend while he will turn with disgust from the deceptive copperhead when peace shall crown our efforts to sustain our Country - I know southern men too well to believe they can ever respect the Northern doughface or lickspitter copperhead -

There are noble men in the southern army whom to know is to esteem them - You know at once they are too honorable to be dishonest (but have been deceived by false unprincipled designing men who would rejoice at the prospect of honorable return of allegiance to their country once again fraternally united) - I am confident this will come

I have as yet heard nothing from my papers; hope to soon - Will let you know immediately the result - I have been offered the privilege of going into the hospital at Baltimore with the wounded from here with an opportunity to remain the greater part of the winter - but my affairs at home and your poor health will not allow me to indulge in a thought of it - I told the Med Director so - and consequently hope to be released - Cannot tell how soon - Hope soon

I got the Pansy in Estellas letter put in by Cousin Carrie - Tis far sweeter than southern flowers for me - I intended to have got some from two Quaker ladies who visit the wounded in my hosp occasionally and sometimes bring beautiful flowers to them and send them in this letter - I will in my next if I can -

How pleased I am that the girls are improving in Music I cannot express - I hope they will have some good pieces to play for me when I get home How happy we will all be wont we If Ma only gets her health - Well I will not anticipate too much - I sometimes do not realize my fondest hopes and indeed do not always expect to - I am quite well it is 11 o'clock P.M. must stop

So good bye all, Yours &c Benj. A. Fordyce

Chapter XIII
Words of Gratitude

Dr. Fordyce' concern for his patients and their sur-
viving relatives is demonstrated in Walter Morse'
letters of gratitude to Mrs. Fordyce and to Dr.
Fordyce.

─────────

[Stationery]:

Office of
A.N. Wood & Co's Portable Steam Engine Works
Eaton, Madison Co. N.Y. Dec. 10, 1864

Benj. A. Fordyce, Surgeon, 19th A.C.
Winchester Va

My Dear Friend   Thanks to your kindness I was enabled to leave town soon after you left me - My pass was needed at the pickets: we arrived at Martinsburgh late in the evening so I did not find the body of my brother until the next morning when it was brought to the Express Office. At Baltimore I met an older brother on his way to Winchester, but he turned back with me and we reached home on Thurs evening: the remains of brother Alfred came on Saturday and were found to be kept perfectly and in good order. It was a great comfort to all the family that they were permitted to see the body in so good order.

I never tire in telling them of your kindness and unwearied care for Alfred and of your attention and hospitality for myself. All the family wish me to express their thanks and gratitude with my own, but I feel as if the best I could say would be but a poor expression of what we all feel toward you: it will be happiness for us, if we are ever able to be of service or comfort to you or any of your family. We are all perfectly satisfied that you did all that could have been done for Alfred, and it will ever be a comfort to us to know that he did fall under your immediate care.

I hope Doctor Fordyce that you will soon get a leave to visit your family. and that they may be spared to you and with you in a happy long life. I hope too that you will receive your reward for faithfulness in promotion in the service.

My Mother has spoken of writing to you, and I presume she will do so: With kind regards,Yours very truly,   Walter Morse

---

[envelope to Mrs. Benj. A. Fordyce]:

Eaton N.Y. Dec. 10/64

Mrs. Benj. A. Fordyce

I had just written a letter to Doctor Fordyce, when I noticed in the papers that the 19th A.C. were on the way southward, or to Washington: I wod be glad to send the letter to the Doctor, but not knowing how to direct it I take the liberty to enclose it to you wishing that you would forward it.

Doctor Fordyce told me that yourself and a daughter were in poor health. Please accept my kind regards and my sincere wish that you may both be restored to health, and all be kept for an early reunion with husband and Father away.

This I feel deeply - although a stranger to you all at home - from the great regard I have for Doct. F., and his great kindness to my brother and myself under circumstances of peculiar trial and anxiety. I have talked with my fathers family so much about Doct. F. that it will be a great pleasure to any of us if we may sometime meet with any of your family: hoping that this may sometime be permitted I remain

Yours respectfully   Walter Morse

Chapter XIV
Life in Ward B

Dr. Fordyce continues his service to his patients as he describes life in Ward B of the hospital in Winchester. He waits patiently for an answer to his application for relief from duty, sells his horse but receives no payment, counsels his family, and is heartened by the news that Sherman has captured Savannah. Thus end Dr. Fordyce' letters to his family in New York State. However, the copy of his receipt for the return of his Instrument Case is ample proof of the magnitude of the event on the day that he laid down the burden of responsibility that he had carried for eighteen months.

Sanitary Commission   Winchester Va. 19th A.C. Hospital
Dec. 10th 1864

My dear wife

I have just heard indirectly from my application to be relieved by resignation - It has been shelved for the present somewhere at Head Quarters and I hasten to inform you lest you remain too uncomfortable at our old home a longer time than your health will permit -

I think you had better let Mr Baldwin keep the horse and keep your fodder by all means Get Mr Congdon to take care of the old cow or sell her, and close up everything - Kill your pig pack it and keep it

Then, if you will not be too much burthen to your parents go there - keep all outside property snug - Write to me often of your health as my prospect of being relieved will depend almost wholly on that -

I cannot think but that my resignation will be accepted yet - This hospital will be broken up and then if at all it will come through - I expect pay again in a day or two and will send you some so that it will come safe I guess - Buy and get any and every thing you and the children need - I hope to earn enough to make you all comfortable and intend to save it. I hope you will get what you want

I wear cheap clothes as it will answer to wear here. The rebs in last battle got my valise some clothing and all my woolen stockings - I have obtained 2 pair first rate stockings since and do not need any I should write for some of your good things but boxes are so often broken open that I probably should not get them - and I live well enough at 75 cts pr day now

I would not stay at the old place too long and get sick.

I shall write to the girls in a few days if I do not soon hear from my papers -

I hope to hear that you are all at your fathers in your next

You must take things cool - I am obliged to Close up your barns entirely locking everything up - Have nobody around the premises except such as you want there

There is a great want here of good Surgeons - I do not know but they think I am good for something so they keep me some get leaves of absence at almost any time, but I am not of that sort

I hope you are as comfortable as when you last wrote - The girls too & my boy George

Well I must stop it is after 11 o'clock I have been to Masonic Lodge &c   Yours as ever Benj. A. Fordyce -

(PS) I am quite well.

Ward B. 19th A.C. Hospital

Winchester Va Dec. 16th 1864

My dear wife

I shall not address the children as I intend to send a few lines to the girls in this as they are so good to write to me often - I received a letter from them and you today dated Dec 10th and am sorry to learn that the girls are sick with chicken pox I hope not dangerous - You do not say anything respecting your own health so I hope you are more comfortable

You say you have not yet received the money sent by Major Altons Clerk - Well I wrote to him immediately on receipt of your letter dated Nov 29th and he forwarded to me the receipt from Adams Express Co for the same dated Nov 2nd showing that everything had been done in good faith on his part and promptly done too I enclose the receipt as also the one for $250 49/100 more that I sent from here You must send the $350 receipt to the express office as soon as you can conveniently by some careful business man, who will not surrender it up but will take necessary steps to inform company that the money has not been received - I think it will be found for you very soon after -

The money was in 7 $50 bills bearing 7 3/10 pr cent int so you will observe it is a very good kind of note to keep as the interest is payable semi-annually - 1st interest is due on 5th February for 6. mos - I would like to have you keep them to look at occasionally - The draft on the treasury I will send you an order to draw as soon as I learn you have received it -

I am quite well though I get tired when it comes night - I have 52 sick and wounded now under my charge - I sent off 30 day before yesterday and am filled up again so soon -

My papers I have not yet heard from them but cannot help but think they will come after a while all right - I could with but little effort now obtain a better position I think but I do not want it - I am proud of the 160th N.Y. Vols and do not wish to leave them while in the service - I have expected to hear from my papers every day - I cannot

---

Chapter XIV - Life in Ward B   *237*

tell the cause of delay - I must close - write as often as you can - I have not recd pay for my horse yet - when I do, shall send it home - Give my love to all - Yours most truly   Benj. A. Fordyce

───────────

[Letter in same envelope]:
Estella and Abbie,
My dear daughters

I thought I must write you a few lines Well now I have commenced I do not know what to write - We had some firing at the front today of heavy artillery - Our nigger came after me to come to dinner and was so frightened he looked quite white shall I say No! not fairly but quite nervous - Well I can assure you it did sound a little soldier-like - One hundred heavy guns were fired in honor of Shermans great victory who it is reported has captured Savannah & 15,000 prisoners - If this be true is it not glorious

Well we rejoice some when we have good news as you see by this - If there was to be a fight I should want to see how we come out - I should not want to be here - I would rather be nearer or further off - The boys have comfortable log huts with fireplaces and enjoy themselves well as a general rule - Some are sick of course - They are in good health generally -

Now about the weather We have had some severe cold weather here - Last week was very cold some had their feet frozen It has thawed up and rained some since and the mud is up to a bodys A-double as Abbie used to say - So you may know it is pretty deep -

I have not been to meeting since I came to Winchester so you cannot expect much improvement in me but I have been to meeting since I have been in the Army - Last time I went to Church was the day before the battle of Winchester and I thought if it operated so I would not venture again soon - but I don't know but it will do to go before long now - what do you think about it?

Tell Ma that I say you and George may have something nice for Christmas or New Years if I do not get home - I hope to come and bring you something myself by that time but do not place much dependence upon it -

I should be pleased to come home I can assure you

I wonder if George eats any apples for me or drinks any cider for me - I should like to step in and see how he would perform - Would not we have fun for a spell though - If I do get home and am well I am going to rest a while if possible - and go round and see some of my friends a little -

I have no time here to visit even officers except they are sick - I have constant invitations to visit citizens here at their houses but have no time and do not go - There are some fine Quakers here who have often invited me to call but I have never had time - I mean to go and see them, however - I must stop

Write often   Yrs truly   Benj. A. Fordyce

York Hosp   (Rebel)
Winchester Va   Jan 11th 1865

My dear little Abbie

I have not written to you in some time and know you will be pleased to hear from me provided I can think of anything interesting to write - I have not received any letter from home of later date than Christmas so cannot write of home matters, but must write of things here - I am yet in charge of the Rebel wounded in a building as large as three of our Meeting house in Venice and three stories high - I have thirty-four of the most severely wounded left under my care some eight with thighs amputated and twelve with thighs broken with Gun shots and other bad wounds to look after They are generally doing well -

You can tell Grandma that one of my nearest neighbors are a family of excellent Quakers that I go to visit occasionally so as not to forget entirely the plain language - One of the young women has just come in to see me on account of someone breaking into their house last night - They called the guard and the robber made his escape without obtaining anything - I shall do all I can for the protection of the family from further molestation - I think they will be careful in future how they call on them as a little line from me will insure their protection - A medical friend has just called on me. I must stop a little time - 12.M. You would laugh I think to hear the manner of expression used here by the people it is so different from what you are accustomed - One case where a rebel captain was wounded I asked his mother if it had discharged much in last 24 hours She replied that she got "right smart" matter out of it - At another time she said he had a "heap of pain" in his knee - When any of them are asked how they feel; if comfortable they reply "tolerable, sir" if improving they are "getting on right smart" If they express a partially doubtful condition They say "I reckon" - Yankees say "I guess" Things are seldom expressed as we hear them at the north - These are the common expressions with hundreds more in all conversations I hear that seem very odd.

I had hoped to come home and see you before this but I find coming home depends more on others than myself - I am very anxious to come and see you all and take some charge of my own private affairs as well as my family but I cannot promise much - I shall continue to try till I come - I shall write to Estella on her birthday if I don't get away before - Jan 12 A.M. I have not yet heard one word from my resignation which was forwarded on the 30th Dec Why I cannot tell - If you were all well I should not care to come home and everything else all right & comfortable for you - I do not really want to come home on Leave of Absence for 15 days or so short a time as is given if I cannot come home for a longer time than that I prefer to stay my time out - This leaving home two or three times I do not fancy - If I can do no better however will try to come a few days - shall write to Estella tomorrow.

From your affectionate father Benj. A. Fordyce

Winchester Va Jan 15th 1865

My dear wife

I have recd no letter from home since yours of 25th Dec - I am not yet quite well have heard nothing from my resignation - Started it a mo today - I go to Frederic, Md. tomorrow with a lot of patients to return next day if the weather is favorable - I have rec'd no pay yet for my horse have not seen the man more than once since I sold him - although he is in our Brigade - He is able abundantly and has sent no word that he wanted to pay me but has been 15 miles away nearly all the time of late - I may see him tomorrow - I go by the command - I got me some stamps yesterday - $1 worth I have all the money I need for the present - Do not want too much - Live well enough now really hope they will let me come home I shall ask for Leave of Absence if this last does not go through -

It is late I must retire as I have some 30 hard cases to load all serious wounds & amputations and all rebels - When I told them I was going with them they all wanted to go - some are so bad I leave them - I hope you are all well.

Love to all, Yours as ever,   Benj. A. Fordyce

(PS) I crowd this in Estella's envelope.
(PS) The man I sold my horse to is:

H. L. Dewey, Q.M. 8th Vt. Vols.

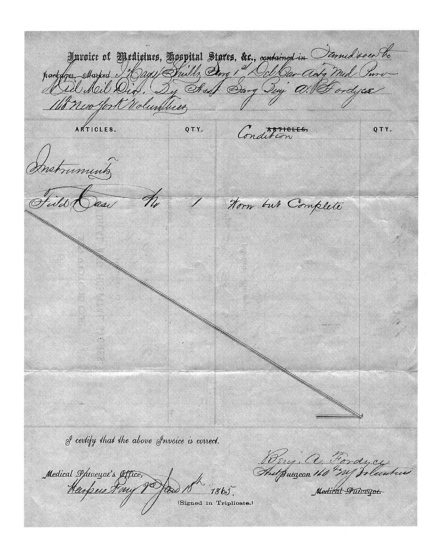

Invoice of Medicines, Hospital Stores, &c., contained in *Turned over to*
packages, Marked *Major Smith, Surg'n 1st Del Cav Acting Med Purv*
Mil Mil Dis. By Asst Surg Bvy A. Fordyce
110 New York Volunteers

ARTICLES.	QTY.	Condition ~~ARTICLES.~~	QTY.
Instruments			
Field Case No	1	*Worn but Complete*	

I certify that the above Invoice is correct.

Medical Purveyor's Office,
Harpers Ferry Va Jan 18th 1865.
(Signed in Triplicate.)

Benj. A. Fordyce
Asst Surgeon 110 N.Y. Volunteers
Medical Purveyor

[This simple document, penned in Dr. Fordyce' fluent hand and signed with a flourish, speaks eloquently of his final act as he departed his service to his country. He returned to his family in Scipio, New York State to take up an active and dedicated life in his community. LPH]

Chapter XV
Decoration Day - 1886

On the twenty-fifth anniversary of the opening of the War, Dr. Fordyce addresses his fellow citizens in the Village of Union Springs, NY where he had taken up residence to continue his practice of medicine. Time has not dimmed his horror of the War and he brings home to his listeners the magnitude of the slaughter.

―――――――

Why are we here today? "What has caused this commotion .... motion.... motion, our country through?" is a line of an old political song of the Whig party sung by thousands in 1840 all over this country which aided wonderfully in the election of Wm. Henry Harrison to the Presidency of the United States - But we are not here to sing political songs nor with political purposes - We had a war of independence once - also a war to protect our citizens from British assumptions - If we are permitted to look back to events in our countrys history which transpired 25 years ago one of which that perhaps more than any other, aroused the people of the whole northern states almost to frenzy was the firing upon Fort Sumpter by Secessionists of South Carolina necessitating the call of the President to the people to Arms to put down rebellion against the government - Those who were incredulous before of the extent of disaffection in the southern states were now appalled by the certainty that Civil War was already inaugurated - The first blow had been struck and the thunderings of the approaching terrible storm were too distinct for further doubt and disbelief - War had really begun and the call for 75,000 volunteers (at that time considered an immense army) was filled in one week - More than 100,000 being and urged upon the President for acceptance -

Yet this immense army by authority of Congress in July 1861 was permitted to be increased by 500,000 more subject to the Call of the President and subsequently to an almost unlimited number by volunteering and draft so that the whole number called into service in the Army was nearly 3,000,000 men - or reduced to a standard of 3 years men - 2,320,000+

Of this Army there were killed in battle	61,362
" " " that died from wounds	34,721
" " " " " " Disease	183,287
Total that died	279,376

This enormous army took about 12 percent of the entire population of the free states and 50 percent of all men liable for military service over 18 and under 45 years of age - These statements are approximately accurate - If they vary from the exact number as taken from the Census of 1860 they are too small an Estimate - What an army & what a cause that should require such a number of soldiers!! Eleven (11) out of thirty-one (31) states were in open rebellion against the Government and by preconcerted action were already in the field at the commencement of the war with immense armies already armed for the conflict - Of the twenty (20) remaining states several were sparsely settled and of small population and to a dangerous extent surrounded with and peopled by Hostile Indians ready upon any pretext to disturb peaceful relations with tomahawk and scalping knife the thinly settled portions of the state rendering these states more or less helpless in the great struggle for perpetuity of our national boundary and existence - The Indians too at this particular time had been incited to more than usual vindictive demonstrations by incending agents from the South - So this great civil contest must be carried through by the never populous & wealthy northern states -

When we from history learn that in the war for Independence there were enlisted about 120,000 men in all during the 7 years war and in the war of 1812 to 15 the entire Militia of all the states was called out amounting to 440,000 men of whom, but few were put in actual service   The war with Mexico in 1846 to 48, was 101,282 United States soldiers and volunteers - In the Revolutionary war the casualties were something over 25,000 including killed, wounded & sickness

In 1812 & 15 casualties killed	1877	wounded	3737
Mexican War do "	1049	"	3420

In the War of the Great Rebellion we have the
almost incredible number of   61,362 killed
in battle and that died from wounds   34,721
That died from disease   183,287
Making the aggregate loss of life from
                    Service in the war 279,370 -

This equals one for every 9 of those who were enlisted in the army
of the Rebellion - What an army of dead men! The very best always
of those who went into the field -

If these men had all been buried in graves allowing only three feet
to each one (which is certainly small enough room for a grave) and
the graves were placed in one row they would reach a distance of
158 1/6 miles or the entire distance from here to Albany in a straight
line - Now allowing seven feet for the length of a grave and 4 feet for
alleys between the graves at the head & foot - it would require 212
acres of clear ground to give this amount of limited space to each of
our dead soldiers - What an immense field to be decorated with
flowers today!

But this is not all - There were many counted missing who have
never yet been found - Whose graves will never be discovered and,
if ever decorated will be covered through the laws of nature by the
hand of an invisible God -

Others too were buried on the fields of battle where they fell or from
hospitals of the enemy where they died of wounds or sickness, whose
graves are unmarked and only known to those whose duty simply
required their bodies to be put out of sight - Many were thus buried-

After the battle near Mansfield La under Banks last expedition up
the Red River on April 8th 1864 which was fearfully contested by a
portion of our scattered forces confronted by three times their
number actually engaged and posted on grounds chosen by the
enemy in a very advantageous position for attack and defense that
portion of 13th Corps in advance three or more miles of the main
Union forces was obliged to sustain the principal shock of the battle-

The killed and wounded was something over 600 on our side with the loss of 1500 prisoners - Although the Confederate loss of killed & wounded was by their admission and reports greater than our own loss of prisoners captured was ten times as many as we took of the enemy - with sixteen other surgeons I was among the prisoners - was immediately paroled to assist in the care and treatment of our wounded prisoners and will add that I was treated with great kindness and by ordinary gentlemanly behavior was furnished with all necessaries for the comfort of the wounded that could be expected with the facilities they had in this part of the country - All the wounded who could not march of our army were captured - As Genl Banks retreated one way in the night and the rebels the other way so that the two armies were fifteen miles apart at 7 o'clock next morning - The wounded were left between the two armies almost destitute of care and food - But the discovery was made early by the Confederates and pursuit of Banks immediately made and another battle fought about twelve miles from the first the next day at Pleasant Hill in which they were met by nearly an equal number and thoroughly beaten - Again Banks retreated leaving his wounded in the hands of the Confederates - With the further result of this campaign we have nothing to say many felt there was great inefficiency shown by the commanding officers -

The dead were left on the battle field until decomposition & fetor of the bodies compelled their burial having no other attention given them than that of the hogs that run wild in the extensive pine woods of that region and are nearly as fleet as a deer living on carion and wild roots disregarding entirely the fact that the bodies of those they were eating at this time were those of Union soldiers - These bodies were gathered in piles with [.....] in hollows in the [.....] and covered with dirt no graves being dug for them - Their flesh became food for the hogs & wild animals of this woody region - This part of Louisianna is covered with pine woods with only an occasional clearing between trees for more than 100 miles - Roads running thro woods winding over sandy sabine crop [.....] - At one of these clearings the battle was fought - The armies occupying the woodland one on either side respectively - When the 13th Corps preceded by an escort of Cavalry and flying artillery got well on to this clearing the attack commenced by the Confederate Army under Gens. Mouton Green &

Taylor whose forces were in front in the form of a semicircle in the woods on elevated ground surrounding this clearing with the most advantageous position that could be chosen -

At the opening of the fight our men fell like hail from this enfilading fire - But this division of the 13th Corps was made up of Western Regiments of marksmen who volunteered for a purpose and although outnumbered 3 to 1 and fairly in a trap fought with bravery never excelled until their ammunition was exhausted and they were completely surrounded before they surrendered - There were the remnants of whole companies without a single cartridge among them - Indeed I never met one of them who was captured that had a cartridge left - The casualties were fearful on both sides - Gen Mouton and several Confederate Colonels & other officers were killed on the field and a large number of soldiers killed & wounded - On our side - several Brig Genls were wounded and Colonels Captains Lieutenants and all the officers of the Flying Artillery with every gun of several batteries captured before our tardy forces could be brought up to check the conquering Confederate Army - They met the advancing Confederates at near sun down and were in line of battle in the woods on the east of the clearing when the 13th Corps had been gobbled up and under shelter of the woods and a rise of ground in front reserved their fire until the enemy flushed with their easily acquired victory were within 12 or 15 rods of our men when upon the signal being given every man aimed at the enemy and fired at the same instant a sheet of flame over a mile causing fearful slaughter of the ranks of the enemy who were instantly repulsed and could not be rallied to renew the attack and after three or four rounds retreated precipitately - The loss of the enemy at this point was nearly as great as their disasters of the earlier part of the battle -

From this point after three or four hours both armies retreated in opposite directions leaving the wounded and dead of both on the field - At this point is where our army should have pursued the enemy and they would certainly have recaptured nearly all the men and guns lost in the earlier part of the day - But other military tactics prevailed and the opportunity was irretrievably lost -

This impartial/imperfect history of this particular engagement I have given from actual observation and participation in it believing it might be of interest to you but more particularly to give you some idea of the suffering of soldiers during battle as well as the necessary disposition of the bodies of those slain in the engagement -

The wounded were taken to Mansfield 5 miles distant - A portion of them are already accounted for but the wounded who died afterwards were better cared for - Many of them recovered after long weary days of suffering - Of those who died I made this memorandum which I found a few days since among papers brought home with me from the cemetery where they were buried - This record has never before been published

The little village of Mansfield is situated in the western part of Louisianna about 45 miles from Shreveport a thriving village on the Red River in the extreme Northwestern part of the state the most important place in the N.W. part of the state and the real objective point of Banks' expedition -

The Cemetery was east of the village about 80 rods surrounded by the ever present pine woods of this region and shaded by a few scattering pines left for this purpose - I was permitted to select a vacant space near the N.W. corner for burial of Union Soldiers -

I find that while a prisoner at Mansfield La I made the following memorandum of burials -

The record of the 1st burial was that of
1   Lt. J. W. Barr - Com'dt 6th Chicago Lt Artillery
                         Wounded by ball passing through temples
                         Died April 9th 1864 -
2nd Capt C.E.Dickey - Adjutant Genl of Genl Ramsoms Staff
                         Wounded through head
3   Capt Chapman of Genl Franklins Staff
                         Amputation Both legs by cannonball thro
                         horse
4   Capt L. Waldo   Wounded thro Rt thigh
5   Capt Coulter   In 3rd row of Graves
6   Capt Dimmitt   Thigh   do
7   Capt Mullin   Leg & Shoulder   do

[Then followed a long list of privates filling 3 rows for 15 or more rods in length - LPH]

After the afternoon battle the first losses upon both sides were realized the commands were left of nearly equal strength each seeking for more advantageous positions for attack and defence - That of Banks to get away safely as fast as possible and that of the enemy to harrass and weaken or capture as many as possible of Banks' Army - This retreat was continued with about equal disasters to either side until Banks reached his base of supplies on the Mississippi River - Soon after this Banks was relieved of his command in this department and I think with a general feeling of relief throughout the country -

~

[A scant seven years later on June 3, 1893, Dr. Fordyce' life was cut short as he gave unstintingly to the care of his patients, including his own son, during an epidemic of Scarlet Fever. LPH]

Epilogue

Among the carefully preserved family memorabilia was a "Memoriam" extolling the exemplary life of Dr. Fordyce. No author or origin of the chronicle is included, yet it appears that it may have been published in it's leather-bound form by a member of the Cayuga County Medical Society of which Dr. Fordyce was a member. Excerpts from this volume follow:

"Let it always be remembered to his credit that when a grave case was in his hands, and the matter at issue was something more serious than the indigestion produced by an unwholesome supper, there was no physician in the world more tenderly patient than he. Scores of cases might be cited from his record in which people were brought back from the gates of death, or at least enabled to live and not die, by means of his long-suffering care and watchful knowledge. When a case of this sort was in his hands, no one could have guessed from his manner that he had anything else to think of.

"In looking back, however, on his life and character it is not his patience and still less is it his capacity for anger, though both are to be counted among his virtues, but the almost inexhaustible geniality of his nature which strikes the attention first and holds it longest. . . . He was genial with all sorts and conditions of men because it was not possible for him to be anything else. There were few among his neighbors who did not thoroughly enjoy a chat with him, although many of them, it is certain, failed to catch more than half his meaning. He frankly enjoyed the people around him, and they as frankly enjoyed him.

"Another thing which contributed very largely to his popularity was the strong sport-loving element in his character. Nothing delighted him more than recounting to an appreciative companion the adventures which befell him on his fishing expeditions, and to the very last he showed an almost boyish enthusiasm in the successes of Union Springs, on the lake and on the ball-ground.

"The writer's only purpose has been to convey to others, his own high appreciation of B. A. Fordyce as a physician of much more than average ability, as a thinker of much more than common power, as a man who, if there could have been added to his almost invincible common sense some touch of the diviner fire of genius, might have made for himself a famous name."

Appendix A
Medical Background

Dr. Fordyce' responsibilities to the armed forces of the Civil War included care of both the sick and the wounded men. His letters reveal the illness that plagued the soldiers as they tried to adapt to new surroundings, the horrors of war and the diseases that were rampant about them.... Dysentery, Pleurisy, Chronic Diarrhea, Epilepsy, etc. As the war progressed, care of the wounded assumed a greater role; and oftentimes the doctors assigned to that responsibility were ill equipped to assume the mantle, either by their medical qualifications or by their dedication to their country's cause.

When on December 1, 1844, Dr. Fordyce was granted recognition by Geneva College for his having completed the requirements for Surgery, could he have imagined that some twenty years later he would be putting that knowledge to such a test in a war that had torn apart his country and destroyed the lives of so many of his fellow Americans?

Dr. Fordyce' library survived him and remained in his son's home for future generations to witness his efforts to further educate himself in the field of surgery: Included among his leather bound volumes we find *Gunshot Wounds, Treatise, or Reflections*, by Henry Francis LeDran, published 1743 by John Clarke, under the Royal Exchange Cornbill, London, England. It must have inspired him to achieve the success that he attained. Nevertheless, how ill-equipped he must have felt for the awful task of binding up the wounds; yet how deftly he employed his knowledge as demonstrated by the reports that have survived in national records.

Dr. Fordyce carried in his wallet the cards that certified to his having attended a course of lectures and successfully passing the requirements for various disciplines of study. Among these cards we find the following:

GENEVA MEDICAL COLLEGE
Surgery
by Frank H. Hamilton

For Benj. Allen Fordyce, Dec. 1, 1844

However, he nourished the constant desire and hope for the opportunity to improve his education as witnessed by the exchange of correspondence found among his papers:

Brooklyn, 108   Oct. 26, 1860

Benj A. Fordyce

My Dear Doctor - I am sorry to discourage you in your praiseworthy attempt to receive the [.....]a little of the Medical profession, but I know of but one way in which you are likely to succeed, namely, by attending a second course of lectures at some Medicine college. This college has never conferred an Honorary Degree nor is it probable that it will except under very extraordinary claims.

Can you not find it convenient or possible to spend four months with us next Spring? It would give you both recreation and instruction perhaps.

Whatever [.....] in my power to do for you I will do with great pleasure.

Very truly yours,
F. H. Hamilton

The following letters from J. P. Barnum, who was serving his country from Dr. Fordyce' own Cayuga County, NY, continue the reference to Dr. F. H. Hamilton and indicate the lack of education that prevailed in the military where on occasion ill-qualified men were promoted to the rank of Surgeon.

U.S. General Hospital
Cor 51st & Lexington Av. N.Y.

Dr. B Fordyce Jr
Dr Sir

I arrived in town this Morning. Met Dr. Flint who received me kindly gave me a note to Dr. Mott. Waited in his anteroom [....] 3/4 of an hour. Dr. Mott came to the door and beckoned me to come into another room. had a pleasant chat found him a gentlemen (but bussy) he wrote me a note and showed me to the door without much ceremony found the note contains an appointmt of Ast. US. Surgeon in the [....]

God bless him and you
Yours in haste
J. P. Barnum

I told him I had studied but 8 mo. & was perfectly ignunt of my duties

Two months later, Dr. Fordyce received another letter from J. P. Barnum:

U.S. General Hospital
Cor. Lexington Av & 51st St
New York, Dec. 2^{d} 62

Dr. B Fordyce Jr
Dr Sir

I think if you do not want those books (on your own term as I told you before leaving) you may send them to S. R. Grey 38 State St Albany. as Freight.

If you want them I shall not be particular with you. Or if you wanted to let me have the money on them. I could in the fl[...] mak a fine thing of them.

I am now acting assistant to Dr. Austin Flint and consider myself fortunte in securing the position for he spares no pains in forwarding me. I will write you a full accout in my next. Shall soon receive a small salery Respects to all

Yours in haste
J. P. Barnum

———————

U. S. SANITARY COMMISSION

Louisville, Ky. April 1863

Benjamin Fordice, M.D.
　　My Dear Doctor:

I am quite ashamed of my long silence but I have really been so bussy that it has seemd almost impossible for me to steal away time enough even to address you.

I am now on duty in this Department as Surgeon in Charge of the transportation of sick and wounded soldiers by R.R. We have a train of Hospital Cars on "Louisville & Nashville" R.R. & Branches. 60 car on the Chatanoga R.R., several in in Ohio & Memphis and in fact on most of the roads now in our possession. I have as yet been so fortunate as to suit my Superior Officers, and if a thorough attention to my business will do it you may be assured that I shall try. Am now receiving the pay of ful surgeon and most of my expenses beside. Please to let me know the amount of that note as I have forgotten and am antious to pay it.

To Dr. Austin Flint and Dr. C. R. Agnew a particular friend of his I am indebted for my place. Dr. F. wrote me a most flattering recomendation and letters of "Introduction" to his friends here. I mention this that you may know that I have not brought your name into disrepute by refusing to "honor the draft" you made on them on my account.

On the Tenn. side of the R. R. Dr. Frank Hamilton Med. Inspector Army of the Cumberlands is my Superior. Dr. H. is boarding at the same place with me at Nashville & on learning of my former place of residence asked for most of the Doctors in Cayuga Co. He inquired particularly for you Sayed a great many pleasant things of old time & when I told him that I was a student of yours remarked "I shall have to adopt you as a grandson immediately on his account"

We are in enemys country danger is on every hand No week passes but that on the R.R. some train is attacked by the Rebels Armed men move arround its whole line. Every bush may contain (and often does) a foe. A week ago Friday the train on which I was was burned and 9 of our guards killed & 6 severely wounded. beside an almost equal loss on them. 40 men from Hospital at Murphisborough were under my charge it made a busy time. but by keeping my head clear & cool I escaped being carried off with all the balance of the passengers Saved my own men from Parole and a long march. Got 91 men in a Hospital extemporised from a neighboring farmhouse. Wounds dressed all in about 13 hours and with but one nurse. A Pretty Good Job?

I think I did a good thing for on my return to Nashville I was presented with a splendid "Pocket Case" of Instruments. By the Medical Director then Much to my surprise but gratification.

Remember me to all the friends at Venice. Please dont scold about the writing on this sheet.

I remain yours most obd'y
J. P. BARNUM

Direct to "Case Sanitary Commission Louisville

Further evidence of Dr. Fordyce' dream of additional education is indicated in his Nov. 19, 1863 letter to his wife, where he wrote:

"I have a kind of notion that if I do not return to Venice to practice medicine, that I shall go with my family to NYC or Philadelphia, spend a year to further educate myself and then locate in some city, or go to Oregon, provided I can obtain a desirable position and spend the reminder of my days in some such way, if practicable and I get home all safe."

Although circumstances prevented further formal education, Dr. Fordyce' alert and eager mind prompted him to develop his talents and to produce some outstanding reconstructive surgery.

The Department of Defense, Armed Forces Institute of Pathology, Washington, DC, have provided detailed information from *The Medical and Surgical History of the Civil War*.[10] Here we find several reports of successful surgery performed by Dr. Fordyce together with a detailed description of a case where, as a result of wounds suffered in the battle of September 19, 1864, the left arm of Sergeant J. Mills, jr. Co. D, 8th Vermont, was amputated at the shoulder.[11] (It is agreed that surgery grows more critical as it progresses upward in the extremities, the importance of a shoulder amputation is apparent.)

Reference to Dr. Fordyce' letters to his wife at the time of his performing the amputation for Sergeant Mills provides an interesting link to the statistical information. In a September 25, 1864 letter he describes the September 19 battle near Winchester, Virginia, when he was in charge of Ambulances and wounded. He writes: "We had an awful battle here but how we whipped them." On October 2, 1864, a few weeks after the September 20 surgery on Jacob Mills, he modestly describes the operation and its successful outcome, prefacing his description with the words, "Since the battle here I have performed some Surgical Operations that are even here considered a little better than some others."

Shortly after the September 19 battle, Dr. Fordyce was at the front during the battle on October 19 and narrowly escaped death himself when a bullet brushed the hair on the back of his neck.

His life was spared to permit him to care for those whom he described in his October 30, 1864 List of Sick and Wounded for Ward B. Hospital, First Division 19th Army Corp. Several of the names of these soldiers appear in the case histories that are outlined in *The Medical and Surgical History of the Civil War*, published in 1990 at Wilmington, North Carolina by Broadfoot Publishing Company.[10]

Excerpt from
The Medical and Surgical History of the Civil War
"Injuries of the Upper Extremities"

Chapter IX, page 616
Case No. 1590

FIG. 480.-Cicatrix after an exarticulation at left shoulder, as it appeared a year after the operation.

"Sergeant J. Mills, jr., Co. D, 8th Vermont, aged 21 years, was wounded at Winchester, September 19, 1864. Assistant Surgeon J. Homans, jr., U.S.A., from a Nineteenth Corps field hospital, reported: 'Gunshot fracture of the left arm; amputation at the shoulder joint; favorable.' On the following day he entered the depot hospital at Winchester, and was transferred to Frederick, November 12th. Acting Assistant Surgeon W. B. McCausland noted: 'Wounded by a minie ball. Admitted into this hospital from Winchester for amputation of the left arm at the shoulder joint, the result of a gunshot fracture of the left humerus, upper third, involving the joint. Arm amputated September 20, 1864, at Morgan's Mills, Virginia, by Assistant Surgeon B. A. Fordyce, of the 16th New York. Flap operation. Condition at time of operation good. November 12th, wound perfectly healthy; simple dressings applied. November 20th, wound nearly healed; discharge slight; simple dressings continued. November 28th, transferred to Brattleboro. On leaving the hospital he was in perfect health, with the exception of a very slight discharge from the wound.' The patient, after treatment in hospitals at Burlington and Montpelier, was finally discharged from service, October 12, 1865, and pensioned. The disability was rated total. This pensioner was paid March 4, 1875. Dr. H. Janes, formerly surgeon of volunteers, of Sloan Hospital, Montpelier, contributed the photograph of the patient, represented by the cut (Fig. 480), taken at the date of the soldier's discharge."

The Medical History of Sergeant Mills sprang to life in that excerpt from *The Medical and Surgical History of the Civil War* and prompted further research which produced both an inspiring life story and a photograph of Dr. Jacob Mills. The grandson and greatgrandson of Revolutionary War veterans, he was born November 18, 1842, in Topsham VT. Upon his return to civilian life after his honorable discharge, he had spent a busy and exemplary life, first in Vermont and then in the state of Montana where he established a Methodist church in the frontier town of Great Falls. He was both an inspiring minister and a very successful business man, as well as a philanthropist. He was quoted as saying that the only things that his wound would not permit him to do was drive four horses and fasten his own shirt cuff. In November of 1870 he married Jennie Forrest Mills, fathered three children, and died October 29, 1925 in Montana at the age of seventy-six.

In spite of the scenes of death, maiming and destruction that he witnessed daily, Dr. Fordyce found time in his busy life to write to his wife and to his children. He brought comfort to his patients and to their families, as witnessed by the December 10, 1864, letter of gratitude that he received from Walter Morse of Eaton NY. His responsibilities far exceeded those generally assigned to an Assistant Surgeon; yet he performed them willingly as his contribution to bringing the war to an end.

Appendix B
Early Letters from the Front

*Dr. Fordyce corresponded with his friends and neigh-
bors who had already committed themselves to the
cause of the War....witness the letters written to the
doctor prior to his entrance into the conflict. They
reinforce our understanding of the conduct of the
campaign and illustrate the esteem in which Dr.
Fordyce was held by all who knew him.*

═══════════

Camp Fisk Walker, Centerville, VA

Feb 2nd 1863

Dr. B. A. Fordyce
Dear Sir

Yours of a late date, came duly to hand, assuring me of your
promptness. I thought you would write, after a time. This is the
second year of the Rebellion, the second month of the year, and the
second day of the month, and also the second time I have been in
VA. soil,

Now for business. You speak of the Town Bounty, now due me from
the Town of Venice, & in regard to it I will say. So long as the Town
of Venice has honest, legal, binding, debts to pay, obligations as
binding in the sight of an honest man as if 2/3 of the tax payers of
the Town had taken their sacred oaths to fulfill. I mean as doubtless
you are aware, repudiation. It is the same spirit, which I am fighting
to conquor, and by which so many mothers mourn their sons
untimely loss.

You may say there is no parallel between the two, but, I tell you, the
greater difference is this, The South have the more honor, being
stimulated by a more noble impulse, the desire of dominion while
the spirit of repudiation, has only money in prospect.

Six months in the service and no pay, and not much prospect, but I will never ask, or receive, as a gift, a single cent, from my town. I did not enlist for pay, nor was "the bounty" any inducement, duty was the motive, forever.

You must not misunderstand me, for it may seem strange, that a person in my circumstances, should refuse $50, a large sum for a poor man, in these times, but I cannot accept it.

You are aware, that I am a free thinker, and express myself with out reserve. and in summing up in regard to this matter, I will say if I am allowed to dictate what should be done with the $50, let it be applied to educate the poor, that they may be brought up to respect truth and honesty, to hate Rebellion, and detest "Repudiation."

I cannot see how B. A. Hull can be discharged while absent without leave, farther than what I have stated, I know nothing.

Lester Sherman, I have not seen since he left on that pleasure trip to Chicago.

Some friends from Cayuga County made us a visit last week. Theo Meiller, Robert Millen, Mr. Lester, Mr. Bothwell, Mr. Hewitt, and Mr. Chadwick. It seemed good to see so many of old familiar faces again. You must excuse me, for taking up so much room by business in this letter.

We are getting a good drill in picket, about these times, having been thus employed for nearly two months, or ever since we have been in Valust.

It tries a fellows stuff, to sleep on the snow and live on hardtack. A person after being out in the wet a good many nights begins to feel a little rheumatic and I am afraid by Spring it will tell on our constitutions if we have any left.

I hope your Singing Schools will prosper and succeed, as I write the boys are singing in one of the tents.

"The flag shall yet wave, o'er many a grave, Before we are in Richmond." This is true.

Write soon, and I will reply as punctually, if I have time.

My respects to your wife and all inquiring friends.

> Yours Truly
>> M. W. Murdock
>> Lieut. 111th Reg. N.Y.V.

———

Camp Hayes Centerville Va
April 29" 1863

Dr. B. A. Fordyce
> Dear Sir or Dr.

Yours of the 25 inst came to hand last evening and as you desird hasten to reply Lester Sherman received $10.00 from you and is making it. [.... ... ...] I am entirely at a loss to know who you refer to in your letter when you say you are afraid some one is playing sharp with him He has acted very much as he has desired having been left by the ears while on the way to Chicago and roamed at large for nearly six months or more I think you need have no fear of sharpers unless he is [bo...] to [....]

If I were you I should send him very little money for what such boys get is only thrown away I merely offer these suggestions that you can act as you see fit Good warm Spring weather is again the "Gen Order" No infinite lately promulgated There being no news to write I will close with my respects to all inquiring friends.

Respectfully your Friend
> M. W. Murdock
> 111" Reg N.Y.S.V.

Hampton Va Augt 21 62

Deryl Hunter
　Der Sir

I have just heard to day of the death of Lewis Freeman on the 19th
We just arrived here and I was in the village I see one of our boys
who is in the hospital and he told me I was very much supprised to
here that he was there I felt vary sure that he must be dead before
this but he has lived up to this time I have not heard the peticulars
and will not be able to go to see about it as we ship this afternoon I
do not know where we shal go to

He died at the General Hospital Fortress Monroe You had better
write to Capt. Cowan about his pay as he will know about it as quick
as he gets official account of his death

Direct your letters as before Washington DC Gen Smith Division
[....] Nevill is well and sends his best respects he feels very sorry
that he was not here soon enough to see him before he died We are
very busy now and have but little time to spare you must excuse
the shortness of this accept this from your friend
Yours truly
Sergt Steele

Medical Directors Office
Fort Monroe. Va. Sept. 19/62

Mr.
　Benj. A. Fordyce
　　　Venice. Cayuga. Co. N. Y.
Sir
Your communication of the 9th inst. is received. In reply I would
state that Lewis E. Freeman died at the Chesapeake General
Hospital. near here on the 18th August of Typhoid fever.

Very Respectfully
Your Obt. Servt.
Rufus H. Gilbert
Surgeon & Medl Director.

Camp near Williamsport Md
Sept 21st 1862

Dear Sir

Your letter of the 9th ulto is just recd - A few days since I recd the official notice of the death of Lewis C. Freeman. He died of Typhoid fever at Chesapeake General Hospital near Fort Monroe Va August 18th 1862 - The Surgeon says "Freeman had no effects except an empty portmanie and a small parcel containing needles thread &c" - He had pay due from January 1st 1862 up to the date of his death - By addressing Ezra B. French Second Auditor Washington D.C you may obtain a circulation giving all the instructions necessary to draw his pay &c - It was with deep regret I learned of his death. He was an honest upright man & an Excellent Soldier He lived thro all the privations of a Captivity in Richmond contrary to my expectation & was doing well at Fort Monroe till by some means he procured some cheese which he ate unbeknown to his attendants causing a Relapse from which he could not rally

Very Respy Yours
Andrew Cowen

Sunday Morning - December 1862

Dr. Fordyce
Dear Sir -

I have just called at your house and found you not at home - I understand that you are a member of the Masonic Fraternity and it is concerning that institution that I wished to see you. While in the army I took the first degree of masonry intending to take the next two as soon as time would allow - but our regiment was ordered away immediately. and I have never since had an opportunity to take them. Now I wish to know if I could take them in your lodge - and if so would there be any additional fee? Any information on this subject which you can give me will be considered a favor by

Your friend
N. J. Hotchkiss
East Genoa N.Y.

Headquarters 1st Brigade
Caseys Division, Fairfax Seminary
Virginia, 6 Miles from Washington
Dec 9th 1862

My Dear Sir

Your communication in regard to Private Bishop A. Hull has just reached me, and I hasten a reply, In regard to yourself my dear Doctor, I never had a shadow of a doubt of your Patriotism or zeal in behalf of our beloved country, I know you to well for that, But in regard to Hull, he has I know give you false statements, That has not a shadow of truth in them, In short he is a bad fellow, During the whole time he has been in the Service he has been a worthless thing, and always an idle shirk, While at Harpers Ferry during our three days bombardment he pretended to be lame and laid about the hospital out of harms way, while my brave fellows was under galling fire from shot and shell, he hid himself under the roof of the hospital a mile from his Regt, But after the surrender he was as well as any man, on our March to Frederick, he had no lame leg then, but marched with his Regt twenty miles in one day, and then deserted, Now doctor those are facts, The rascal has grossly deceived you all, He has never been worth his salt in the Regt but is a lazy idle fellow, and meant to desert, He had better come and report himself forthwith if he knows what is for his interest. I have now an officer detailed in Cay Co. to pick up him and other deserters in that and Wayne counties. The 111th Regt is in my Brigade and encamped directly in front of my Head Quarters, I occupy for my Quarters the house of Bishop Johns, near Fairfax Seminary. He is now a rebel Episcopal Bishop, who left his house finely furnished, Which has been since the war opened, used as head quarters for Brigade and division commanders, the 111th Regt has good Sibley tents, most of them have stoves, and board floors, so that my boys are pretty comfortable The weather here is very cold and snow covers ground, We are between Washington and Alexandria, can from my Quarters see both places, and also the Potomac, By nature it is a beautiful place, but War has made it a desolate place,

I am Doctor, Truly Your Friend

G. Segoine, Col. Comdg

To Doct. B A. Fordyce   1st Brigade Caseys Division
Direct to "Case Sanitary Commission" Louisville

Camp Reno. Brashear City.

La. March 4th. 1863

Mr. Fordyce   Dear Sir

having a small amount of money by me and wishing to put in good hands for safe keeping I thought I would write to you and ask you to take charge of it for me. I will send you what I can spare of my wages, and you may let it out to good men. or you can use it yourself and I will pay you for it.

I am well as usual and so are the rest of the boys in this company. it is fine warm weather here and we have as good times as a soldier can expect.

Please write soon and oblige your most obedient servant
                              Wesley G. Husk
N.B. I can send the money by express and there will be no risk to run
direct your letter to
Wesley Husk   New Orleans
                  La. Co D. 75th N Y. Vols.

Margaretta Oct 24, 1862

Mr. Dr. B. Fordice Sir

I send those few lines to you to let you know my presents wants & condshon I am in want of money enough to defrey my expenses home which I think twenty dollars will do I am a perold prisoner and here sick with the chil fever I want you to send the money as soon as this comes to hand as I have not a cent of money to help myself with and I am here sick on the mersey of straingers without a cent of money and not able to do any thing. Please send your letter to Sandusky City, Ohio

                  Yours truly,
                  Lester Sherman

Camp Hays Centerville, VA
April 14th, 1863

Mr. B. Fordice, esqr

I have just come back to my Regiment and I thought I would write a few lines to let you know that I came through all right. I see Captain Mead in Washington he was on his way home on a furlough, I presume he will be back soon, I came back without any money and I want you to send me 25 dollars as soon as you get this. I have no money with me and I shall have to depend on others till you send it, David Gray wanted me to let him have some money; but I have concluded that I shall need it myself, so you can keep the remainder untill I call for it, we escpect to move from here soon, we had orders to be ready to march yesterday morning; we have been ready ever since but we have not been called on yet but we excpect to be soon dont delay any time in sending the money, I remain yours truly

Lester Sherman

Direct to, Mr. Lester Sherman
        Co. I 111 Regt N.Y.V.
        Washington D.C.

rec'd Apr 20th
Camp Hays Centerville, VA
April 30th, 1863

Dear Sir

I received your letter a few days ago, with 10 dollars in it and I have signed the receipt I want you to keep all the money that I put in your care, untill I call for it I shall send you 10 dollars a month of my wages and I want you to keep it for me, no matter what papers any one show you, unless it is an order from me, in any future time.

I send for 25 dollars and you sent me 10, I wanted to get me a watch, but as you did not send all I sent for I want you to get a watch worth about 15 dollars, and send it to me and you can send a receipt and

I will sign it. I want you to send a dollars worth of postage stamps for I cant get any here. I want you to send me what I send for, and send the receipt of all you send me and I will sign it write as soon as you get this.

Yours with respect
Lester Sherman

Direct to Mr Lester Sherman
Co I 111 Regt N Y. SV
Washington D.C.
P.S.
Bishop Hull is owing me 6 dollars and I want you to collect it for me

---

Camp Hays Centerville VA
May 6th 1863

Dear Sir

I now take my pen in hand to write a few lines to you, and I hope it will find you well as it leaves me at present I sent a letter to you a few days since requesting you to send me a watch worth about 15 dollars, and if you have not started it by the time this reaches you I want you to send me about 5 dollars in money with it and I presume that will last me till I get my pay. tell me if the folks are all well when you write, everything is very dear down here, boots is worth from 10 to 12 dollars per pair and every thing else in proportion We have not moved from Centerville yet, but we had orders to be ready to march two or three days ago, but I suppose it was on account of General Hooker making a move, just as the first order was,

Give my best Respects to all and receive the same yourself
from Lester Sherman
to Mr. B. Fordyce

Camp Hays Centerville VA
May 17th 1863

Dr. Fordyce, Sir
I am well as usual and enjoy camp life very well We have a very nice camp always dry and trees set out in front of each tent, makes

---

it quite pleasant in heat of the day Everything is growing around here finely and grass is large enough to mow in some places altho there is not much farming done. I am out of money and I wish you would send me five dollars and about fifty cents worth of stamps as they are hard to get. When I draw pay from the Government I will send to you ten dollars per month as that is about what most of the boys send altho they have to send home for some of it again before they are paid, We have had orders to march several times but are here yet altho we would like to move just for a change Hoping to hear from you soon and receive the money I close Give my Respects to Mrs. Fordyce & rest of family & friends I subscribe myself

Respectfly Yours
Lester Sherman

Camp Hays, Centerville, Va
May 26th 1863

Dear Sir

I received your letter of the 21st with the 5 dollars and stamps, with much pleasure, as I have been sick nearly two weeks, and have not been able to eat my rations, I dont know how I should have got along, if some of the boys had not lent me money to buy what I wanted to eat, I feel a little better just now. but I am very weak yet, I had about spent the 5 dollars before I got it I sent a letter a little while ago by Morrel Fitch to have you send me 20 dollars, but as you have sent me five you neentnt send but 15 more or else you can tell me when you write again which you had rather do, send me 15 dollars more, or have me give an order for 15 dollars to a man living in the town of Morau I have bought a watch of a boy here and he had rather have the money paid to his father than be paid here to save the risk of sending it by mail let me know as soon as possible if you have not started it before you get this, please to write as soon as you get this, this is from

Lester Sherman
Co I 111 Regt N.Y.V.
Washington, D.C.

Appendix C
B. A. Fordyce, the Author

The flowing script of Dr. B. A. Fordyce' letters to his family and all of his communications to his superiors in battle, speaks of his keen interest in the written word. His interest in the education of his daughters and encouragement of them to write legibly and cogently reflects his earlier experience as a teacher in the Quaker school where he met the student, Emeline Slocum, his future wife. His letters, without exception, were neatly and precisely penned, even under the most trying circumstances ...while camped in tents on the battlefield or late at night after long days of surgery or hospital supervision was blessed with a vision of the scope and immensity of Life and Love and War.

It is, therefore no surprise to find among Dr. Fordyce' papers copies of his earlier writing:

Venice Dec. 22nd, 1848

Thoughts While Attending A Funeral
For the Social Album -

The morning of the 25th of October 1847 was indeed an Autumn morning; wet cold and dreary - Almost every fireside was surrounded by its entire domestic circle, owing to the nearly impassable condition of the roads - Nature seemed [....]ally in mourning - The trees were bereft of their foliage, showing early preparation for the rude frosts of winter - The verdure of Natures carpet was partly faded by the scorching frosts of Autumn, only to return with the mild reign of Spring - Flora too with her annual plants was a severe sufferer - The crown of her beauty, i.e., the beautiful and variegated corollae of her flowers were withered forever.

The toll of the church bell announced the approaching funeral procession - Another of the original pillars of the glorious liberty of our Republic hath passed through the dark vale, and gone to his final rest - The age of the deceased as is the custom was struck on the bell; and many who were curious enough so to do, counted; One, Two, three, four, and on, and on they counted till the extreme age of a century and eight years were told - The coffin was carried into the Church and the black pall covered over it - A short and appropriate sermon was delivered in which the principal topic presented was, that, though isolated instances of remarkable longevity may occur among us, that the allotted time of three score years and ten years may be exceeded, yet the cert[...] that the "insatiate archer death" is ever on our track with the strong arm of Omnipotence for[...]ally, behooves us all to be every ready to make capitulation on the most favorable terms.

What an eventful series of years in the history of the world thought I, has that body which now lies cold and inanimate before this assembly passed through - How closely allied his life with the early history of our country! But eight years younger than George Washington and frequently in his company it seemed rational that he might bear some of the impress of the Father of his Country to his latter years - And so indeed it was, the old mans highest delight seemed to consist in his last days in rendering a just tribute of esteem for the unchangeable goodness of George Washington - Born at a time (1739) when the Kingdoms of Europe were at war with each other in vain attempts to settle the claims to territory in America; when too, the Indians were endeavoring to expel and exterminate the whites from this continent, the reason is at once evident why so great a share in the history of our government during his life is marked by sanguinary conflict - We cannot notice but few of the points of history and these very briefly connected with his life.

He well remembered Braddocks defeat (1754) by the Indians the grief of the settlers in the provinces and particularly the border settlers seemed without bounds when the tidings came that the flower of the British veteran troops sent to America to aid in resisting the savage cruelty of the Indians had fallen victims to the merciless tomahawk and scalping knife - To hear the old mans recital and see him act the scenes in his second childhood were enough to chill ones blood - The dismay of defeat and the joy of success quickly giving place to each other on the almost fleshless face of the old man were really interesting to notice.

The great earthquake that struck Lisbon were sensibly felt throughout the world and was distinctly remembered by the deceased.

Millerism it is true was [.....]at this time known but prophets of the same kind had just then put forth their belief that the millennium was at hand, and thousands then believed with fear & trembling - If Miller, the old man said, could have a few earthquakes to aid him he certainly would obtain many more converts - In the revolution he was an actor - He was taken prisoner at Ticonderoga then exchanged and lay in the hospital at Lake George many weeks sick - After recovery he again joined the army after the surrender of Burgoyne at Saratoga Springs - Almost every event connected with the struggle for liberty from the throwing the tea overboard at Boston to the making the treaty of peace at Paris was fresh in his memory-

He has seen our country pass from colonial and Provincial governments under Great Britain, Spain and France to an independent great and powerful nation of the earth - He lived to see eleven presidents peaceably elected, He lived through fourteen presidential terms of office and to see the time when eight of the presidents should precede him to the grave and nearly half a century after Washington had gone to the tomb - Much in the history of other nations might be mentioned but we forbear - The Silent earth now cover the remains and they are rapidly returning to the dust from which they were formed. Peace be to his dust.

B. A. Fordyce

[Tucked into the preceding letter were Louise Coulson's comments to add life to the following:

"This is Ebenezer Parkes - d. Oct. 24, 1847 age 107 years, 9 mo and 4 days. Buried at East Venice Cemetery, Town of Venice. Her map pointed the way to the grave's present day location."

=========

Funeral of Juliet Valentine Clark - March 27, 1842

On the morn of 27 March 1842 the sun rose clear and threw her resplendent light oer a slumbering world . Twas Sunday; and at the season of the year when a Sunday at home passes off drearily with the young whose airs are always restless especially on this day but still always awake to the liveliest anticipations of future felicity - Could an idle spectator gazing around on those who present themselves before his view discern the inmost thoughts of every soul on this day and the manner in which each thought is ushered into existence a more delightful drama would be presented to his view than would be possible to exhibit before him at the most magnificent of our theatres - - - - - - - - At the solicitation of a young friend we started on horseback to attend the funeral of a young lady who had recently died - We traveled slowly towards the place of our destination viewing the landscape on the eastern banks of the beautiful Owasco and admiring the sublime scenery which met our gaze on all sides till led to exclaim —

A place not beneath an angels pride,
But fit for the seraphs of heaven to reside -

Here in rather a secluded though picturesque place we were informed that we had arrived near the place of our destination by the immense number of horses and carriages which were tied around a small but comfortable and commodious dwelling - Every thing was characteristic of the residents of the place having been bereft of some fond object of their cares and affections by the cruel hand of death - All around was a grave death-like silence save now and then the neighing of some uneasy horse or the cooing of a few doves in a barn nearby - - - - - The house was crowded to overflowing - The pastor of a neighboring church soon arrived and the services commenced - His theme was appropriately "on the mortality of human life" - He endeavor impress on the minds of his audience the ambiguousness of human existence also to show them that the wheels of time were wafting them on to that bou[...] from which no traveler can return - He endeavored to show them that human life was as variable and fleeting as the winds of heaven and that a preparation for future existence was necessary to their well being in eternity - He was a well formed and fair proportioned man about 45 years of age and his appearance was well calculated to impress upon the minds of his audience the solemnity of his subject - The services were ended and the coffin was brought out of the door and opened as is the custom that the spectators might see the remains of a respected friend - After the spectators had satisfied their curiosity in looking at the corpse the mourners were seen issuing from a door in the front part of the house to take a last view of the relics of their beloved relative - The first was the bridegroom of the deceased who had been bereft of the idol of his affections 27 days after he had vowed before the hymeneal alter to love cherish and protect her; Secondly the parents, and brothers and sisters of the deceased followed each other in succession and lastly the more distant relations: There were no mock mourners there tears were sure to flow copiously from the eyes of those who possessed the strongest of hearts from those whom fear could not awe nor the severest hardships fatigue - But oer a lovely sister dead, "As did tears feelingly and fast" - - - The procession moved slowly towards the churchyard to deposit the remains of Juliet C___k in the earth that they might return to the dust from which they were taken - - -

Juliet C___ the daughter of Joseph &
and wife of E.C___ aged about 24 years died at the house of her father on Sat. 26th March 1842 at 2 o'clock A.M. - She was a young woman of more than ordinary talents connected with considerable beauty added to this an irreproachable character; polite in her behavior; modest in her deportment, and engaging in all her manners; industrious and enterprising in the performance of all her duties; an ornament to society; who but two weeks before her death was the very picture of health and a few months before had fallen into the enchanting snares of cupid and 27 days before her death

---

stood before the hymenial alter pledging herself to one who was deserving of being like her with a prospect of long and happy life But alas! how vain and flickering is human life - In three weeks she was the victim of dire disease - A ray of hope beamed forth that the progress of the monster would be intercepted but to hope succeeded despair its hold was too firm - The skill of the attending physician was baffled and no desired effect was produced by any remedy which he applied They all seemed to irritate the disease and hasten the dissolution of the patient - On the sixth day another physician was called but the disease had raged so far that no relief could be given to the patient and on the morning of the seventh day after she was taken her spirit took its flight and winged its way to the regions of bliss to the god who gave it - - - Thus departed one who has left many relations to mourn her loss and friends to lament their bereavement of her society——-

F C G (?)

[Juliet, daughter of Jos. & Mary Valentine, wife of Eri Clark (cousin of B. A. Fordyce), died March 25, 1842, age 25, buried Stewarts' Corners Cemetery, Town of Venice, NY. LGC]

Venice Dec.   1860

"Hands Off"

This is perhaps an American expression claiming Young America for its complete and thorough introduction into general use - yet world wide in its application - From the little dealer in Candies to the dealer in nations and men though their wares are held in the most attractive manner before the gage of the world if examined minutely [.....] closely the gentle and many times polite admonition is given if not in words absolutely in action "hands off" - From the cradle of the tender infant to the monument surrounded by evergreens in the cemetery, remembrances of the strong tie that binds the living to the departed the curiosity of the inquisition is really held in restraint by the positive injunction "hands off" -

Appendix C - B. A. Fordyce, the Author

The boy pursuing the butterfly hat in hand attracted by its gaudy plumage and graceful undulating flight - The man straining every pore of mind and body to attain worldly honor for the applause & congratulations of his fellows though successful learn equally when the butterfly is crushed by rude handling and all its beauty spoiled in its death & the honors attained bring a world of bitter envy & raw corous hate how much wiser & better it would have been to observe the rule "hands off"

The boy that handles black iron in the smith's shop - The pickpocket caught with fish hooks surrounding his neighbor's pocket - The confidence man disining an accomplice explaining the nature of his business or a policeman - learn that they have made a slight mistake by reason of excessive curiosity handling

Self Defence is one of the first developed manifestations of animated nature - scarce a creature in all creation but what to a greater or less degree possess the means of self-protection

Some to an incredible extent when compared to the apparent necessities of their condition - for instance the Rattle Snake which gives positive warning of his hostile intentions if you approach too close & whose bite is so fearfully fatal to all animal life -

The Cobra the Masuawger(?), & indeed nearly all the animals of the serpent kind - Carnivoural(?) animals - birds of prey are powerful in their means of defence and attack -

No creature so helpless in all the varieties of animal life for defence or escape as man unaided by the gift of Reason yet when so enlightened no power short of infinite seems capable of interposing obstacles to his successful progress -

This brings us to the second part of this subject - viz. Respect for the rights of others   This is a principle recognized by all forms and practices of Law & Government - acknowledged admitted and taught by all the varying systems of Theology; is allowed by all scientific teachers and investigators to be paramount in importance to all other matters of interest combined; is the inherent principle impressed on the mind from earliest youth to the farthest extreme of age -

Whether we view encroachments on individual rights in the boy at school forcibly appropriating his neighbors slate to his use or in a Napoleon Bonaparte by aid of military power assuming the Imperial throne of France - Whether from the scale of the robber of a neighbors poultry yard to Alexander the Great who appropriated whole Kingdoms to his use whether from the command of the Brigand Chieftan or Pirate Captain to the Duty levied on glass, tea, paper and Painters Colors by Geo the III The principle is unalterable-

Indeed in all the exercises of Arbitrary and tyrannical power when brought to the bar of the faithful historian for trial and adjudication before the enlightened world the judgment of a just indignation is rendered against them and the admonition is given with a thousand fold force to all seeking the right of others "Hands Off" -

From the bloodthirsty Hayman who so heartlessly murdered Magyar men women and children in cold blood in Hungary to Maximillian the Mexican leader & conspirator of today each receives notice "Hands Off" - The one by the indignant operations of Manchester in free and enlightened England - the other by the recommendation of the President U.S. in his last annual message urging the interference of our government in favor of   [.....] the constitutional President of the Mexican States -

In Indian history it is related that a child in one of two tribes of Indians entertaining the most friendly relations to each other found & caught a grasshopper while at play with children of the other tribe a desire to possess was entertained by the child of the neighboring tribe & force was used to obtain it when the Kindred children of the first interfered the squaws took up the matter adopting respectively the sides of their kindred and the loss of a tolerable amount of hair was lost with such other use of hands and finger nails as would make the most positive impression on their antagonist leaving scratches and marks in abundance as evidence of valor Strife was sectional yet - When the warriors of the respective tribes returned from their hunting and fishing excursions the matter was related to them then strife became general - Immediately both parties made preparation for the conflict The Indian council, the war paint the tomahawk & knife were all brought into immediate requisition - The subtle cunning of the savage was arrayed against equally sly & adroit opponent - The number of warriors in each tribe were about equal being two hundred on a side by general consent the contest was to be made on Lake Erie - Both parties were provided with boats one of bark the other of dug out or log canoe

The conflict commenced hand to hand with Tomahawk & Knife a warrior wounded & thrown overboard was instantly drowned boats were sunk the lake appeared a sea of blood at last the contest was ended the warriors of one tribe were all killed of the other twelve only remained to tell the sad result What a frightful termination of childhood covetousness for a grasshopper much better had the little ones been taught the rule Hands Off

But a few years since for a little difference in church matters so slight indeed that it should certainly have been all over looked and compromised by all desiring the good of those interested the whole civilized world was shocked by the military display in the frightful bombardment of Sevastapol the which no military effort recorded in history is worthy of comparison The Allied Armies of England France & Turkey against the immense army of Russia each worthy of the other in military prowess & skill - i.e. the great powers of the world in deadly conflict for a matter so small as not to be worthy of note by the most minute historian unless it were to properly exhibit the extreme sensibility of national honor - Thousands on thousands of persons inocent in every respect of any participation in the cause of this conflict lay groaning at one time in the streets of Sevastopol in the agonies of Death - Property of untold worth was destroyed a writer describing the battle to the Emperor of Russia says that the French & English bombardment by their artillery looked as if all the fires of Hell were let loose on the city - not even a semblance of resistance could be made the rapidity of the firing the continued roar of the heavy artillery alternated with the screams & groans of wounded & dying the steady & rapid advance & charge The demonic pandemonium itself seemed to [....]-

Italy so long ground beneath the Tyrany of Austria rises in her might under the [.....] of Victor Emmanuel assisted by Garribaldi and asserts her rights and again assumes her place among the nations of the Earth notifying Austria in a most sensible manner "Hands Off" - -

South Carolina stands like the boy with a chip on his shoulder warning his companions not to knock it off or they catch it - calculating by bluster and threats to remain scathed act as she will - She really acts as though she believed the rest of world was made to help her catch & hold her niggers and if perchance we refuse to be hound & bark on the track of her negroes she tears her hair throws up ashes and swears she will blow up all the rest of Gods creation and tear especially the United States into fragments   My impression is she had repress a little ebulitive of her passion and for the present at least keep her "Hands Off" -

Endnotes

(1) Imagine Emeline.... bereft of her lifelong companion after two years of widowhood, caressing this mahogany link to her family and the past.... seeking to preserve it for future generations by writing its identity in one of its drawers.

(2) Louise Gayton Coulson, the name expresses the cadence of her speech....the directness of her approach to life, to history and to her Family heritage, The Fordyce Family. From the moment that her voice came across the telephone wires, it was apparent that a treat was in store. That telephone call initiated a relationship that continued until the time of her passing in 1991.

While she was still on this earth, Louise Coulson devoted countless hours of research into the historical records of the Central New York area; and as she abstracted the data, she gleaned notes that related to her family, to Dr. Benjamin Allen Fordyce. Countless letters she penned, sharing the nuggets that she had mined from those ancient county records; and it is these that enhance and illuminate the correspondence between Dr. Fordyce and his wife, Emeline and their three children.

One can now imagine her delight in finally meeting in heaven all those departed ancestors who had been such close companions in her lifetime. All of her dreams come to fruition in that transition into Eternity. Mrs. Coulson's comments will be found bracketed and identified with her initials LGC.

(3) Excerpted from "New Jersey Militiaman in Revolutionary War was Pioneer Settler in Scipio," *The Cayuga County Farm & Home Bureau News* (September 1951): 12.
"John Horton Fordyce - 1835-1862 - Three years after he married Louise Close, young John Horton Fordyce enlisted in Company E of the 138th New York State Volunteer Regiment as a private, after refusing the captaincy of the company. Nine weeks later, on November 13, 1862, he died, near Washington, D. C., at the age of

27. Surviving him, besides his wife and parents, was his only child, George Fordyce, who had been born on September 30, 1860. This boy had first been named after George Washington, but when his father went off to the Civil War he told his wife he thought that President Lincoln would be a great man and if so he wanted his son named after him. So "Lincoln" was added to the boy's name later. The homestead, incidentally, contains a great many pictures of the martyr president, Abraham Lincoln."

John Horton Fordyce was Louise Gayton Coulson's great grandfather (John Horton Fordyce[1], George Lincoln Fordyce[2], Rebecca Walton Fordyce[3], Louise Gayton Coulson[4]).

(4) Monday May 29, 1865, Adv: "Dr. Benj. A. Fordyce Having recently removed from Town of Venice to Village of Union Springs would respectfully inform citizens of the village & vicinity that he will attend calls in his profession if desired. Has been engaged in practice of medicine for last 20 yrs. & had extensive experience in operative surgery during last 2 yrs. while serving in the army."

(5) In 1906, after the completion of his term as Cayuga County Sheriff, George Fordyce purchased the house at 4 North Cayuga Street in Union Springs and detailed Edward Cater for the renovation and remodeling. From a nineteenth century country-Gothic structure there arose a new creation. A bay window appeared on the south side; the north wall was extended. Plate glass glistened from new and enlarged windows. The interior was expanded to accommodate a library and parlor, in addition to the sun-lit living room. The room above became a billiard room. And, wonder of wonders, the house boasted the first bathroom in the village. This necessitated the development of an intricate water system with two huge cisterns to store the rainwater that pored off the steeply pitched roof that was added.

Gone was the simple beauty of the cherry handrail and the flight of steps leading up from the front door. To the back stairs it was relegated, while a new flight ascended to the front hall above, with butternut paneling and an angular staircase to update the decor to the Mission styling recently introduced. The mantle in the living room was a brooding mass of paneled Mission grandeur, encumbered with mirror and shelves.

The tall walnut entrance doors were removed and stored away in the barn. In their place appeared a massive oak door graced by a leaded and beveled glass window. The suns of succeeding years never failed to seek out those graceful curves of sparkling beauty and to transform into rainbows the inner reaches of the house, giving rise to the thought that possibly through that magic of nature flowed the spirit that endeared it to everyone who called the house his home.

(6) It is interesting, when reading of the Murdock Family at home in New York State, to refer to the letters received by Dr. Fordyce from Lt. M. W. Murdock as he served in the 111th Regiment of New York Volunteers of the Northern Army at Centers, Virginia in February 1863. A copy may be found in Appendix A - Early Correspondence from the Front.

(7) LGC Note: The mockingbird is grey and white, or a brownish gray. Could this be a clue that BAF was a little color-blind? His interest in the birds interests me - though anyone would be interested to hear a mockingbird sing! - because his father was interested in birds, and was the one who awakened the interest in George L. Fordyce, 2nd cousin of George S. Fordyce, and 29 days younger in age. By the turn of the Century, when bird study began to evolve to studying the birds "with a glass, not a gun" - to study its habits and characteristics with a telescope, instead of shooting it to "study" it - GLF was in the vanguard of ornithologists in this observation of birds, and made many contributions to this knowledge, as well as his work on migration of birds and the annual Christmas bird censuses. This interest began when he was age 9, and BAF's father started him on a life-time route.

(8)

Head Quarters 1" Division 19" A.C.
Franklin. La. February 15" 1864.

SPECIAL ORDERS
NO. 15   (Extract)

3. Assistant Surgeon BENJAMIN A. FORDYCE, 160th New York
Volunteers is detached from his regiment, and assigned to the
Medical Charge of the Batteries of this Division.

He will reciept to Assistant Surgeon STUB for the Hospital
property & Stores, belonging to the Batteries.

By Command of
Brig. Gen. Emory
s/ _____(illegible)
A. A. General.

C.C. 160th N.Y.V.
thro - C.O. 3" Brigade

(9)

Head Qrs. 19 Army Corps of U.S. Forces
Western Louisiana   Franklin
Mar 7" 1864

Special Orders
No. 66   Extract,

5. Assistant Surgeon Fordyce 160th N.Y. Vols. is hereby ordered
to report to Surgeon Sanger Medical Director 19" Army Corps for
duty in charge of General Hospital at Franklin

By order of Maj. Gen. Franklin
s/ John P. Baker
Captain & A.A.A.G.

(10) - *The Medical and Surgical History of the Civil War* (Wilmington, NC: Broadfoot Publishing Company, 1990): 10:616, 626, 6434, 700, 702, and 725; 11:56, 238, and 252; and 12:501. The information supplied through the foregoing references was supplied through the generous assistance of the Archivists of the Otis Historical Archives of the National Museum of Health and Medicine.

(11) *The Medical and Surgical History of the Civil War,* vol. 11 (Wilmington, NC: Broadfoot Publishing Company, 1990): 238. "Injuries of the Lower Extremities, No. 982 - Morse, A.A., Pt., D, 114th N. York, age 25 Date Oct 19, 1864, Operation - Left, circ.; Operator - A. Surg. B. A. Fordyce, 160th N.Y.; Result - Died Nov. 13, 1864; exhaust'n, Autopsy."

Index of Fordyce Letters

Date	Location	Author	Recipient	Political	War & Battles	Camp Life	Medical	Southern Scene	Northern Scene	Black Reference	Letters of Special Interest	Page
Oct 26 1863	Venice NY	Estella	B A F							x		96
Oct 26 1863	Venice NY	Abbie	B A F							x		97
Nov 03 1863	Vermillion Ville LA	B A F	Emeline	x	x	x	x		x	x		97
Nov 08 1863	Sabbath Evening	Emeline	B A F	x						x		101
Nov 08 1863	Venice NY	Estella	B A F							x		103
Nov 09 1863	Venice NY	Abbie	B A F							x		103
Nov 09 1863	Vermillion Ville LA	B A F	Wife/Children	x	x	x		x	x			104
Nov 15 1863	Vermillion Ville LA	B A F	Emeline		x	x		x	x			107
Nov 19 1863	New Iberia LA	B A F	Emeline	x	x			x	x			109
Nov 20 1863	New Iberia LA	B A F	Abbie				x			x		111
Nov 27 1863	New Iberia LA	B A F	John B Strong	x	x	x				x		112
Dec 05 1863	Sherwoods NY	Estella	B A F							x		113
Dec 06 1863	Sherwoods NY	Abbie	B A F							x		114
Dec 06 1863	Sherwoods NY	Emeline	B A F							x		115
Dec 14 1863	New Orleans LA	B A F	Wife/Children				x		x			117
Dec 18 1863	New Iberia LA	B A F	Wife/Children				x	x	x	x		118
Dec 26 1863	Sherwoods NY	Estella	B A F							x		120
Dec 27 1863	Sherwoods NY	Abbie	B A F				x		x			121
Dec 27 1863	Sherwoods NY	Emeline	B A F						x	x		122
Dec 27 1863	Sherwoods NY	G Slocum	B A F							x		123
Dec 30 1863	New Iberia LA	B A F	Wife/Children				x		x	x	x	124
Jan 03 1864	Sherwoods NY	Emeline	B A F					x		x		126
Jan 04 1864	Sherwoods NY	Estella	B A F							x		127
Jan 10 1864	Franklin LA	B A F	Emeline	x	x			x			x	128
Jan 23 1864	Franklin LA	B A F	Wife/Family	x	x	x						130
Jan 23 1864	Franklin LA	B A F	Abbie				x		x		x	133
Jan 21 1864	Sherwoods NY	Abbie	B A F							x		134
Jan 24 1864	Sherwoods NY	Emeline	B A F							x		137
Jan 24 1864	Sherwoods NY	Estella	B A F							x		139
Feb 07 1864	Franklin LA	B A F	Wife	x	x	x						140
Feb 15 1864	Franklin LA	B A F	Emeline				x		x	x		142
Feb 18 1864	Franklin LA	B A F	Wife/Children	x	x	x	x	x				145

Date	Location	Author	Recipient	Political	War & Battles	Camp Life	Medical	Southern Scene	Northern Scene	Black Reference	Letters of Special Interest	Page
Feb 22 1864	Franklin LA	B A F	Resignation		x		x					147
Feb 25 1864	Franklin LA	B A F	Wife/Children		x	x	x			x		148
Mar 10 1864	Franklin LA	B A F	Wife/Children		x	x	x	x				151
Mar 13/14 64	Franklin LA	B A F	Estella/Abbie			x		x		x		152
Mar 13 1864	Franklin LA	B A F	Wife/Children		x							153
Mar 20 1864	Brashear LA	B A F	Emeline/Abbie			x	x	x		x		154
Mar 23 1864	Venice NY	Emeline	B A F				x		x			156
Mar 30 1864	N'Orleans-On Board	B A F	Abbie		x			x				159
Apr 02 1864	RedRiverLA-On Board	B A F	Emeline		x			x				161
Apr 03 1864	AlexandriaLA OnBoard	B A F	Wife/Children		x	x		x				161
Apr 09 1864	Mansfield LA	B A F	Parole of Honor		x							163
May 03 1864	Mansfield LA	B A F	Emeline	x	x		x					163
Jun 04 1864	New Orleans LA	C C Dwight	John B Strong		x							167
Jun 12 1864	Mansfield LA	B A F	Capt Montgomery		x							168
Jun 19 1864	Morganzi LA	B A F	Emeline		x	x	x	x		x		168
Jun 20 1864	Morganzi LA	B A F	Daughters			x	x	x		x		170
Jun 21 1864	Morganzi LA	B A F	Emeline		x	x	x					172
Jun 26 1864	Morganzi LA	B A F	Abbie			x		x				173
Jul 05 1864	Algiers LA	B A F	Wife/Children		x	x	x	x				173
Jul 08 1864	Algiers LA	B A F	Emeline			x	x					175
Jul 19 1864	Fortress Monroe VA	B A F	Emeline		x	x		x				180
Jul 20 1864	BurmudaHundred VA	B A F	Wife/Children	x	x	x	x	x				181
Jul 29 1864	Washington DC	B A F	Emeline		x		x					183
Aug 02 1864	Monocacy MD	B A F	Abbie		x	x		x	x			185
Aug 05 1864	Monocacy MD	B A F	Emeline		x	x	x					186
Aug 08 1864	Halltown VA	B A F	Emeline	x	x	x	x	x				188
Aug 14 1864	Middletown VA (near)	B A F	Estella		x			x	x			190
Aug 20 1864	Charlestown VA(near)	B A F	Emeline		x	x	x	x				191
Aug 23 1864	Halltown VA (near)	B A F	Emeline		x	x	x	x			x	192
Aug 25 1864	Halltown VA (near)	B A F	Wife/Children	x	x	x	x					194
Aug 30 1864	Charlestown VA(near)	B A F	Wife/Children		x	x	x		x			197
Sept 01 1864	Charlestown VA(near)	B A F	Wife/Children		x	x	x					198

Index of Fordyce Letters